Alternative to the Bread of Affliction

Alternative to the Bread of Affliction
— *And Other Essays* —

Walter Brueggemann

FOREWORD BY
Theodore J. Wardlaw

CASCADE *Books* • Eugene, Oregon

ALTERNATIVE TO THE BREAD OF AFFLICTION
And Other Essays

Copyright © 2024 Walter Brueggemann. All rights reserved. Except for brief quotations in critical publications or reviews, no part of this book may be reproduced in any manner without prior written permission from the publisher. Write: Permissions, Wipf and Stock Publishers, 199 W. 8th Ave., Suite 3, Eugene, OR 97401.

Cascade Books
An Imprint of Wipf and Stock Publishers
199 W. 8th Ave., Suite 3
Eugene, OR 97401

www.wipfandstock.com

PAPERBACK ISBN: 978-1-6667-3516-1
HARDCOVER ISBN: 978-1-6667-9196-9
EBOOK ISBN: 978-1-6667-9197-6

Cataloguing-in-Publication data:

Names: Brueggemann, Walter, author. | Wardlaw, Theodore J., foreword.

Title: Alternative to the bread of affliction : and other essays / Walter Brueggemann ; foreword by Theodore J. Wardlaw.

Description: Eugene, OR: Cascade Books, 2024. | Includes bibliographical references and indexes.

Identifiers: ISBN 978-1-6667-3516-1 (paperback). | ISBN 978-1-6667-9196-9 (hardcover) | ISBN 978-1-6667-9197-6 (epub).

Subjects: LCSH: Bible—Criticism, interpretation, etc. | Bible—Hermeneutics. | Church and social problems.

Classification: BS1192.5 B825 2024 (print). | BS1192.5 (epub).

VERSION NUMBER 02/14/24

Scripture quotations are from New Revised Standard Version of the Bible, copyright © 1989 by the National Council of the Churches of Christ in the United States of America. Used by permission. All rights reserved worldwide.

For the well-beloved
Erskine Clarke
teacher, historian, editor, colleague

Contents

Foreword by Theodore J. Wardlaw | ix
Preface | xi

1. Alternative to the Bread of Affliction | 1
2. Preaching the Psalms | 7
3. On Tenacious Parenting | 21
4. The Litigation of Scarcity | 27
5. Twin Themes for Ecumenical Singing: The Psalms | 46
6. In the "Thou" Business: The Travail of Biblical Language ... Again | 57
7. Reaping the Whirlwind | 82
8. The Poem: Subversion and Summons | 98
9. The Impossible Possibility of Forgiveness | 104
10. On Appearing before the Authorities | 118
11. Getting Your Sibilants Right: The Evangelical Shibboleth | 126
12. Do the Numbers | 133
13. Awaiting the Verdict | 140
14. At the Death of Peter Knauert: Peter amid Remembering and Hoping | 145
15. Advantage McEnroe | 151

16	What Does It Mean to Be Human?	159
17	When the Music Starts Again	161
18	The First Great Commandment	168
19	A Little Evangelical Geography	181
20	Toward Perfect Health	188
21	Peace: The Fruit of the Spirit	191
22	Three Key Moves toward White Extremism	201
23	A Retrospect	211

Bibliography | 219
Name Index | 225
Scripture Index | 227

Foreword

WALTER BRUEGGEMANN IS REGARDED widely across several decades as the most influential Old Testament scholar and theologian in America. The son of a pastor in the German Evangelical Synod of North America— a predecessor denomination of the United Church of Christ—Brueggemann has cut a theological swath that bears great similarity, by the way, to two other remarkable American theologians of an earlier era—Reinhold Niebuhr and H. Richard Niebuhr. Like the Niebuhrs, Brueggemann began his academic career at Elmhurst College and earned his Bachelor of Divinity degree at Eden Theological Seminary. He went on to earn his Doctor of Theology degree from Union Theological Seminary in New York, was ordained in the United Church of Christ, and, as of now, has published over a hundred books and numerous scholarly articles, and has preached in churches and universities around the world.

Dr. Brueggemann began his teaching career at Eden Seminary, and ultimately served at Columbia Theological Seminary in Decatur, Georgia, where he is now the William Marcellus McPheeters professor emeritus of Old Testament. He and his wife Tia currently reside in Traverse City, Michigan. He remains active as a highly-regarded teacher and preacher in constant demand in lectureships and in pulpits.

The Church, though, as his dear friend Erskine Clarke has said, is finally Brueggeman's "natural habitat." For him, the pastoral life has always been integral to his teaching ministry. "Perhaps this is why, even as a young professor at Eden," Brueggemann has said, "I slowly joined the circle of itinerant preachers, as I followed in the wondrous footsteps of Barbara Brown Taylor, Tony Campolo, Jim Forbes, Tom Long, and Will Willimon—a most distinguished company of preachers" (p. xiii).

He continues to share his insights boldly from pulpits, Church School seminars, and so many other settings where the topic is likely to be outreach and empathy on behalf of a hurting world. Central to this proclamation is an outrageous claim from Rev 11:15: "The kingdom of this world has become the kingdom of our Lord and of his Messiah, and he will reign forever and ever."

This is an important book that begs for your attention, and here is why. It is a critical and faithful collection of essays, biblical study, lectures, themes that run deep as we migrate from ancient history to the present situation in which we find ourselves, relentless scholarship seen through the travails of eyes and ears alert to the horror and hope of our time, prayers . . . and, dear reader, even a poem!

However, the reader should not approach this book as one looking for a central theme. Instead, what Brueggemann is doing is to offer us bits and pieces of his brilliant mind. These essays, written across a number of years, some of which have been published in a variety of significant publications, represent something of a bread-crumb trail allowing us to follow along in Brueggemann's intellectual journey.

For instance, in the book's namesake, "Alternative to the Bread of Affliction"—Brueggemann begins the first chapter by describing for the reader the meaning of the phrase "the bread of affliction." It is an apt description of the social condition of the plight of the Babylonian exiles described in Isaiah 55.

"They are displaced persons under duress," he writes. "They are outsiders who must hustle to measure up, who will never be good enough to be accepted; their lives were bitter and their bread tasteless in their mouths . . . These displaced Israelites were no strangers to the bread of affliction" (p. 1). Eventually, Isaiah the poet offers an alternative: "Come buy and eat; come buy wine and milk, without money, without price" (p. 3). "He offers free food that is quite unlike the costly junk food of Babylon . . . No more bread of affliction!" (pp. 3–4). Brueggemann weaves this text toward the liturgical setting of Lent, and the feast of the eucharist, and in the "holy of holies" the very presence of the bread is transformed into the bread of deliverance, the bread of emancipation. "Savor and chew and swallow," says Brueggemann, "and remember those who know only the bread of affliction . . . Savor and chew and swallow along with your neighbors. This is an invitation for all of us who are hungry and thirsty for God's newness!" (p. 6).

Elsewhere in this book is a chapter titled "The Poem: Subversion and Summons," which anticipates the new David—the new possibility of shalom. David, this new ruler, possessing wisdom and understanding, will break the monopoly of the powerful and will rule for the meek. "What we usually have," writes Brueggemann, "is authority with knowledge but no wisdom, with data but no understanding, the kind of power that governs on behalf of the billionaire club, so that the rich get richer" (p. 100). But hopeful eyes are trained on unthinkable things like no infant mortality, no economic displacement, no oil spills despoiling creation. They are looking beyond the world they are familiar with, and are training their eyes on the coming advent.

> "The wolf shall live with the lamb,
>
> > the leopard shall lie down with the kid,
> >
> > the calf and the lion and the fatling together,
> >
> > and a little child shall lead them." (p. 101)

"The poem is about Advent," writes Brueggemann. "And we dare to say, we confessing Christians, that the poem concerns the Christmas baby who refuses Rome's rule of force and religion's rule of code, opening the world to healing, forgiveness, and joy." "So try this in Advent," says Brueggemann. "Depart from logic and memo and syllogism, and host the poem." (p. 102).

I have joyfully endeavored to lift up a couple of chapters in this amazing book. They cover so many profound and contemporary topics that are utterly informative and, finally, are inspiring to any person of faith looking for how such faith can be stronger. My hope is that this new book might challenge and encourage you to read it; no, to devour it! If you have not yet discovered Walter Brueggemann, this book is a great place to start.

As I think of the kind invitation to write this foreword, I regret that, but for one week-long seminar when Walter Brueggemann accepted the invitation to work with me and some twenty other pastors (all of us in the first third of our ministry, knowing a few things about preaching and wanting to know more), I missed the opportunity to sit in any number of his seminary classrooms. That was simply because I had chosen another seminary from which to prepare for ministry. But I have delighted in hearing so many friends—all of them pastors now—speak of the impact Walter Brueggemann has had on them. Over and over again, they use words like "pastoral." One of my dearest friends, who did have the opportunity at Columbia Theological Seminary to be formed, class after class, by the scholarly biblical theology of Walter Brueggemann. She has told me that, beyond his scholar's intellect, he also carried with him a pastor's heart and visible concern for the ups and downs of being students. "His pastoral life," she said, "was integral to all of his teaching."

One of the ways that one can measure Brueggemann's enduring pastoral impact is by the prayers he prayed at the beginning of each class he taught. Generations of his students have remembered those prayers and, more than once, have remarked on the deeply spiritual awareness those prayers demonstrated. That awareness has always characterized Bruggemann's presence and leadership in the Church. As this book amply demonstrates, it still does.

Theodore J. Wardlaw
Advent 2023

Preface

I CANNOT REMEMBER A time when I did not think some about preaching. My dad was a pastor; he invited "feedback" from my brother, Ed, and me at Sunday dinner. We no doubt were quite forthcoming about our half-informed "feedback." In college I regularly shared leadership of the liturgy at St. Paul UCC in Elmhurst where regularly I listened to the erudite sermons of Edwin J. Koch. In seminary I received my only B-plus in preaching from the formidable Frederick Schroeder. (My other preaching teacher in seminary was the equally formidable Ernest Nolte, who preached the ordination sermon for Ed and me). When I graduated from seminary and was ordained, I entered a graduate program at Union Seminary in NY; during those three years at Union I preached regularly in a small UCC congregation in the Bronx. After I had joined the faculty at Eden Seminary, after a good bit of work, I slowly joined the circle of "itinerant preachers" as I followed in the wondrous footsteps of Barbara Brown Taylor, Tony Campolo, Jim Forbes, Tom Long, and Will Willimon—a most distinguished company of preachers. Later I published some collections of my sermons plus a few expository studies of preaching in the Old Testament.

I have also happily been on the receiving end of good preaching. Occasionally a preacher will voice some uneasiness that I am to be in the congregation. My response to that is honest and prompt: "Everyone needs to hear, repeatedly, the news of the gospel." No matter how familiar it is, every time "the old, old story" is sounded in our hearing yet again, it may become for us "the new, new song." I have sat "under" good preaching over time, including my present congregation, Central United Methodist Church in Traverse City. I have been "on both sides now," speaking and listening. I am grateful on both counts for the difference such voicing continues to make for me and my life.

Preaching has been a mainstay of the covenanted people of God at least since the work of the Deuteronomic tradition in ancient Israel. Gerhard von Rad, terms Deuteronomy "preached law."[1] Along with the book of Deuteronomy, its sermons are sprinkled through the royal history of 1 and 2 Kings as an interpretive commentary on the royal line. That practice was extended and verified by the several sermons in 1 and 2 Chronicles.[2] In the New Testament a core text on the centrality of preaching is the exclamation of Paul in a series of rhetorical questions:

> But how are they to call upon one in whom they have not believed? And how are they to believe in one of whom they have never heard? And how are they to hear without someone to proclaim (*kerussontos*) him? And how are they to proclaim (*keruzosin*) him unless they are sent? As it is written, "How beautiful are the feet of those who bring good news!" (Rom 10:14–15)

Paul of course is quoting Isa 52:7:

> How beautiful upon the mountains
>   are the feet of the messenger who announces peace,
> who brings good news,
>   who announces salvation,
>   who says to Zion, "Your God reigns." (Isa 52:7)

The poet asserts that the reign of Babylon under Nebuchadnezzar was decidedly penultimate and could not be sustained. The good news of the displacement of Nebuchadnezzar is that the covenanted people of God were permitted homecoming (see 2 Chr 36:22–23). The decree of Cyrus, the Persian ruler, implements the good news of YHWH. The words of Isaiah summarize the work and possibility of faithful preaching: "Your God reigns!" That is all; but that is everything:

> Your God, YHWH, who covenanted with Israel, rules!

---

1. Von Rad, *Studies in Deuteronomy*, 16.
2. See von Rad, "The Levitical Sermons in I and II Chronicles."

Your God, YHWH, who calls the worlds into being, governs!

Your God, YHWH, who defeats the power of evil—not excepting Babylon and Rome—reigns!

Your God, YHWH, is carried by the "messenger" who has beautiful (i. e., "welcome") feet and a buoyant voice.

Preachers are often tempted to entertainment, or didacticism, or banality. But the work is otherwise. The work is simply to attest, yet again, over and over, that this God wills only good in the world, finally has prevailed and will prevail.

In the long sweep of Christian history, it is Martin Luther who has most boldly grasped the centrality of preaching for the life of the church. For good reason Luther asserted that "right preaching" is a *sine qua non* for a faithful church. Indeed, he set preaching in parallel to "sacraments rightly celebrated" as the certain means whereby God's grace is performed amid the congregation. It is from Luther that we get the intractable "three point sermon":

—The human condition;

—The saving work of the Gospel;

—The shape of the new life in the Gospel.

It is too bad that this "three point sermon" of Luther has been in so many ways trivialized. The serious sacramental force of the sermon has been fully appreciated and articulated by Karl Barth who asserted that the Word of God takes three symmetrical forms, *the elementally generative Word of the creator* (see Ps 33:6), *the Word embodied in the life of Jesus of Nazareth*, and *the Word proclaimed in the congregation*. It is breathtaking and mind boggling to ponder that the preached word has the same generative, transformative, salvific capacity as does the creating word of God, and the fleshed word of Jesus! For all of our attention to visual imagery in our society that all too readily holds our attention, there is something very different and elusive about *spoken-heard* utterance that takes place in a moment and may reverberate with forceful assurance and summons for a long duration in the ears, memories, and lives of the congregation. What a mouthful to say with Paul, "Faith comes from what is heard"! I suppose, moreover, that it is fair to say that Freud, with his face-to-face therapy, in some way is a secular recognition that utterance—spoken and heard—is indeed generative of new reality. It must be so, in contrast to the endlessly repetitious ads to which we are much too readily subjected. Thus faithful preaching is indeed a word from "elsewhere," from outside the grip of the congregation or the horizon of the preacher. It is a word from the revealed-imagined world of evangelical construal that intends, every time, to divest our closed world of both domination and despair. And then to imagine that this generative, emancipatory word is entrusted to preachers, most of us who are more or less ill-suited to the wonder and burden of such utterance.

I am fortunate indeed to have had, over a long period of time, access to the pages of the *Journal of Preachers* as a venue for my writing. The articles reprinted here are a collection of some of my articles in the *Journal*. And of course, over that long stretch I have been graced by and grateful to the editor of the *Journal*, Erskine Clarke. He has been uncommonly receptive to my work. I am grateful to him (and to his cohorts at the *Journal*, notably Jet Harper and Rosemary Raynal) for their receptivity to my work. Beyond that, of course, I am indebted to the readership of the *Journal*, mostly working preachers, who have been willing to engage my work in responsive ways.

I am pleased to dedicate this collection, with thanks, to Erskine Clarke. In doing so I have no doubt that I speak for a multitude of the readers of the *Journal* and for the long run of his students who with me would be eager to express their gratitude to and appreciation for Erskine. We have been blessed as a company of colleagues, he would no doubt agree, by doing the faithful work of preaching.

I end this brief comment by reference to the conclusion of the book of Acts over which I get chill bumps every time I read it:

> He [Paul] lived there two whole years at his own expense and welcomed all who came to him, proclaiming the kingdom of God and teaching about the Lord Jesus Christ with all boldness and without hindrance. (Acts 28:30–31)

As we know Paul had been through many toils and snares, not least from the authorities in the Roman Empire. Finally he settled in Rome after is long hard travels. In his "retirement," what he did was "proclaim the kingdom of God," the very same words introduced by the evangelists (see Mark 1:14–15). He managed to pay his own way, thus not dependent upon any other resources. That freedom permitted him to be "bold." Of course, most preachers among us do not have such funds. Paul is, nevertheless, a model for the church. The work is to continue to proclaim the rule of God. It is to declare, over and over,

> The kingdom of the world has become the kingdom of our Lord and of his Messiah, and he will reign forever and ever. (Rev 11:15)

Of course this is an outrageous claim every time the preacher proclaims it. It was an outrageous claim when Paul declared it, or when Mark wrote of it, or when Moses addressed Pharaoh, or when Isaiah spotted "beautiful feet." It is always an outrageous claim that contradicts "the facts on the ground." But we know better. We know better, because we have witnessed the drama of Good Friday when Rome prevailed, and we are witnesses to his resurrection that is the final word on Rome or any other would-be absolute that would deny the governance of the emancipatory God. It is a ready move in the church to traverse *from the pulpit* of such proclamation *to the altar* where we boldly confess:

Christ has died;

Christ is risen;

Christ will come again.

In such an utterance we dare to assert the truth of our lives, a truth that defies all other claims. We have been given our theme; now it is time, yet again, to muster our boldness, stamina, and courage for our moment of fear, hate, injustice, and violence.

Walter Brueggemann
October 13, 2023

1

Alternative to "the Bread of Affliction"

Fifth Sunday in Lent

ISAIAH 55

I WANT TO TELL you about a biblical phrase, "the bread of affliction." The phrase refers to a social condition in which you eat your bread and live your life under great pressure, because there are deep demands on you, quotas to fill, deadlines to meet that may break your heart or your back (see Deut 16:3; Isa 30:20). That pressure may sour your taste for bread and squeeze your life into despair.

I.

In our text in Isaiah the Israelites are exiled into Babylon. They are displaced persons under duress. They are outsiders who must hustle to measure up, who will never be good enough to be accepted; their lives were bitter and their bread tasteless in their mouths. They had to live a life they did not want to live under the pressure or of Babylonian power, and Babylonian culture, and Babylonians expectations that were uncompromising.

These displaced Israelites were no strangers to the bread of affliction. They could remember all the way back to the days of slavery in Egypt under Pharaoh. Pharaoh imposed heavy demands on them, making more bricks while they had to gather their own straw. Their lives back then were bitter and hopeless, and the bread they ate tasted like cardboard at best.

Or if we fast-forward from Babylon, later on the Jews under the Roman Empire ate the bread of affliction. Their land was occupied by Roman soldiers and Roman tax collectors, and their cultural, religious identity as Jews was under assault. It is no wonder that they lost their appetite for the bread of affliction served up by Rome.

It turns out that the story of God's people is a story of the bread of affliction . . . *right now* in Isaiah in Babylonian exile, *back then* in Egypt under Pharaoh, and *later on* under the Roman Empire. Every time it was the bread of affliction. Everywhere afflicted by bread that does not nourish!

Surely it is true: everyone knows about the bread of affliction. Everyone knows about impossible quotas to fill, impossible deadliness to meet, impossible tasks to perform, impossible expectations to meet. It might be the expectations of one's family. It might be the pressure and hassle of work. It might be the vexation caused by one's children. It might be money worries or unbearable debt and the trap of poverty. It might be the endless vexation of premiums and copayments and deductions. Or it could be worse, no health coverage at all, or no home, or no food, life in a food desert without a grocery store. But of course the bread of affliction is not evenly distributed.

- Poor people eat more bread of affliction than do wealthy people.
- Women eat more bread of affliction than do men.
- Blacks eat more bread of affliction than do whites.
- Gays and lesbians eat more bread of affliction than do straights.
- Palestinians eat more bread of affliction than do Israelis.

But the bread of affliction is everywhere. It must be chewed and swallowed and accepted when we have no capacity or leverage to do otherwise. That was how it was back in Babylon, and how it is every day among us.

II.

So imagine the displaced Israelites in Babylonian exile, unhappy, sad, humiliated, in despair. And then, right in the middle of the bread of affliction comes this poet Isaiah. He came, as our best poets do, out of nowhere. Maybe he was sent by God as some poets are. Maybe the unbearable circumstance of his people evoked him. Or maybe he had an irrepressible urgency and he had to speak. What we have from him is his abrupt, staggering, disruptive utterance. He called out to his displaced people fed up with the bread of affliction: "Yo, you hungry; yo, you thirsty." In his poetry he asked them some questions that he intended to get their attention: "What are you doing? Why do you let the Babylonians feed you such bad stuff? This is what he said:

> **First question:** *Why do you spend your money on that which is not bread and does not nourish?* Why do you eat the junk food of the empire? Why do you let the dominant economy shape your appetite and propel your life in distorted directions?
>
> **Second question:** *Why do you labor for that which does not satisfy?* Why do you use your energy and intelligence toward goals that when you achieve them are empty of meaning and purpose? Why do you let the dominant economy of Babylon send you on wild goose chases for no good reason?

These are not really questions. Isaiah is not waiting for them to answer. These are in fact reprimands. The poet is scolding his people for letting the junk food of the empire propel their life and energy for the purposes of the empire and not for their own good.

III.

And then—take a deep breath!—the poet offers an alternative:

> Come buy and eat;
> Come buy wine and milk,
>   without money, without price. (Isa 55:1)

He offers free food that is quite unlike the costly junk food of Babylon. It is God-given food unlike the offer of Babylon or of Pharaoh or of Rome. He uses "bread" as an image of an alternative life, no longer governed by the fake bread of affliction. He invites these vexed, sad, exiles to recover their faith and live with the abundance and the freedom given by God. It's all free!

This is the news to the exiles. God offers alternative bread and alternative milk, and alternative wine and alternative life. The poet says:

> Listen carefully to me and eat what is good;
>> delight yourselves in rich food. (Isa 55:2)

No more bread of affliction!

This offer of alternative is what the God of the gospel has been doing all along. Way back in Egypt with Pharaoh and his bread of affliction, the alternative was the sweet taste of manna, the inexplicable bread of the creator God. The story goes like this in the wilderness:

> Some gathered more, some less; those who gathered much had nothing over, and those who gathered little had no shortage; they gathered as much as each of them needed. (Exod 16:17–18)

This is what the same God of the Gospel will do later on when Jesus comes to a hungry crowd in the wilderness. They were hungry because they had been fed the bad food of Rome. And now Mark reports:

> Taking the five loaves and the two fish, he looked up to heaven, and blessed and broke the loaves, and gave them to his disciples to set before the people . . . All ate and were filled; and they took up twelve baskets full of broken pieces and of fish. (Mark 6:41–43)

There was enough free bread left over for all twelve tribes of Israel. In the work of Jesus, God offered these desperate folk an alternative life of abundance.

This is how God works:

> Against the parsimony of Pharaoh, God sent *abundant manna;*
>
> Against the imperialism of Babylon, God sent *free bread and free milk and free wine.*
>
> Against the predatory power of Rome, God sent the *surplus bread given by Jesus.*

That same bread is on offer outside the zone of greedy system of fear.

But, says the poet Isaiah, to receive that alternative abundant bread we have to leave the empire. So Isaiah imagines a great procession of God's people marching out of Babylon back to their identity of faith:

> You shall go out in joy;
>> you shall be led out in peace. (Isa 55:12)

And all along the parade route of those who will leave the pressures of empire, like the parade crowd on Front Street, will be gathered to watch the parade home the mountains and the hills and the trees, all of creation; they will sing and dance and clap their hands in joy. They will celebrate God's people coming back to their true identity and their sanity. But in order to get the bread of life, we have to leave the demands and the rewards of the empire and its 24/7 rat race.

IV.

So we have this text in Lent. This poetic text is an invitation to people like us to recognize how much we have gotten comfortable with the bread of affliction, how much we take as normal the mighty pressures of consumerism, the empty promises of convenience, and the insatiable demands of the 24/7 rat race into which we induct our kids and our grandchildren, all in the name of wellbeing, the assurance of success through the rat race, and the hint of our superiority through our race or ethnicity or nationality, all of which comes with the junk food of empire. Lent is *a chance to notice*. But also *a chance to depart* too much fear, too much anxiety, too much anger, too much rush, too much greed. It is not about giving up chocolate for Lent, even if that is good for our bodies. It is about giving up our taste for the bread of affliction and receiving the better bread of God's abundance.

Well, I suspect that some of you are like me. You do not any longer eat much bread of affliction, because you have arrived at the abundant blessings of God's goodness. So have I. If that is true for you as it is for me, then consider this. Some among us know mostly the bread of affliction, do not know of the abundance, abundance in health care, abundance in housing, abundance in food, abundance in good schools. Those of us who no longer have the taste of the bread of affliction in our mouth are invited in Lent to share that good bread of abundance with those who dwell in affliction, by ministries of charity and compassion, by the good work of justice, by the embrace of the neighbor, all of whom have entitlements to good bread. We have entrusted to us the free bread of God's abundance; it will defeat the bread of affliction every time it is shared.

Lent is a time to repent of our taste for the bread of affliction, even if we have gotten used to it. So Isaiah can say in this poem:

> Seek the Lord while he may be found . . .
>
> for my thoughts are not your thoughts. (Isa 55:6a, 8a)

God has other thoughts and other intentions of wellbeing for us. "My ways are not your ways."

God has other ways for you and me than the bread of affliction.

And now we arrived at this dramatic moment when we taste the alternative bread at this table. This alternative bread offered to the exiles is given again. It is the bread of deliverance. It is the bread of emancipation. It is the bread of joy and freedom. It is the bread that defeats the bread of affliction. It is the same bread that he gave when he took, he blessed, he broke, he gave! With a surplus of life-giving nourishment!

As we eat this bread, remember the bread of affliction that seduces us. Savor and chew and swallow, and imagine us on our way out of the rat race of empire. Savor and chew and swallow and remember those who know only the bread of affliction. Keep them in mind as they are invited along with us. This is an amazing offer at this table. Like the poet said to the exiles: you who are hungry and thirsty, come without money and without price, delight yourself in God's newness. Savor and chew and swallow along with your neighbors. This is an invitation for all of us who are hungry and thirsty for God's newness!

Central United Methodist Church

April 7, 2019

2

Preaching the Psalms

John Calvin famously begins his Psalms commentary with this opener: The book of Psalms is "An anatomy of all parts of the soul."[1]

I.

My alternative way of saying what I think is an equivalent to Calvin's verdict is this: The Psalms are the voicing, in a highly stylized way, the emotional extremities of our lives in the presence of God and in the presence of the congregation.

The act of preaching, I propose, is the reperformance of this voicing:

—It is *a voicing*; it is for out-loud utterance in speech and song. It requires self-announcement.

—It concerns *the emotional extremities* of our lives, the heights of elation expressed in awe, wonder, praise, and thanks, and the depths of doubt, alienation, despair, need, and abandonment. The two great genres of hymn (with thanksgiving) and lament (protest and complaint) reach beyond the reasoned civility of Enlightenment rationality into our concealed recesses where our fear and hurts dwell from which energy and courage may arise. These emotional extremities that are, in a reductionist technological society, an embarrassment are here known to be the real substance of life and rich grist for faith.

---

1. Calvin, *Commentary on the Book of Psalms*, xxxvi–xxxvii.

—The voicing is in a *highly stylized* way. Thus Psalm study is largely constituted by analysis of genres, of recurring patterns of speech. That is what makes the Psalms so repetitious. They consist in the regular, trusted ways of speaking that the community has found reliable and apropos for identifiable venues and circumstances of life. Attentiveness to the Psalms consists in the capacity to host these patterned speeches knowingly and imaginatively, so that the community that uses them faithfully becomes, in the phrasing of George Lindbeck, "a cultural-linguistic alternative": "this is the way we talk in this circumstance."[2] We know what to say and to whom to say it. This familiarity with the patterned way of speech helps to *voice* and to *form* raw emotion into a manageable, usable, transportable utterance to which repeated appeal can be made. Such stylized practice evokes familiarity and therefore some comfort, in such usage, the same familiarity and comfort that we find in the stylized usage of liturgy, in the stylized give-and-take of "therapeutic conversations," and in the familiarity of television commercials.[3] Mostly we do not have raw, undisciplined utterance in these Psalms; the patterns, however, assert the legitimacy and value of such utterance of extremity.

—This stylized voicing is *before God*.[4] The Psalms may indeed serve a psychological function of catharsis and are often taken as such. But at bottom the Psalms are a theological transaction, a dialogic engagement in covenant that knows that God is on the other end of such song and speech. Thus emotional extremities are not only *voiced*; they are *submitted* as an offering of self to God. The voicing of elation before God (praise, thanks, wonder) is done in a conviction that God receives what we offer, wants such praise, and is pleased and enhanced by it. The voicing of anguish before God (lament, protest, complaint) is done in an awareness that God hears and honors such utterance and answers them as the case may be. Thus the Psalms are a patterned way of giving one's life (and the life of the world) over to God. Such an offering of self and world is not unlike the offering of bread and wine in oblation. We are received by God and

---

2. Lindbeck, *The Nature of Doctrine*, 32–41. Lindbeck comments: "Thus the linguistic-cultural model is part of an outlook that stresses the degree to which human existence is shaped, molded, and in a sense constituted by cultural and linguistic forms . . . This stress on code, rather than the (e.g., propositionally) encoded, enables a cultural-linguistic approach to accommodate the experiential-expressive concern for the unreflective dimensions of human experience far better than is possible in a cognitivist outlook" (34–35).

3. See Brueggemann, "The Formfulness of Grief."

4. See the full exposition of this phrase by Stroup, *Before God*.

given back, blessed and broken, now infused with sacramental force. It is like that with our lives and with the life of the world. When our lives are honestly uttered over to God (in elation and in anguish), they are handed back to us with emancipated power and reconciled energy. God's very act of receiving and answering has transformative effect as, in a lesser key, does every interpersonal exchange that is done in honesty.

—This practiced, patterned speech is done in *the congregation*. It is obvious that the great doxologies are for congregational (temple?) use. It is entirely credible that the laments are not designed for the great congregation. They may have been for quite personal use or, as Erhard Gerstenberger proposes, for family or village "rituals of rehabilitation."[5] But even in such "private" usage, the matter is still congregational. Even alone, one prays as a member of the congregation from whom the patterned speech (codes) has been appropriated. One never does a Psalm alone, but always in the company of those who share this patterned speech and therefore this faith.

The utterance and the singing of the Psalms is an act of participation in the on-going work of the community that consists in the honest ceding of self and world, with all of our gifts and wounds, over to the mercy and majesty of God. In the full practice of the Psalter, nothing is withheld from God. Thus Calvin can say, "All parts of the soul," all parts of the self, all parts of the world, are given over to the mystery of God. Preaching is simply the act of making possible this reiterated work of giving our lives to God and so becoming fully ourselves in and through the act of yielding. I propose, for the preaching task, that we consider in turn *plot* and *character*, the two primary ingredients of a narrative rendering of reality.

II.

There is, of course, no tight, all-comprehensive plot in the book of Psalms, just as there is no tight, all-comprehensive plot for any of our lives. It is nonetheless useful to trace out in a rough way *a coherent plot-line* in the book of Psalms that may roughly correspond to the plot-line of our lives. As we learn in Anatomy 101 (on which see Calvin above), there is a recurring commonality in the plot-line of human life; so it is in the Psalms. We each experience that plot-line in our lives in distinctive ways, but the commonalities are evident. Particular psalms give

---

5. Gerstenberger, *Der Bittende Mensch*.

voice to the plot differently, but the pattern persists and recurs. When we perform that plot-line in the book of Psalms (or any part of it), pastorally, liturgically, or in preaching, we are roughly performing, before God and the great congregation, the plot-line of our lives. I got the idea for this from Claus Westermann, the greatest of Psalm interpreters of the last decades. In his analysis of Songs of Thanksgiving (Pss 30; 31; 40; 66; 116; 138), Westermann has observed that in the stylized practice of Israel giving thanks eventuates in telling the story of the experience of the speaker, for which Psalm 30 is a choice example.[6] The speaker of that psalm tells in sequence:

> how he was in a static condition of prosperity (vv. 6–7a)
>
> how he was plunged into dismay by God's hiddenness (v. 7b)
>
> how he made supplication to God (v. 8)
>
> how he asked questions of God in an attempt to motivate God to act on his behalf (v. 9)
>
> how he addressed God in petition (v. 10)
>
> how God turned his life to well-being (v. 11), and
>
> how he arrived at his present new condition of praise and thanks (v. 12).

Westermann sees that Israel's characteristic way of giving thanks is to iterate the story of what has gone on in life and how that relates to God, that is, the God hidden, the God who hears, the God who turns! This is a) the pattern of the Psalms, and b) the recurring story of our lives lived in faith.

Readers who are familiar with my own work may recognize that my way of rendering that recurring narrative is under the rubric of, "orientation/disorientation/new orientation."[7] Of this taxonomy I have suggested that some of us can maintain a status of well-being over time, but soon or late we find ourselves moving into and sometimes out of disorientation.[8] The practice of Israel in the Psalms is to tell that entire tale, including

---

6. Westermann, *The Living Psalms*, 166–200; Westermann, *The Psalms*, 73–83.

7. Brueggemann, "Psalms and the Life of Faith."

8. Janowski, *Arguing with God*, has provided a full exposition of the drama of the Psalms under a three-fold rubric: I. From Life to Death; II. Interlude: The Gate of the Abyss; III. From Death to Life. This study will be the reference point for subsequent discussion.

what is sometimes voiced as God's failure to maintain covenantal fidelity. The disorientation may have many causes (in the book of Psalms not least the destructive work of "enemies"); but in any case this is the truth of our lives in a recurring way, indicating Calvin's "all parts of the soul." This is the truth of all parts of our life, personal, interpersonal, in the larger community and in the public life of the world. It is the plot-line we live out in various ways, a plot-line already scripted and given stylized expression in these poems. Given that we have this script that reperforms the common narrative of our lives, it is as though we know "beforehand" the narrative path of our lives, give or take peculiar by-ways for each of us.

Of course the full narrative exposition does not occur in all of the Psalms, or even in most of them. It is likely that Westermann has identified all of the best cases of the full story in the Psalter. What the Psalms do, rather, is to tell this paradigmatic story of trouble and rescue in bits and pieces, just as most of us sense the move of our lives, not in a grand sweep, but in bits and pieces over time. But the community has discerned that the bits concerning gifts and pieces concerning wounds amount to a coherent tale of our life in the world with God.

Thus I propose that, without forcing matters, it is of great heuristic value to treat each Psalm as though it were a part of the larger story that must be performed over and over. Thus sometimes we get only the complaint that sometimes remains unanswered, as in Psalm 88! Sometimes we get only praise and thanks without an acknowledgment of antecedent trouble. And sometimes, happily, we get only the glad affirmation of statis of well-being. That is,

> sometimes we get only *orientation,* the Psalms we most love;
>
> sometimes we get only *disorientation,* the Psalms the church tends to neglect in its denial;
>
> sometimes we get only *new orientation,* when we are taken by surprise, as in the ultimate surprise of Easter.

It is of immense importance in the life of a congregation to see that the Psalter is a script for this common reality. It will, moreover, be of great value in a congregation to recognize that in various ways at various paces we are all (liberals and conservatives) living through this. We are all living through it, according to this script, in the deep awareness that God is engaged with us in the plot-line. In the congregation where I worship,

- Here is a well-off couple for whom all is well, and then a granddaughter abruptly and unmistakably is marked by a disease that is more than an inconvenience.

- Here is a church leader, skilled in the mysteries of digital communication, who loses his home via unemployment.

- Here is a woman in our church, coming out of great loss in her life, who tenaciously oversees our regular engagement with homeless families whom we host.

- Here is an older guy who is bewildered by the strange emerging world and knows some sadness about it.

- Here is another older guy living in happy statis, sending sermon notes to his grandchildren every week, having no doubt that the center will hold.

- Here is yet another older guy too long alienated from his beloved older son, and can only grieve and hope.

- Here is a set of grandparents who have stood by while their tiny granddaughter has undergone a series of surgeries for a brain tumor . . . and with great positive outcome!

- Here is a young man who went off to college after a high school rendezvous with drugs and alcohol, and who is now soaring in an excited education as the world comes freshly alive for him.

- Here is the mother whose sophomore in college had a psychotic break, regrets having moved in with her mother-in-law, has lost her closest relative to untimely death, and wonders why God is "doing" this to her.

- Here is a widow who spent all she had to provide nursing care for her husband, prepares for a second hip replacement, and continues to love God and neighbor without resentment.

The list goes on; there is more than I know in our congregation, because I go to the "late" service that gathers mostly older people. The congregation is peopled by personal *tales of stasis* of well-being, by *plunges into dismay*, and by being *newly surprised by joy*. All of these narratives are brought to church each time we meet, wanting those tales to be honored and wanting them exposited in terms of gospel faith. Each of these persons is occupied with the specifics of "my" circumstance. For each of them, it is an important question, "What shall I do with this failure, with this hurt, with this gift, with this possibility?" The extremity has become defining (how could it not!). But one cannot just sit on it, because we are meaning makers. We are bound to wonder and then to interpret. One must process the reality and the extremity that comes with it, twist it and turn it to see what all is pertinent. The Psalms provide a script for a gospel exposition that honors specificity along with the discovery that we, as a community, have been here with this wound or this gift or this stasis before. We are part of the procession of story-tellers and story-performers.

The cases I have cited are personal and familial. But of course the Psalms are concerned with public issues as well, and members of my congregation are alert to and engaged with public issues. The Psalter celebrates good "citizenship" and calls it "righteousness" (see Ps 112). The Psalter knows about greed and bribes and war and poverty. It also knows about generosity and justice and bids God to that task. It knows that the practice of economic justice for the needy and poor generates social stability and prosperity, as in Ps 72. It knows that at every turn in the drama of personal and public life, the ups and downs are venues in which God is discerned as present or absent, as faithful or fickle. The plot is about open-ended dialogic interaction, of giving and receiving, of falling and rising, of dying and living. The capacity to process our life through this dynamic interactive plot permits us to be human in a blessed way. Without this plot repeatedly performed, we might end in a reductionist fanaticism or in a cold arrogant autonomy. This script tells us otherwise about ourselves. It is through this script that we may practice solidarity and express in common what we sense so acutely and directly about our lives:

> Before our Father's throne we pour our ardent prayers;
>
> Our fears, our hopes, our aims are one, our comforts and our cares . . .
>
> We share our mutual woes, our mutual burdens bear,
>
> And often for each other flows, a sympathizing tear.[9]

The pastor knows about this. I always astonished at the intimacies of life that are shared with the pastor. The preacher's task is to situate these particularities in the larger narrative that is the truth of our life, a life ceded over to God who receives, hears, and sometimes answers.

---

9. Fawcett, "Blest Be the Tie That Binds."

III.

Along with plot, the second ingredient for good dramatic art is *character*. Here I want to ask, "Who is the character who speaks in the Psalms?" Sometimes it is the voice of the community, sometimes it is the voice of a single speaker, an unidentified "I." In fact the voices that spoke first in the Psalms are anonymous, despite much interpretive speculation. Given that anonymity that is lost in traditions that were not concerned with copyrights, we have a great deal of freedom to identify and characterize the voices of the Psalter.

One strategy of interpretation that achieved canonical status is through the "superscriptions," the notes that stand before Psalms that purport to identify the speaker. The most prominent of such superscriptions are those that assign Psalms to David (Pss 3; 34; 51; 52; 54; 57; 59; 60; 63).[10] Of these the best known and most used is Ps 51 for which the superscription is: "A Psalm of David when the prophet Nathan came to him after he had gone in to Bathsheba." The superscription draws the psalm close to the narrative of 2 Sam 11–12. Thus we are able to say that the psalm presents David who has violated the commandments (on killing and adultery), who stands under severe divined judgment, and who here speaks a deeply moving and apparently deeply felt repentance. It is this tradition that has helped to establish the popular notion of David as the "author" of the Psalms.

It is, however, generally agreed that the superscriptions are "secondary." That is, they are added much later in the tradition and do not provide clues to origin or to original speaker. Thus the on-going interpretive tradition has generated the "character" who speaks in the Psalm: "The Psalm titles do not appear to reflect independent historical tradition but are the result of an exegetical activity which derived its material from within the text itself."[11] Two matters become clear as we ponder the interpretive move from an "original" anonymous speaker to an "historical" identified speaker in the superscription. First, the Psalms are *acutely specific*. They treat particular circumstances, particular crises, and particular verbal responses to circumstance and crisis. But second, that specificity is *transportable*. The Psalm could move from circumstance to circumstance, from emotional extremity to emotional extremity, from speaker

---

10. Childs, "Psalm Titles and Midrashic Exegesis."

11. Childs, "Psalm Titles and Midrashic Exegesis," 143. See also Childs, *Introduction to the Old Testament as Scripture*, 520–22.

to speaker. The poetry of repentance in Ps 51 is quite specific, but it is belatedly transported to David.

In fact, when we read the Psalms liturgically or devotionally, we also engage in such transport, though we seldom reflect on the process. Thus with the beloved Ps 23, we do not know the original speaker of the poem. We easily assign it to David. In our reading, however, we do not linger over David; we readily transport the psalm (without critical reflection) to our own circumstance, to our own valley of the shadow of death, to our cup running over, and our own dwelling in the house of the Lord forever. The Psalms have identifiable genres. But they are not generic. They are specific and we engage in agile interpretation in order to make them our own specificity.

Since, as Brevard Childs notes, "one senses the variety within the canonical process," through which the Psalms are "often greatly refashioned for use by the later community," I propose that the preacher contribute to "the variety of different hermeneutical moves" and continue the refashioning for later use.[12] By this I suggest that the preacher assign new superscriptions to the Psalms in order to give the Psalms new contemporary currency. Such a new specificity may pertain to someone in the congregation or someone outside it. The new superscription might be shared with the congregation, or if it is too intimate for that, used only to free and feed the imagination of the preacher without public identification. I came to this awareness and possibility when, long ago, I was teaching Psalm 109, a Psalm of immense vengefulness. It was and is my pedagogical habit to ask the class, "Who is the speaker here?" I was not asking an historical-critical question, but rather was inviting pastoral imagination. Thus we read Ps 109:9–13:

> May his children be orphans,
>   and his wife a widow.
> May his children wander about and beg;
>   may they be driven out of the ruins they inhabit.
> May the creditor seize all that he has;
>   may strangers plunder the fruits of his toil.
> May there be no one to do him a kindness,
>   nor anyone to pity his orphaned children.

---

12. Childs, *Introduction to the Old Testament as Scripture*, 22.

> My his posterity be cut off;
>> may his name be blotted out in the second generation.

When I asked, "Who is speaking here?" Linda answered quickly and confidently: "This voice of the Psalm is a woman who has been raped." Her answer caused a long pause in the room. Linda's verdict, of course, is not historical-critical. It is personal, intense, and contemporary. And, of course, Linda is right, though I would not have thought of it. That is exactly the character who speaks here, one deeply offended and violated, but with courage to speak out and demand that God's punishment should be commensurate with the violation she has suffered. The psalm, moreover, ends with deep affirmation of the steadfast God who attends to our violations.

> Because your steadfast love is good, deliver me . . .
> For he stands at the right hand of the needy,
>> to save them from those who would condemn them to death.
>> (Ps 109:21b, 31)

The preacher may never tell the congregation about such a contemporary connection. But simply entertaining such an interpretive context will greatly illumine, because the preaching task is to tell the story reflected in the psalm: a) with *great specificity*, and then b) to invite *transport* of that specificity to other specificities.

I believe that the heuristic generativity of such new superscriptions might be especially useful with some of the angry psalms of vengeance.[13] Very many church people might say and genuinely affirm that they have never been that angry and would never pray that way. But then a very different superscription might transport the force of the psalm away from us to someone else, perhaps a mother in Baghdad whose son has just been killed by a bomb . . . or an inner-city mother in the United States with the same loss through neighborhood violence. Such a transport might be an effective strategy for getting our minds off ourselves and transposing the psalm into an intercession, to pray with and alongside those who require prayers that we would never utter for ourselves. Because the Psalter is the voicing of emotional extremity, the church has available here access to the deepest anguishes and highest elations that must be voiced, even if they are not always grounded in our own immediate experience. We

---

13. On these Psalms, see Zenger, *A God of Vengeance?*

do "share each other's woes," the scope of such sharing of woes is further opened by these poems beyond "our own kind."

And of course the same applies to the great hymns of exultation and elation. Thus for example, the gladness of Ps 65:9–13 celebrates the gift of rain upon which life depends:

> You visit the earth and water it,
>   you greatly enrich it;
> the river of God is full of water;
>   you provide the people with grain,
>   for you have prepared it.
> You water its furrows abundantly, settling it ridges,
>   softening it with showers, and blessing its growth.
> You crown the year with your bounty;
>   your wagon tracks overflow with richness.
> The pastures of the wilderness overflow,
>   the hills gird themselves with joy,
> the meadows clothe themselves with flocks,
>   the valleys deck themselves with grain,
>   they shout and sing together for joy.

Perhaps the superscription might be, "A congregation in Texas after the breaking of severe drought." Or perhaps the wonder of a coherent peaceableness would be reflected in Ps 85:10–11 that might serve any reconciliation in a family or in a congregation or in a great national "Truth and Reconciliation Commission." The superscription might be "When Peter and Andrew found a peaceable settlement of their father's will":

> Steadfast love and faithfulness will meet;
>   righteousness and peace will kiss each other.
> Faithfulness will spring up from the ground,
>   and righteousness will look down from the sky.

Or the familiar table prayer of Ps 145:15–16 might serve "The Dedication of New Food Coop":

> The eyes of all look to you,
>   and you give them their food in due season.

> You open your hand,
>> satisfying the desire of every living thing.

In such a context, the sharp warning of v. 20b, "All the wicked he will destroy," is a wake-up call about environmental violence that will not be tolerated. I suggest that when interpretive transport teems with new characters in emotional extremity, the possibilities for the preacher are limitless. The preacher permits the psalm to voice the great wounds and the great gifts of the day.

IV.

Plot and *character* are interpretive features that will do generative work for the preacher. *Plot* is the directional flow of life that we all have in common that moves willy-nilly from a stasis well-being to trouble and sometimes to new possibility. *Character* is the identification, in quite specific ways, of endless stream of God's creatures who face the daily realities of gift and wound. The preacher is to narrate the plot, often only a bit or a piece of the entire narrative. The preacher's task is to draw the Psalm close to a specific character, or better, to draw our character close to the Psalm and thereby to have our own sense of self reconfigured and repositioned. The characters in these Psalms are rich in emotional extremity and are invited to enter as full participants in the plot at the appropriate access point.

But matters of plot and character cause us finally to notice that the Psalter is *God-occupied*. God is often addressed here as "thou," sometimes in glad doxology as we have seen in Ps 65:9–13, sometimes in bitter denunciation over infidelity. Thus Psalm 44 might be read "National Rage after 9/11."

> Yet you have rejected us and abased us,
>> and have not gone out with our armies.
> You made us turn back from the foe,
>> and our enemies have gotten spoil.
> You have made us like sheep for slaughter,
>> and have scattered us among the nations.
> You have sold your people for a trifle,
>> no high price for them.

> You have made us the taunt of our neighbors,
>> derision and scorn of those around us.
> You have made us a byword among the nations,
>> a laughing stock among the peoples . . .
> All this has come upon us,
>> yet we have not forgotten you,
>> or been false to your covenant. (Ps 44:9–17)

The plot draws our life and the life of the world into intense interaction with God. As in the model text of Psalm 30, God is everywhere in the sequence of the standard plot:

> implied in the stasis of prosperity (vv. 6–7a)
>
> hidden in dismay (v. 7b)
>
> addressed in supplication (v. 8)
>
> questioned as to motivation (v. 9)
>
> petitioned to act as God is able (v. 10)
>
> acknowledged as the agent of "turn" (v. 11)
>
> praised for transformative action (v. 12).

Without God . . . no poem! And with the poem, only this particular God! Thus the plot is an artistic portrayal of the way in which life is performed in intense engagement with God.

The character of God is rich and supple. This is not a God who can be reduced to the certitudes of one-dimensional fundamentalism. Nor is this a God who can be safe and "non-interventionist," as some progressives prefer. This is a God who is an active agent, endlessly elusive, on occasion available, celebrated frequently as "faithful and steadfast," but known as well to be unfaithful, not steadfast, fickle, absent, neglectful. This is a God who "can do all things," so we hope for this God as an ally in the daily contest of our lives; but sometimes the same character is remote and indifferent, and so Israel (and we) may be relentless toward God. Even though there is no divine response in Ps 88, the calling on God never quits. God's hand must be forced! The psalm might be entitled, "The daily urgency of Sam who could not find a job:

> O Lord, God of my salvation,
>> when, at night I cry out in your presence,

> let my prayer come before you,
>> incline your ear to my cry . . .
> Every day I call on you, O LORD;
>> I spread out my hands to you . . .
> But I, O LORD, cry out to you,
>> in the morning my prayer comes before you. (Ps 88:1–2, 9, 13)

This particular superscription is evoked by the recognition that unemployment is eventually ostracizing; I may be shunned by friend and neighbor (vv. 8, 18).

In *the performance of the plot* and in *the tracing of the character of God*, the preacher sketches out *a God-occupied world*. This is a God for whom no secret can be hid. This is a God who is nearby and not far off (Jer 23:23). This is a God with whom life is intense, wondrous, demanding, open-ended, and hope-filled. This is a God who is a compelling to match for the emotional extremity of our life in the world. The wonder of God matches our elation; the absence of God corresponds to our anguish. This God makes possible and makes necessary the full disclosure of how it is with us.

All of which means that the Psalter has on offer a remarkable alternative to the flat, reductionist world of denial in which we are mostly expected to live. Such a world, we imagine, is manageable . . . or cannot be managed. We imagine that we are on our own and can do as we please . . . or we imagine we are on own and must run the race-race in order not to fall behind. But the Psalms know better than that. The preacher knows better than that. And when the preacher knows, the church can know, and when the church knows, there can be a subversive, generative enactment of courage, energy, and freedom. It begins when our emotional extremities are honored and resituated in the presence of God from whom no secret can be hid. The dominant world all around us is like a maximum security intelligence community with reams and reams of well-kept secrets, secrets of elation and anguish. But such secrets kill! The telling gives life! That cage of lethal secrecy is interrupted every time we reperform our lives through in a Psalm.

June 5, 2013

3

On Tenacious Parenting

> We will go out with our young and our old; we will go out
> with our sons and our daughters... —Exod 10:9

WE HAVE NEVER BEEN able to determine the historical identity of Pharaoh in the Exodus story. He might have been Thutmose or Ramses. Or he might have been Seti. The Bible has no interest in his identity and does not bother with the question. And the reason for such a lack of interest is that when we have seen one Pharaoh, we have seen all Pharaohs. They all look alike and act alike. Said another way, over the long course of theo-economic history, many different persons are cast as Pharaoh and take on his persona. Thus in reading the Exodus story, we do well to ask, "Where is Pharaoh showing up?"

I.

As portrayed in the Bible, Pharaoh is an agent of *greedy productivity*. He cannot have enough—enough of wealth, enough of power and control, enough of self-aggrandizement. His passion is always for more, in his case, *more* bricks in order to build *more* granaries in order to store *more* grain. Grain in the ancient world was a mark of power and wealth because everyone has to eat. James C. Scott, *Against the Grain*, has shown that a monopoly of grain was the basis of the earliest empires of the Near East. Pharaoh's greed for more was ruthless and unending. He commanded his slaves:

> Get to our labors (Exod 5:4)
>
> Let heavier work be laid on them (v. 9)
>
> Complete your work (v. 13)
>
> You are lazy (v. 17)
>
> You shall not lessen your daily number of bricks (v. 19)

Pharaoh will not be satiated!

Concerning the prophetic imagination of Ezekiel, Pharaoh must boast about his wealth, even to claim that he is a self-starter. The Nile River is in fact the source of his wealth but in his self-deception he can imagine he invented the Nile:

> My Nile is my own;
> I made it for myself. (Ezek 29:3)

He overestimates his power and prowess and consequently becomes a polluter:

> You consider yourself a lion among the nations,
> but you are like a dragon in the seas;
> you thresh about in your streams,
> trouble the waters with your feet,
> and foul your streams. (Ezek 32:2)

II.

Pharaoh's proud success characteristically depended on cheap labor that was reduced to a tradable commodity. Such a supply of cheap labor, in his case as in the case of US wealth, is slavery. But it could alternatively be low wages that keep workers dependent, in debt, and devastated into despair. It is no wonder that Pharaoh's Israelite slaves "groaned under their slavery and cried out" (Exod 2:23). Such cries of course did not matter to Pharaoh. He was interested only in the bottom line of production. As bricks became more valuable and more required, the production quota could readily increase because slaves are allowed no bargaining power.

For good reason Pharaoh feared the loss of his supply of cheap labor, even as slave owners in our Old South feared slave rebellion and passed laws for the return of escaped slaves. Thus the story of the Exodus turns on tension between *the intent of the Israelite slaves* to depart Pharaoh's Egypt and *the ruthless resolve of Pharaoh* to prevent such escape. Pharaoh's fear of such an escape led to his irrational policy of violence:

> When you act as midwives to the Hebrew women . . . if it is a boy, kill him. (Exod 1:16)

He was prepared to kill the children in order to retain his labor force! The outcome of his policy was to pollute the Nile, the very source of his life and property:

> Every boy that is born to the Hebrews you shall throw into the Nile. (Exod 1:22)

Like every Pharaoh this one reduced vulnerable threatening people, when necessary, to a readily dispensable commodity.

III.

As the story goes, the long arc of history governed by YHWH is against Pharaoh. He slowly came to recognize that his absolutist policy of violence was unsustainable. As a result, he entered into calculating negotiations with Moses in order to concede as little as possible. His ruthlessness is matched by his unblinking cunning. The narrative identifies three ploys of negotiation by Pharaoh.

First, Pharaoh will permit the slaves to worship "your God" (the God of emancipation), but worship must be in his land and so kept under close surveillance (Exod 8:23). Moses must of course refuse the offer because worship of YHWH cannot take place under Pharaoh's supervision.

Second, Pharaoh will allow the Israelite slaves to go and worship YHWH, but then adds an unexpected question that toys with the slaves: "But which ones are to go?" (10:8). Pharaoh intends to hold back some as hostages. Moses resists with a statement of uncompromising resolve, refusing to leave anyone behind (10:9). He refuses to bargain anyone away, not "our young or our old, our sons and daughters, our flocks and herds." Pharaoh responds that he will never let "your little ones" go. The conflict concerns the protection of the children of the Hebrew slaves, a protection linked to YHWH and inimical to Pharaoh's cunning ruthlessness. Committed as he is to brutal transactional processes, Pharaoh can never appreciate such non-negotiable human solidarity, particularly as it pertains to vulnerable children.

Third, Pharaoh further conceded that even the children can go, and only "flocks and herds" (their wealth!) will be kept hostage (10:24). This is yet another bargaining ploy that Moses must refuse. In each of these proposals Pharaoh reluctantly concedes more and more.

Our interest here concerns the second ploy of Pharaoh concerning the children of the slaves. Moses is totally committed to the children; no doubt the slave mothers and fathers were adamant in their protection of their children. Moses in effect declares to Pharaoh, "We won't go until we all go." In Exod 10:26 Moses avers that not a hoof of an animal will be abandoned to Pharaoh, much less our children. So the issue is joined. Will the children of the vulnerable be separated from their parents as pawns in a rapacious policy of greed? Or will passionate solidarity prevail against the separation policy of Pharaoh?

IV.

Pharaoh never "was" but always "is." It take no imagination, in our context, to see that this narrative pertains to our contemporary Pharaonic policies that treat the vulnerable as disposable and that regard cheap a labor force as a dispensable commodity. It takes no imagination to see that a lustful passion for wealth, control, and security draws toward irrationality that in the end will be self-destructive. Of course the parents of the separated immigrant children among us do not imagine that they are reiterating this old drama. And those parents back in Egypt for whom Moses spoke did not understand that they were sketching a paradigm for our later use. Both sets of parents, then and now, simply acted out parental solidarity that cannot be defeated by the ruthless cunning of Pharaoh. It is an old tale now being reiterated before our eyes. Now as always, a deathly outcome of such insanity for such Pharaonic power is certain.

Before our very eyes now acted out is lethal, self-destructiveness with which the fear and greed of Pharaoh never reckon. We are watching tenacious parenting that evokes important engaged allies. Pharaoh did not know, then or now, that this pathos-filled drama of fear and greed collides with the will and purpose of the God who cherishes, champions, and sides with every child, no matter how vulnerable. When we do such faithful imaginative reading, we may wonder where the Bible-thumpers are who are so enthralled by fear and greed that they miss the drama before our very eyes.

V.

The God of all children is presented in Scripture as one with tenacious parenting instincts. Of course there is the waiting, welcoming father of the Prodigal Son (Luke 15). Long before that, however, Israel (this company of slaves) is marked as God's own son, the first born (Exod 4:22), to whose emancipated wellbeing God is committed.

Amid the crisis of exile when Israel as God's beloved child was under threat, this tenacious divine parent as "all in" for the child:

> When Israel was a child, I loved him,
>> and out of Egypt I called my son . . .
>
> How can I give you up, Ephraim?
>> How can I hand you over, O Israel?
>
> How can I make you like Admah?
>> How can I treat you like Zeboiim? (Hos 11:1, 8)

> Is Ephraim my dear son?
>> Is he the child in whom I delight?
>
> As often as I speak against him,
>> I still remember him.
>
> Therefore I am deeply moved for him;
>> I will surely have mercy on him, says the Lord. (Jer 31:20)

> Can a woman forget her nursing child,
>> or show no compassion for the child of her womb?
>
> Even these may forget,
>> Yet I will not forget you. (Isa 49:15)

Tenacious parenting at our border replicates God's deepest tenacity that bends the arc of history toward vulnerable beloved children.

The God of vulnerable children long before anticipated the resolve of Sir Lancelot in Camelot:

> If ever I would leave you, it wouldn't be in summer . . .
> But if I'd leave you, it wouldn't be in autumn . . .
> And could I leave you running merrily through the snow . . .
> If ever I would leave you, how could it be in springtime . . .

Oh no, not in springtime, summer, winter, or fall
No never could I leave you at all.[1]

YHWH sang that song early on for the slaves; and now parents at the border, echoing the Lord of all borders, sing it about their children. And we join them in active resolve. "No never"!

Columbia Theological Seminary
June 30, 2019

---

1. Lerner and Loewe, "If Ever I Would Leave You."

4

The Litigation of Scarcity

THE BIBLICAL CLAIM OF "abundance" is a hard sell in a world that is frightened, insecure, prone to hoarding, and alarmed about running out. The fact that it is a hard sell requires us to think well about how we are now to factor out that claim in our practice and in our preaching.

I. THE DEEP CLAIM

The Bible makes the deep, pervasive, and defining claim that life in God's creation is life that can be lived is a life that can be received and enjoyed in glad abundance. That claim, first, is rooted in the conviction that the God of the Gospel is the creator God who holds the whole world in God's own hand, and wills abundance for all creatures. That claim, second, is grounded in the derivative conviction that God has ordered to be a gift that keeps on giving. The earth is watered,

> giving seed to the sower
> and bread to the eater. (Isa 55:10)

> And God is able to provide you with every blessing in abundance, so that by always having enough of everything, you may share abundantly in every good work. As it is written,
> He scatters abroad, he gives to the poor;
> his righteousness endures forever.

> He who supplies seed to the sower and bread for food will supply and multiply your seed for sowing and increase the harvest of your righteousness. (2 Cor 9:8–10).

This deep claim stretches from its beginning in the initial authorization and empowerment of creation by the creator:

> Let the earth put forth vegetation: plants yielding seed, and fruit trees of every kind on earth that bear fruit with the seed in it . . . Be fruitful and multiply and fill the waters in the seas, and let birds multiply on the earth . . . I have given you every plant yielding seed that is on the face of all the earth, and every tree with seed in its fruit; you shall have them for food. And to every beast of the earth, and to every bird of the air, and to everything that creeps on the earth, everything that has the breath of life, I have given every green plan for food. (Gen 1:11, 22, 29–30)

The claim reaches all the way to the identification of the Good Shepherd who lays down his life for the sake of the sheep: "I came that they may have life, and have it abundantly" (John 10:10). Thus we may consider the entire sweep of the gospel drama—from creation to the specificity of God in Jesus—to be a drama of generous, life-sustaining abundance.

More concretely we might recognize that this sweeping drama of abundance is given narrative specificity in *two great moments of abundance* that, in both instances, contradict the facts on the ground in an exhibit of the creator's capacity to refuse the killing scarcity that is so evident all around.

In the Old Testament the great narrative of abundance is the manna story in Exod 16. That narrative is remembered as having occurred in the "wilderness." The wilderness is marked by two decisive features. On the one hand the wilderness is beyond the reach and control of Pharaoh and his guarantee of food according to his storehouses of confiscation. On the other hand, the wilderness is marked by an absence of viable life support systems. There was there no viable supply of bread! (We may take "bread" as the most elemental requirement for human sustenance as it is the most elemental gift given by the creator.

In this quite remarkable circumstance—beyond Pharaoh and without viable life supports—Israel is surprised by gifts beyond explanation or imagination. First there were quail (Exod 15:13). Third there was water from rock (Exod 17:6)! But second, there was bread! It was just there in the morning after the dew (16:14). It just came (long before grits!). The narrative does not explain anything. The Israelites never expected it, as is evidenced by their wonderment, "What is it?" The Hebrew phrase of the question, *man-hu*, became the name of the bread! The bread is *man-hu-manna- "what is it"*? They wondered when they got the bread. It turned out to be wonder bread! Moses response to their wonderment is terse: "It is the bread that the LORD has given you to eat" (16:15). It is as though Moses wanted to say, "Don't ask for explanations; enjoy the surprise." And they did! Moses instructs, "Gather as much as each of you needs." And they did. Moses did not say "Only two per customer." Each gathered enough to be sated; the bread was administered in perfect abundance:

> Some gathering more, some less . . . Those who gathered much had nothing over, and those who gathered little had no shortage; they gathered as much as each of them needed. (16:17–18)

There was enough; everyone ate to satisfaction:

> He made water flow for you from flint rock, and fed you in the wilderness with manna that your ancestors did not know, to humble you and to test you, and in the end to do you good. Do not say to yourself, "My power and the strength of my own hand have gotten me this wealth." But remember the LORD your God, for it is he who gives you power to get wealth, so that he may confirm his covenant that he swore to your ancestors, as he is doing today. (Deut 8:15–18)

To be sure, the bread of abundance comes with a caveat against greed and hoarding that may be propelled by fear of scarcity. Some failed to heed the warning of Moses. Perhaps not unlike Pharaoh, the great hoarder, they hoarded the bread with the hope of enough for the next day. But of course, gift-bread cannot be stored up. They foolishly stored it up. And 1) it bred worms, 2) it smelled bad, and 3) it melted. The question "What is it" was foolishly answered, "Its mine!" That misunderstanding of wonder bread soured the gift. It did not, however dim the force of the narrative, for that memory of abundance came to occupy the doxologies of Israel:

> He rained down on them manna to eat,
>   and gave them the grain of heaven.
> Mortals ate the bread of angels;
>   he sent them food in abundance. (Ps 78:24–25)

> They asked, and he brought quails,
>> and gave them food in abundance.
> He opened the rock, and water gushed out;
>> it flowed through the desert leek a river. (Ps 105:40–41; see 107:4–9)

Eventually the manna memory became anticipatory for later poets for a good life in the land of free food (Isa 55:1–2).

That paradigmatic Israelite memory of abundance has it counterpart in the gospel narrative that reiterates the story of abundance through the life of Jesus. Jesus was in a "deserted place" (wilderness!); he found there a hungry crowd with "no leisure even to eat" (Mark 6:31). He fed them in a place that was without any viable life support system. He performed his magisterial verbs whereby he provided abundance where there had been none. He voiced his four life-giving verbs:

> He *took* the loaves;
>> He *blessed* the loaves;
>>> He *broke* the loaves;
>>>> He *gave* the loaves!

There is no explanation, only narrative memory, no generalizations, only the immediacy of the moment. But what a moment: all ate! All were filled! There were left-overs of twelve baskets of bread, enough for the twelve tribes of Israel. (Unlike Moses, Jesus seems not have minded good leftovers!)

And then again in Mark 8. Again there was a crowd without enough to eat (Mark 8:2). Again he had compassion. Again he enacted his dominical verbs:

> He *took* the loaves;
>> he *thanked* for the loaves;
>>> he *broke* the loaves;
>>>> he *gave* the loaves.

All ate! All were filled! There were seven baskets of bread left over, enough for the seven nations of the traditional roster of nations beyond Israel.

There was enough *for the twelve tribes*; there was enough for *the seven nations*. There was enough! Since that moment, moreover, the church has reiterated this drama of grateful abundance, uttering his lordly verbs: "He took, he blessed, he broke, he gave." It is a dramatic act that defies the scarcity of the world. Divine compassion, in a sacramental way, refuses the evident scarcity of the wilderness! To paraphrase, On these two narratives hang all the law and the prophets, the gospels and the epistles!

> For you know the generous act of our Lord Jesus Christ, that though he was rich, yet for your sakes he became poor, so that by his poverty you might become rich. (2 Cor 8:9)

I must add a note about the social context of "abundance" in the Bible. The world of the Bible is a small agrarian economy. It consists in peasant agriculture that supported and sustained a small urban population that clustered around the "urban elites" of king, priests, and scribes.[1] This economic reality suggests that abundance consists in agricultural produce, that is, the "grown produce" that sustains life in its most elemental needs.

Such a claim of abundance does not readily or easily transfer from the elemental prospects of a small agrarian economy to an industrial or technological economy that specializes in things manufactured. It is an illusion simply to transfer the assurance of abundance from *grown produce* to *things manufactured* that reach beyond elemental creaturely needs to mastering management. Wendell Berry astutely characterizes the difference between the "periphery" of agriculture and the "center" of industrial-technological order:

> It is still true that the center is supported by the periphery. All human economy is still land-based. To the extent that we must eat and drink and be clothed, sheltered, and warmed, we live from the land. The idea that we have now progressed from a land-based economy to an economy based on information is a fantasy.
>
> It is still true that the people of the center believe that the people of the periphery will always supply their needs from the land and will always keep the land productive; there will always be an abundance of food, fiber, timber, and fuel. That too is a fantasy. It is not known, but is simply taken for granted.
>
> As its power of attraction increases, the center becomes more ignorant of the periphery. And under the pervasive influence of the center, the economic landscapes of the periphery have fewer and fewer inhabitants who know them well and

---

1. Boer, *The Sacred Economy of Ancient Israel*.

know how to care properly for them. Many rural areas are now occupied mostly by urban people.[2]

Thus we must honor the distinction between grown produce and things manufactured. Whereas grown produce evokes wonder, things manufactured invites control. It is not possible, then, to extend the claim of abundance to things manufactured as the news of the Bible focuses singularly on the abundance of grown produce (bread). The Bible pushes us back to the most elemental realties of creatureliness, just as the virus does as well.

II. THE ANCIENT ANGUISH

Of course this assurance of abundance, attested in two narratives of wondrous inexplicable food and reiterated in our recurring liturgical dramas, is too good to be true. It turns out, moreover, often not to be true. We may identify two freighted moments in Israel's memory when the claim of abundance was unmistakably contradicted by facts on the ground. (We may recognize that in Christian tradition Good Friday and especially Holy Saturday are such moments when claims of abundance turned out to be, in the experience of faith, null and void).[3]

First there is no doubt that the wilderness narrative in the Books of Moses is the primary matrix of biblical crisis if scarcity. While the outcome of the narrative is magisterial abundance, the defining reality of wilderness is that there was there no bread, meat, or water. The narrative pivots on the awareness that there is no evidence for or guarantee of abundance. That is why this narrative can be reread in many later circumstances of scarcity. When Israel departed the regime of Pharaoh it came to scarcity!

We can identify at least three textual articulations of scarcity in this dramatic moment when Israel entered the wilderness away from Pharaoh. In the book of Exodus, Israel is only two verses into the wilderness when the complaint begins:

> If only we had died by the hand of the Lord in the land of Egypt, when we sat by the fleshpots and ate our fill of bread; for you have brought us out into this wilderness to kill this whole assembly with hunger. (Exod 16:3)

---

2. Berry, "Local Knowledge in an Age of Information."
3. See Lewis, *Between Cross & Resurrection*.

Amid the scarcity that was life-threatening, they remembered the comfort of Egyptian food. They promptly forgot the pain and anguish of brutalizing slavery and yearned for their good old days. The point is reiterated in Num 14:2–4:

> All the Israelites complained against Moses and Aaron; the whole congregation said to them, "Would that we had died in the land of Egypt! Or would that we had died in this wilderness! Why is the LORD bringing us into this land to fall by the sword? Our wives and our little ones will become booty; would it not be better for us to go back to Egypt?! So they said to one another, "Let us choose a captain, and go back to Egypt.

In their crisis of scarcity they did not recall their glad dancing and singing about emancipation. Now Pharaoh's slave camps looked pretty good. Moses response to those who rebelled against his leadership is remarkable, for he asserts that the present inhabitants of the good land of promise are not to be feared. Indeed they are only "bread for us" (v. 9). "Bread" is on Moses's mind as well, and he is confident that they will come to "bread" soon. While the narrative ends in forgiveness for some (v. 20), Moses is brutally judgmental toward those who yearn for a return to Egypt (vv. 22–23).

The third episode of scarcity is the most poignant. In the book of Numbers, the culinary memory of Egypt is vivid and precise:

> We remember the fish we used to eat in Egypt for nothing, the cucumbers, the melons, the leeks, the onions, and garlic; but now our strength is dried up, and there is nothing at all but this manna to look at. (Num 11:5)

The Egyptian menu is contrasted with the anemic inadequate nourishment of manna . . . or so they say! This time even Moses loses patience with the scarcity and sides with the people against the great Lord of emancipation:

> Why have you treated your servant so badly? Why have I not found favor in your sight, that you lay the burden of all this people on me? Did I conceive all this people? Did I give birth to them, that you should say to me, "Carry them in your bosom, as a nurse carries a sucking child," to the land that you promised on oath to their ancestors? Where am I to get meat to give to all this people? For they come weeping to me and say, "Give us meat to

eat!" I am not able to carry all this people alone, for they are too
heavy for me. (Num 11:11–14)

The scarcity is more than Moses can bear and more than he can resolve. We might expect an empathetic response from the Emancipator. God does take careful note of the lament over scarcity:

> You have wailed in the hearing of the Lord, saying, "If only we had meat to eat! Surely it was better for us in Egypt. (v. 18)

But then God responds with a vindictive promise of abundance that will be savage in causing respiratory problems:

> Therefore the Lord will give you meat, and you shall eat. You shall eat not only one day, or two days, or five days, or ten days, or twenty days, but for a whole month—until it comes out of your nostrils and becomes loathsome to you—because you have rejected the Lord who is among you and have wailed before him, saying, "Why did we ever leave Egypt?" (vv. 18–20)

It turns that YHWH lacks empathy for those who gripe about scarcity. And then the Lord changes the subject from *Israel's scarcity* to a question concerning *God's own power*:

> Is the Lord's power limited? Now you shall see whether my word will come true for you or not. (v. 23)

It is a rhetorical question. YHWH had no wonderment about YHWH's own capacity; nor did Israel. The crisis is resolved by the arrival of abundant quail:

> Then a wind went from the Lord, and it brought quails from the sea and let them fall beside the camp . . . about two cubits deep on the ground. So the people worked all that day and night and all the next day, gathering quails; the least anyone gathered was ten homers; and they spread them out for themselves all around the camp. (vv. 31–32)

But the outcome is an unhappy one, because the anger of the Lord was kindled. They got the food for which they had hoped, but with the abundance they got wrath. They were not careful about what they had asked for! The narrative ends in abundance as did Exod 16. In the end, however, the real issue is not abundance. It is coming to terms with the rule of YHWH. Life will be on YHWH's terms that render the issue of scarcity/

abundance of lesser urgency. As with so much of Israel's faith narrative, the matter is less than satisfactorily resolved.

The other great moment of scarcity is the exilic experience of Israel when its leadership was displaced from its assured security and power. The book of Lamentations is a script for such loss of abundance. While the paradigmatic narrative of Moses receives some good resolve, the book of Lamentations, like real life, characteristically awaits resolve. In Lam 2:12 the voicing of deep grief comes down to food. Even the babies go hungry!

> They cry to their mothers,
>> "Where is bread and wine?"
> as they faint like the wounded in the streets of the city,
>> as their life is poured out on their mothers' bosom. (Lam 2:12)

As elsewhere in these long songs of grief, there is no answer and no resolve. The scarcity is left unaddressed. The crisis is reiterated in Lam 4:4–5:

> The tongue the infant sticks to the roof of its mouth for thirst;
>> the children beg for food,
>> but no one gives them anything.
> Those who feasted on delicacies perish in the streets;
>> those who were brought up in purple cling to ash heaps.

Again it is the "infant" and "the children," the ultimate measure of misery. There is no response. There is no offer of deliverance. There is no sign of old promises of wellbeing or feed. The tone of the whole is one of guilt and punishment. This tone makes this scenario quite unlike the Moses narrative in which there are both bread and forgiveness. There is none of that here, because we have moved from a paradigmatic sketch to real life. And in real life, as the Bible knows, there is scarcity.

The real experienced problem of scarcity means that the voiced grief of the book of Lamentations will remain unresolved and open-ended. This is unmistakably clear in the enigmatic conclusion of the final poem. Tod Linafelt renders the verse this way:[4]

> For if you truly have rejected us,
>> bitterly raged against us . . . (Lam 5:22)

---

4. Linafelt, *Surviving Lamentations*, 60–61.

Linafelt judges that the ending is "left trailing off," "remains unanswered," "remains incomplete," and "is left opening out into the emptiness of God's nonresponse." This cold raw reality of scarcity mocks as a deep challenge to Israel's base-line assumption of abundance. A case can be made that the book of Lamentations receives a response and assurance in Deutero-Isaiah, most prominently in Isa 55:

> Ho, everyone who thirsts,
>   come to the waters;
> and you that have no money,
>   come, buy and eat!
> Come, buy wine and milk
>   without money and without price.
> Why do you spend your money for that which is not bread,
>   and your labor for that which does not satisfy? (Isa 55:1–2)

That, however, is not an adequate answer to the unbearable moment of scarcity that is voiced by Israel. We might wish for a more direct and immediate resolve of scarcity. But we do not get such resolve every time, not for sure, and not in his instance. Not every lived reality is well answered by faith, even by the wonder of wilderness manna. Thus the struggle of "The Deep Claim" and the "Ancient Anguish" is a defining biblical reality and task of faith as it pertains to the real life of the world. The hard work of faith is to adjudicate, in a variety of unyielding circumstances, between the deep claim of faith and the quotidian reality of the world. It is in this clash that we live. That hard work requires that we be, at the same time, *fully trusting in the claim* and that we be *fully honest about the anguish*. It is in such circumstance of scarcity that we find out if we are able to trust, when we know that the reality of our life in the world is not readily overcome by our best mantras of faith.

III. OUR CONTEMPORARY DOUBT

We have inherited the task of adjudicating between the claim of abundance and the anguish of scarcity. The task of adjudicating between grown produce and things manufactured does not aim at an exclusionary either/or. But it also does not seek a "middle way" of finding "balance" between the two. The intent, rather, is to ask about the deepest gifts that come from God and sources of our most elemental satisfactions as God's creatures. While we work at the task, moreover, we have ringing in our ears the verdict of Jesus, "You cannot serve God and wealth (Mammon) (Matt 6:24; Luke 16:13). The matter is urgent among us because we now face, amid the virus, an acute reality of scarcity:

> The pandemic has challenged this view of abundance. We don't have enough tests, masks, ICU beds, ventilators. In the coming months we face shortages of jobs, money, food and basic supplies. Scarcity may not be our theology but it is our reality. How should we think—and—preach about God's overflowing providence in a time of scarcity?[5]

Perhaps that reality should not surprise us. Moses had already declared, "There will never cease to be some in need on the earth" (Deut 16:11). Or more familiarly, "The poor will always be with you" (see Matt 26:11; Mark 14:7; John 12:8). The poor of course are the desperate carriers of scarcity. They always have scarcity first. And even now amid the virus, there are those who experience no scarcity of masks, ventilators, or any other requirement (see David Geffen on his yacht! Or note that professional athletes can get tested any time they want). The matter of scarcity is so ordinary and now so glaring that we may conclude that the arithmetic of Thomas Malthus and David Ricardo is decisive, namely, that the earth cannot sustain in abundance and expansive population. There is not enough to go around. Perhaps so; and if true then our usual theology of abundance (that is the basis of "stewardship" in the church) needs to be radically revised. I am not ready to accept that fatalistic judgment. Here are three thoughts that I have had about the present "pandemic of scarcity."

1. It is important to recognize that for many of us this is the first time that it is our scarcity. We have known by the hearing of the ear about scarcity for a long time, but it was not ours. It was always "some orphan in India" or some "disadvantaged" nation or some "less fortunate" neighborhood remote from us. That remote scarcity has long required our attention, but it has not theretofore been experienced by "us" as a theological crisis. Now however, the scarcity is very close to "us," and cannot be disregarded. Now it is a *white scarcity* while we have been content with scarcity among poor Blacks. The indexes of the pandemic suggest no factoring out by race, no privilege for whites. Now we are at *American scarcity*. We have long judged the US as God's chosen

---

5. From a Prospectus for the future planning of the *Journal of Preachers*.

people, or more "patriotically" made a claim of exceptionalism. Thus scarcity ought to be elsewhere because we are without doubt "the richest nation in the world." Now the scarcity is enough to shake some of our confidence in our ready claim of exceptionalism. I suppose, moreover, that one could even say that this now is *male scarcity*, because the virus is without gender distinction while heretofore it may have been that women were generally or vulnerable.

We now recognize that we face *white scarcity, American scarcity*, and perhaps unusual *male scarcity*. Thus I propose it is not scarcity that evokes a theological crisis. It is rather that it is *our* scarcity, and we can no longer assume privilege and exemption. If this is a correct analysis, then the theological crisis is not the loss of abundance (that always occurs somewhere!) but rather our new circumstance in solidarity with others who have long faced scarcity. Thus the problem is not theological; it is sociological and economic, with the inescapable wonderment, "Who gets what?" and "Who decides who gets what?" We are, as *white Americans* placed in a situation that is wholly unfamiliar to us, so that we may ask, "How do we speak of abundance and scarcity when we find ourselves now in the company of those who have live forever in scarcity?" Our loss of privileged exemption may now cause us to embrace Malthus, who in like manner was informed by social advantage that he found under challenge and threat. This means, I take it, not that abundance is not on offer, but that it is not peculiarly on offer to us, thus exposing an assumed privilege that came with vast and expansive consumer comfort.

2. The matter of abundance and scarcity, claim and anguish, is made more complex by the interplay of *things manufactured* and *growth produced*. As long as we have remained focused on produce grown, we have stayed close to the granular quality of creation and have, perforce, remained close to local neighborly reality. As produce grown has become a salable commodity via agribusiness, we have confused produced growth with things manufactured. As a result even crop produce, gardening, chickens, and cattle have come to be mass produced commodities that have been loosened from the felt rhythms of creation that in turn has slackened the link to the local. As we have made the move to regard *the gifts of creation* as *commodities*, it has been an easy step to conclude that our wellbeing consists in an accumulation of commodities, that is, in things manufactured. The marketers have knowingly recognized that growth produced is not a very marketable item; we see very little advertising for grown produce. What we see, rather,

is marketeering for things manufactured, especially the Big Three of drugs, computers, and cars. Thus we are readily seduced into imagining that the promised abundance of gospel faith consists in things manufactured such as drugs, computers, cars, and masks and ventilators. When reasons according to the ideology of commodity, we can only conclude that we face a season of acute scarcity.

If however, the true abundance of human life, or more largely creaturely life, is in relational reality and organic connection to produce grown, we might judge that our God-given abundance is not in things manufactured but in growth produced. Grown produce has intrinsic to it a neighborly component, whereas things manufactured tend toward private ownership, use, and accumulation. Grown produce, moreover, draws us closer to local intentionality that tells against excessive mobility. It is likely the case that in time to come we will not have an abundance of things manufactured that depend on fossil fuel. Things manufactured of course add to our creaturely comfort and convenience but do not in a commensurate way contribute to happiness, even while they damage and deplete the resources of creation to be needed in coming generations. We may end up, in the familiar words of Harry Emerson Fosdick, "Rich in things and poor in soul."[6] It is perhaps not a given that being "rich in things" need result in "poor in soul," but we know enough and have seen enough that excessive reliance on commodities does indeed diminish our functioning in "the image of God" as responsible overseers of the creation. We may think again about the seductions of an imagined abundance of commodities that invite us away from our creaturely vocation. (Even ventilators, it may turn out, may rob us of the dignity and wellbeing of living toward our deaths in embedded serious companionship. It is entirely likely, dear reader, that in a like circumstance this writer would also want a ventilator).

3. A third interpretive thought has occurred to me. Our excessive embrace of things manufactured is perhaps propelled by "the desires of the flesh." Paul's primary catalogue of "the desires of the flesh" is augmented by two subsequent catalogues:

> Now the works of the flesh are obvious: fornication, impurity, licentiousness, idolatry, sorcery, enmities, strife, jealously, anger, quarrels, dissensions, envy, drunkenness, carousing, and things like these. (Gal 5:19–21)

---

6. Fosdick, "God of Grace and God of Glory."

> They have lost all sensitivity and have abandoned themselves to licentiousness, greedy to practice every kind of impurity... But fornication and impurity of any kind, or greed, must not even be mentioned among you... no fornicator or impure person, or one who is greedy (that is, an idolater) has any inheritance in the kingdom of Christ and of God. (Eph 4:19; 5:3–5)

> Put to death, therefore, whatever in you is earthly: fornication, impurity, passion, evil desire, greed (which is idolatry)... anger, wrath, malice, slander, and abusive language from your mouth. (Col 3:3–8)

These several banned behaviors portray an individual who is completely autonomous without any answerability to God or to neighbor (see Luke 18:4). Brigitte Kahl shows, moreover, that such desires of the flesh are not an innate part of the human person, as much of the Augustinian tradition has insisted, but are rather facets of "the law of Rome," "the combat order of Caesar's empire."[7]

> In an up-front attack on the competitive of system of euergetism/benefactions, which, as we have seen, is a key feature of imperial order in a Roman province like Galatia, "works" are declared to be no longer the showcase of the self in the public race for status... The "new" law of Christ (5:6; 6:2) does not abandon Jewish law as such but rather the competitive and combative hierarchy of self and other that is at the core of Roman imperial *nomos*.[8]

It is an easy and obvious move from the "combat order" of Caesar to the iron law of the market in competitive economics that has been so frankly formulated by Milton Friedman.[9] That "law of the market," as in the "order of Caesar," has presented individual competitiveness as the proper ordering and administration of life resources. It is the self under such a mandate who can ignore the neighbor, and who has no limit on self-possession, self-serving, self-sufficiency, or self-indulgence. We are able to see the "desires of the flesh" at work among us that slots the neighbor as a competitor for scarce goods. Once the insatiable self is made the measure of all things, the satisfaction of appetites becomes defining, the accumulation of goods is irresistible, and the hoarding of surplus goods

---

7. Kahl, *Galatians Reimagined*, 270.
8. Kahl, *Galatians Reimagined*, 271–72.
9. Friedman, *Capitalism and Freedom*.

is inevitable. In the midst of the virus we can see this destructive urge at work wherein the states must compete for needed equipment, only to learn that in the end FEMA has "stolen" masks and ventilators away from the states. And even before that it was a greedy concern to escalate the market that led to the nullification of federal planning for a coming pandemic. It is not difficult to trace the route from such "desires" to policy outcomes that are disastrous. It may be that there are not enough to go around. But we need not draw a conclusion about cosmic scarcity. We need only look at the ideology that propels the desires of the flesh to understand how scarcity appears among us. It may well be that the declaration of Moses concerning "the poor always" is true. It may well be that Malthus and Ricardo are correct. I think not. I think rather that our society is addicted to a fearful greediness that causes scarcity where it need not be. It is unnerving that Paul could declare that those who live by the desires of the flesh "will not inherit the kingdom of God," that is, such anti-neighbor action precludes participation in a coming future of generous wellbeing (Gal 5:21). Such practice assures that there will not be twelve baskets of abundance left over; not even seven!

IV. OUR ALTERNATIVE PROSPECT

In the midst of a predatory economy that means to devour all resources and all vulnerable neighbors, the people gathered around Jesus are committed to the practice of abundance that is characteristically demanding, inconvenient, and decisively counter-cultural.

1. We are participants in a contest between *bean-counters* and *story-tellers*. If we rely on the bean-counters, it is easy enough to see that we live in an economy of scarcity. As a result, many economists, following Friedman, can define economics as a study of "the distribution of scarce resources." We, however, do not permit the bean-counters to have the final say about scarcity and abundance. It turns out that abundance is not arithmetic. It is rather episodic and is sustained by story-tellers who remember for us one-off happenings when abundance inexplicably arrived. Thus:

- abundance is the day bread arrived inexplicably in the wilderness;
- abundance is tale of five loaves and two fish, twice performed;

- abundance is free lunches fixed by a single mom of six in our town who has turned her hamburger joint into free food for needy children;
- abundance is an insurance company that waived premiums in order to protect the unemployed;
- abundance is a government action to provide adequate income for those who cannot pay their rent;
- abundance is a bank that defers or cancels student debt;
- abundance is double-shift nurses and doctors who give themselves over to the virus infected.

Abundance is action that defies the bean-counters and insists that in the deepest part of our common life we are not competitors. We are rather generous sharers who risk resources on behalf of neighbors.

Perhaps storytellers can rarely defeat bean-counters. That, however, is our common vocation in the gospel. We believe that most of the time the bean-counters are not only giving us data but are exercising control. And we refuse, at our best, to remain in such a calculus. That leaves us with the worrisome wonderment, "Are such stories true?" And we do not know. We only risk retelling them because we "love to tell the story." So here is a bottom-line story of the conflict of a bean-counter and an alternative actor.

In 2 Kgs 6:8–23 the King of Syria (Aram) is deployed as a threat to Israel. The King of Syria pursues Elisha, the source of intelligence leaks. His army surrounds Elisha's house. Elisha's servant sees the assemblage of horses and chariots outside the house and is frightened. He can count! He sees how many there are. But Elisha, who regularly defies the bean-counters by appeal to alternative resources, assures his servant: "Do not be afraid, for there are more of us than there are with them" (v. 16). The servant is bewildered. He can count *only two of* "*us*," Elisha and himself! But then the servant has his eyes opened. He saw! "The mountain was full of horses and chariots of fire all around Elisha" (v. 17). Who knew? Well, Elisha knew and then his servant knew, and then the King of Syria came to know. And then the story is kept for us, and we get to decide if the story is reliable enough for us to act alternatively. On such tales of abundance the truth of the gospel depends. Such tales rarely persuade a bean-counter. But it did in the case of the servant; and it might again sometime soon; we never know. And when we are persuaded out of our bean-counting mode, all kinds of astonishingly abundant things happen!

2. What may happen is that we come to see that *growth produced* is a more reliable resource than *things manufactured*. In the Elisha story, the things manufactured are chariots, armor, swords, and all kinds of "might." But the tale culminates with the offer of growth produced, that is, "a great festival" reconciliation, of wine and meat and vegetables that overcame the hostility that had evoked the weapons.

In the midst of the virus we are coming to recognize, here and there, that our wellbeing is not defined principally by things manufactured. They make our life more convenient, to be sure, and sometimes more secure. But they do not bring the kinds of satisfaction we most deeply crave. Thus on one page one day in the *New York Times* we get this remarkable testimony to otherwise:[10]

—Sarah Lyall: The other day we had a (non-COVID-related) health scare at my house, and the great outpouring of sympathy and kindness and practical help that flowed over my phone late into the night and through the next day—I will never forget it. With everything going on, our little group is such a small thing, but it feels like a gig thing. It feels like life-line. It feels like love.

—Katherine Rosman: That was the sole purpose of the get-together, to belt out that song off-key and at the top of our lungs. It was cathartic, it was funny, it was energizing. Then we each returned to the new realities of our homes, families and jobs, clinging to the boost that being unfiltered with your friends can give and which goes on and on and on and on.

—John Branch: It's my heightened sense, especially at night. The stars are brighter than ever, the Big Dipper tipped as if pouring out unfamiliar stars looking to be noticed . . . Critters rustling in the ivy, light rain dripping into the gutters, late-night whispers of my teenage daughter . . . I noticed a spot of grass riffling amid the calm sea of blades. It was an unseen mole, chewing on roots. I am numbed to the outside world but a quarantined superhero of the senses.

—Manny Fernandez: Mrs. Burdock told the [second grade] class she wanted to play a game. She would say a word, and then everyone had to find an object that began with the last letter of that word . . . My daughter tore through rooms . . . Things fall apart. Second grade carries on.

10. *New York Times* (April 21, 2020) A15.

—Taffy Brodesser-Akner: I've seen beautiful things: people coming together, the healthy checking on the sick, the able grocery shopping for the stricken, applause for medical workers, but the thing that has stayed with me the most was two weeks ago, when the bat mitzvah of my dear friends' daughter Rose was cancelled . . . A few of the women who are part of the women-only theater group . . . recorded . . . the extremely melodic introduction to the ceremony of calling her up to Torah. It was the most beautiful thing I'd ever seen . . . the story of a girl's cancelled bat mitzvah became the story of much everyone loved her.

There is no need to be romantic about it; we still use our phones and screens. We still require masks and ventilators. In the midst of that, however, we are drawn to another register of reality that is marked by generous specificities we had not noticed. Our pursuit of things manufactured had caused us not to notice. When we notice, we see gift-giving generosity that comes toward us, even in spite of our obduracy.

3. Paul voices an alternative to "the desires of the flesh." He terms them "the fruit of the Spirit":

> By contrast, the fruit of the Spirit is love, joy, peace, patience, kindness, generosity, faithfulness, gentleness, and self-control. There is no law against such things. (Gal 5:22–23)

These are not self-willed virtues. They are gifts that rush upon us by the work of God's Spirit who refuses to be contained within our fearful ideologies. The bet that Paul makes is that the rush of God's Spirit can override the claims of "the flesh." Or to out it otherwise, the urge of abundance will overcome the fearful drive toward scarcity.

It is quite remarkable that Paul's two catalogues of "the desires of the flesh" (5:19–21) and "the fruit of the Spirit" (5:22–23) are sandwiched by his two symmetrical articulations of what is at stake. Before the catalogues he asserts: "For the whole law is summed up in a single commandment, 'You shall love your neighbor as yourself'" (5:14). And after the catalogues Paul urges: "Bear one another's burdens and in this way you will fulfill the law of Christ" (6:2). The self is deeply and wholly bound to the neighbor; there is no other viable existence.

It is the alternative claim of the gospel (as of the Torah!) that connection to the neighbor is a channel for abundance. It turns out that abundance is not simply a gift or a guarantee. It is at the same time a practice. It is the day-to-day exercise of mobilization of resources and energy for the wellbeing of the neighborhood. That sustained engagement, moreover, generates even more resources. Indeed, even the land is more willing to produce more growth when it is regarded as a creaturely mate according to the fruit of the spirit. Or conversely the land is more grudging when it is treated by commodity-based agribusiness. Creaturely response is more positive and life-sustaining in all its parts of God's world when treated according to the generous intent of the creator.

In this season of scarcity, the gospel claim of abundance stands as a powerful counter-cultural insistence. That insistence does not dispute the reality of serious scarcity. It insists only that scarcity is not the deep truth of our life, and that the practice of abundance is an effective mode of resistance to that scarcity. The gospel thus is an invitation:

—to choose grown produce rather than things manufactured;

—to receive the fruit of the Spirit as an alternative to the desires of the flesh;

—to love and tell the stories well.

It is true that Moses declared, "there will never cease to be those in need on the earth" (Deut 15:11). That verdict is most often taken as a statement of resignation and a relief from any obligation to care about those carriers of scarcity. But that is because it is not often enough noticed that in the same instruction Moses also asserted: "There will be no one in need among you" (v. 4). The move from "never cease on earth" to "no one in need" is accomplished, for Moses, through the practice of debt cancellation, that is, the practice of generous neighborly abundance. There is no doubt that the leverage of debt sustains an economy of scarcity.[11] But it need not be so. Jews and Christians are mandated to otherwise. The defeat of the power of scarcity is not an act of magic from above. It is rather an act of neighborliness from below. It is the sum of the gospel ethic. It is a mandate that is sustained by credible storytellers who love to tell the story.

April 29, 2020

---

11. Graeber, *Debt: The First 5000 Years*.

5

Twin Themes for Ecumenical Singing
The Psalms

PERHAPS THE MOST INTERESTING and difficult interpretive issue in the Old Testament (both in the text itself and in our on-going interpretive work) is the adjudication of alternative, competing textual traditions.

I.

These quite distinctive traditions voice different theological passions and expectations, and they reflect very different socio-political contexts. On the one hand there is an interpretive tradition that is rooted in *memories of Moses and the covenant of Sinai* that received dynamic articulation in the book of Deuteronomy. This tradition sought to bring every aspect of social life under the rule of the emancipatory God of the exodus. This was done by the on-going extension of Torah claims from the basic rule of the Decalogue through the book of Deuteronomy. The social rootage of this tradition was no doubt in village life in such "towns" as Tekoa, Anathoth, Moresheth in Gath, Nazareth, and Bethlehem. These villages were inhabited by agricultural peasants who lived a subsistence existence without any margin of safety or well-being. For that reason these peasants knew of great risks and consequently they knew that life had to be lived attentively. This interpretive tradition expressed the passion of a community what was *rigorously normed*, that knew the right way life should be lived, and understood the hard outcomes of a poorly lived life. That community took the tradition of Deuteronomy as both a narrative base-line and as a continuing process of interpretation.

On the other hand there is the textual tradition generated by the royal-priestly-scribal enterprise of Jerusalem, the city that was the economic engine for surplus wealth and the temple site of liturgical imagination that legitimated an economy of privilege and a politics of hierarchal power. This tradition pivots around God's sure promise to David and the celebrated economic success of Solomon, and dared to appropriate the old divine promise to Abraham to which the chosen in Jerusalem claimed to be heirs. These "heirs" could easily accept that their urban prosperity and security were God's gift to them, and they could readily imagine and expect an ebulliently expansive political economy grounded in God's unconditional fidelity.

These two traditions offered ancient Israel very different competing visions of life and faith; both made claim to be the proper and legitimate version of covenantal faith. The adjudication of these traditions is an on-going enterprise in Scripture. Thus for example, In Ps 89:3–4, 19–20, 28–29, the durability of God's promise to David is celebrated and affirmed. In Ps 132, however, the promise to David is severely modified by the "if" of Deuteronomy:[1]

> The LORD swore to David a sure oath
>> from which he would not turn back:
> "One of the sons of your body
>> I will set on your throne.
> If your sons keep my covenant
>> and my decrees that I shall teach them,
> their sons also, forevermore,
>> shall sit on the throne." (Ps 132:11–12)

The unconditional quality of the divine promise is now circumscribed by Torah obedience.

Given these tensions, we imagine that Israel had the hard work of generating a hymnal for all Israelites. The work must have been done in a committee that eventually produced the canonical book of Psalms. Like every hymnal committee this committee had, perforce, reliable

---

1. On the "if" of Deuteronomy, see Brueggemann, *Solomon*, 139–59.

representatives of these several traditions who advocated for their favorite hymn-Psalms. One could imagine that there were debates and arguments that ended, like every hymnal, in compromise. The outcome of committee work in the book of Psalms reflects that tension at the very outset. Psalm one is reflective of the Moses tradition with phrasing that is clearly reminiscent of Deuteronomy. Psalm 1 is not really a Psalm; it is rather a preface (as in every hymnal) that suggests to users of the hymnal how of the ensuing hymns are to be sung.[2] Thus the hymnal committee proposes that all the Psalms should be sung by a community that is rigorously normed according to the Torah of Moses. That orientation pertains, moreover, even in hymns that do not mention Torah. Along the way the hymnal committee has situated specific Torah hymns at strategic places to reassert the Torah emphasis, notably in Pss 19 and 119.[3] The singing of this community is the acknowledgment that its life consists in living in response to the mandates of Torah with the outcomes that result from such a life of glad obedience.

This Torah piety, however, does not singularly dominate the formation of the book of Psalms. This is evident in the placement of Ps 2, surely treasured by the Jerusalem community and its liturgy. This Psalm introduces into the liturgical imagination of Israel that dramatic moment in which God designates and authorizes "my son," that is, the Davidic king (v. 7). It is anticipated that this newly designated and anointed king in Jerusalem will be dominant in the earth, an anticipation quite alien to the Torah-party but surely cherished by the king-party.

Thus at the outset the book of Psalms voices two modes of faith, life, and hope that run all through the Psalter and the Bible. It is possible that the Torah party was not persuaded by the royal claims made in Ps 2. It is equally thinkable that the king-party was not too much moved by the rigorous norming of the Torah in Ps 1. But both Psalms are there at the outset, making the Psalter an ecumenical book that, like every ecumenical effort, requires attentiveness to voices other than the ones we prefer and with which we are most comfortable.[4]

---

2. Childs, *Introduction to the Old Testament as Scripture*, 516, has noted that in the Western Text of Acts 13:33 the quote from the second Psalm is cited as "the first Psalm." This suggests either Psalm 1 was not in purview so that it was not reckoned as a Psalm but as an introduction. Childs comments on the way in which the two psalms are as offered "a part of the introduction to the whole Psalter."

3. See Mays, "The Place of the Torah-Psalms in the Psalter."

4. It is often noted that the first line of Psalm 1 and the last line of Psalm 2 are parallel; this similarity suggests that the two lines form an *inclusio* that intentionally

I have no wish to impose an anachronism or a caricature on the book of Psalms. Nevertheless it occurs to me that without undue strain, it is possible to identify that continuing tension among us. Thus, for example, imagine villagers, rural folk, who are committed to rigorous, social moral norms of a traditional kind. They may look askance at urban folk who play fast and loose with too many norms, perhaps especially concerning sexuality and money. Conversely we may think of urban folk who "live large" and who find old-fashioned morality from "back home" passé and excessively restraining. Imagine a hymn book committee of *rural conservatives* and *urban liberals* who may make a song book together. Each party is willing, perhaps reluctantly, to join in singing of hymns that the other party treasures. Such an ecumenical enterprise amounts to a recognition that neither party, neither the *rigorous normers of conservatism* nor the *bullish expansionist liberals* can have the final word about the collection. Neither gets to sound the final word of truth. That last truth is found in the God addressed in the singing, the One who outflanks all of our favorite formulations.

II.

Psalm 1 is *transactional* in an assertive confident pedagogical style: good behavior yields good outcomes! The Psalm aims to inculcate the young into a set of certitudes acquired by experience, observation, and revelation. The voice of this Psalm knows about the "wicked, sinners, and scoffers because in a rural village everyone knows about everyone; there is no place to hide. These are observable neighbors who are shiftless and unreliable. One can spot them by their careless way with their livestock, by their indolence in letting mown hay get rained on, by seeing how crooked their rows of maze are, plus rumors of unpaid debts.

Anybody can see what happens to such neighbors. They have crop failure. They renege on bank loans. They lose the farm. Or as the poem avers, "They perish" (v. 6). Soon enough they become hapless renters, tenants who stay only temporarily. And the next spring they must move again and find another place to inhabit temporarily. One can easily notice their specific acts of neglect and irresponsibility. But these specific acts amount, in the horizon of the Psalm, to a way of life, a path to walk. The poem uses an agricultural image to characterize them: "chaff," the

---

binds the two Psalms together.

residue from grain that is light and without substance, blown away by any whiff of wind, no staying power.

The instructive voice of this Psalm does not intend to have any children to grow up this way. It is expected and assumed that children in this family and tribe are on the way to becoming responsible, reliable adults who have appropriated for themselves the norms that have caused this family, tribe, and village to prosper.

Beyond flat instruction the poetry of the Psalm playfully engages a metaphor to aid in the pedagogy. It is this playful metaphor that keeps the poem from becoming excessively didactic. The image is of a flourishing tree fed by a reliable stream of water, a noticeable marker in an arid climate. Such trees stand out in contrast to low-life shrubbery that can barely survive in rocky soil. This pedagogy, with a suggestive imagination, urges its addressees to choose that life. Thus one can hear an echo of Deuteronomy in this pedagogy: "I have set before you life and prosperity, death and adversity . . . Choose life so that you and your descendants may live" (Deut 30:15, 19). This is a once-for-all choice about the direction of one's life. But it is a choice made over and over again in actual lived circumstance that concerns political economy and neighborly infrastructure. It is this "over and over" quality that requires us to sing about it over and over. Thus the meditating "day and night" on Torah is an acute and lively awareness that we live in a normed world that will not be mocked with impunity. This introductory paragraph to the Psalter defines the folk for whom the hymnal is intended. This community consists in prosperous rural land-owners who are savvy about agricultural work, who manage a subsistence income to assure well-being, and who know the rhythms of the soil that are credited to the creator God who presides over the landscape with a rigorous unfailing (so the psalm!) reliability.

While Torah instruction focuses on specific actions, such actions have important social outcomes. This ready capacity for responsible living delineates the limits of the "congregation of the righteous." In a rural community, the membership in a local congregation does not change much from generation to generation because the membership consists in land-owners who manage responsibly and transmit the land in good order to the rising generation. In the end, the Psalm is confident that the creator God is the guarantor of an orderly world wherein seed-time and harvest follow reliably; one must be prepared to engage in and rely upon that orderliness. When one disregards or mocks that order, there are practical costly consequences. It is no wonder that the village engages in a rigorous norming. The world is dangerous. And we know in some great part how it works and what is required of us. Imagine this community of Psalm 1 and the Psalms that follows singing together:

> We plow the fields and scatter the good seed on the land,
> But is fed and watered by God's almighty hand;
> God sends the snow in winter, the warmth to swell the grain,
> The breezes and the sunshine, and soft refreshing rain.[5]

The singing community knows about the work to be done; it also knows the terms through which gifts are given.

By the time we get to Ps 19, another Torah Psalm, we are able to sing the Torah of the Lord is restorative:

> The Torah of the LORD is perfect,
>   reviving the self;
> the decrees of the LORD are sure,
>   making wise the simple;
> the precepts of the LORD are right,
>   rejoicing the heart;
> the commandment of the LORD is pure,
>   enlightening the eyes. (Ps 19:7–8)

The Torah, moreover, is more precious than making money:

> More to be desired than gold, even much fine gold;
>   sweeter also than honey,
>   and drippings of the honeycomb. (v. 10)

One might easily imagine that the "wicked, sinners, and scoffers" would not comprehend this calculus. It is, however, precisely this calculus that calls into being the singing congregation that is joyfully, gladly, obediently at home in the creation that God has ordered toward abundance.

---

5. Claudius, "We Plow the Fields and Scatter." I am astonished to find that the hymn is omitted from most recent hymnals including the new Presbyterian hymnal. That omission is likely the work of "urban elites" who regard "plowing and scattering" as remote from lived reality, alas!

III.

When we read Ps 2, the second introductory Psalm, we are in a very different world. Psalm 2 is daringly *transformational*. It anticipates that the Davidic king in Jerusalem will, by power and with full divine authorization, become dominant in the earth and among the nations of the world. Thus in what must have been a liturgical performance (a liturgical performance likely reiterated with regularity) the Davidic king is invested with the full authority of the creator God to work the will of the creator God among the nations. (Happily for the king the will of the creator God coincides with the wants of the urban elite who support the king)! The Psalm (and its liturgical performance) constitute an act of immense imagination, for the promise of the Psalm is completely disproportionate to the actual power and capacity of the Jerusalem establishment. The Psalm and its performance permitted the urban elites to cluster (as always) around the hope of expansion of commerce and international trade that would produce much surplus wealth.

The only way such extravagant imagination can be sustained is to have the royal claim deeply rooted in the doxological reality of the creator God. Thus behind the royal authorization in vv. 6–7 there is the God who "sits in the heavens" and laughs mockingly at the pretense of the nations that think they can compete with the Davidic king (vv. 4–5). Such defiant pretense by the nations (vv. 1–3), in the horizon of this Psalm, is a bad joke. It is because of the unchallenged authority of the creator God that the Davidic establishment in Jerusalem can make its theo-political claim to power and authority over the nations, a claim echoed in ways we do not notice in the final affirmation of Matt 28:18. This authorization leads to a scenario in which the kings of the nations will "wisely" (v. 10) "kiss the feet" in glad subjugation" (v. 12).

It is clear that in this psalm, a second introduction to the Psalter, we are a very long way from the close transactional reasoning of Ps 1. Here there are no commandments given to the king, no Torah on which to meditate "day and night," no warning about the danger of waywardness, and no thought of "perishing" for disobedience.[6] Now the accent is singularly on the potent capacity of the authorized king to

---

6. The single Deuteronomic attempt to curb royal ebullience by an insistence on Torah provides that the king must attend to the Torah in a way that sounds almost like "day and night": "He shall have a copy of this Torah written for him in the presence of the levitical priests. It shall remain with him and he shall read in it all the days of his life..." (Deut 17:18–19).

work his will on the earth. It is anticipated (as in the parallel liturgical affirmation of Isa 9:7) that "his authority will grow continually" without limit or restraint. We Christians have absorbed this expansionist tone by reading the Psalter in "Messianic" ways, so that the expansionist rhetoric pertains to the rule of Christ.

We may notice three emergences from this introductory Psalm that instruct us to read the Psalter with reference to the transformative capacity of the royal regime. First, there are sprinkled through the Psalter a series of "royal Psalms" that variously reflect the centrality of kings for Israel. Among them is anticipation of royal domination in Ps 110:

> Sit at my right hand
>> until I make your enemies your footstool . . .
>
> The Lord is at your right hand;
>> he will shatter kings on the day of his wrath. (vv. 1, 5)

Remarkably it is the Lord, not the king, who will accomplish this on behalf of the king. Perhaps most important is Ps 72 that affirms that the royal commitment to social justice for the poor and needy will cause the earth to flourish:

> May the mountains yield prosperity,
>> and the hills in righteousness.
>
> May he defend the cause of the poor of the people,
>> and give deliverance to the needy,
>> and crush the oppressor. (vv. 3–4)

Second, as we move through the Psalter we notice that the accent on the human Davidic king ebbs and is displaced by celebration of the divine king, YHWH. In the "Enthronement Psalms" (Pss 96–99) it is anticipated that the dramatic enthronement of YHWH in the Jerusalem temple would bring joy in creation as all parts of creation are restored by the new divine rule. The coming of the divine king is abruptly transformative:

> The LORD is king! . . .
> Let the heavens be glad, and let the earth rejoice
>> let the sea roar, and all that fills it;
>> let the field exult, and everything in it.
>
> Then shall all the trees of the forest sing for joy . . . (96:10–12)

No imagination is required to see that the new rule of God, directly (Ps 96) or through the human king (Ps 72) is transformative of "climate change"!

Third, it is worth noticing that the formula of royal designation in Ps 2:7 ("You are my son") is reiterated in the gospel tradition at the baptism of Jesus (Mark 1:11). The gospel tradition attests the authorization of Jesus as king and messiah by the formula, and thereby draws the Jesus narrative into the orbit of royal claim. The gospel narrative does this, even though Jesus seems to resist that designation, perhaps because he is rooted in the Torah tradition or perhaps because the political risk of such claim could not be made too early: This claim for Jesus

> is already to set up a clash between the "gospel" of the empire and the gospel of the kingdom of God . . . We can hardly, then, read Mark's opening lines without recognizing that the Gospel's central character is on a collision course with Caesar.[7]

When the Psalms are read through the lens of Christological claim (as with Augustine and Bonhoeffer), then the force of Psalm 2 becomes most crucial for our approach to the canonical book of Psalms.[8]

IV.

The committee that compiled the book of Psalms refused to choose between these two introductory Psalms and placed them together at the outset as a required guide. It did that even though there was no doubt strong advocacy by both the Torah party and the king party. If either advocacy had prevailed to the elimination of the other introductory Psalm, we would be invited to read the Psalter in very different ways. In its wisdom, however, the committee refused such an option and insisted that both Psalms must be introductions. Both traditions must be given full voice from the outset, because in an ecumenical enterprise no significant voice must be silenced or eliminated.

Thus as we begin the Psalter we have Psalm 1 that is *compellingly transactional*; it intends, by disciplined obedience, to maintain a steady state of social order without radical disruption. We have alongside Ps 2 that is *powerfully transformative*; it insists that the mobilization of the will of the creator via the Jerusalem establishment will generate an economy

---

7. Hays, *Echoes of Scripture in the Gospels*, 92.
8. Byassee, *Praise Seeking Understanding*.

of prosperous wellbeing. As we read the Psalms, it will be useful for the reader (and the reading congregation) to consider the way in which we ourselves variously tilt toward transactional modes of life and faith, or bend toward transformational modes of life and faith.

In her recent fine book on presidential leadership, Doris Kearns Goodwin has shown that our strongest, most effective US presidents have a capacity for combining *transactional and transformative* modes of work.[9] Thus Lincoln was at his most transformational in the Emancipation Proclamation. But as the film *Lincoln* has made clear, Lincoln had to be transactional by coercion, cajoling, and bribery to win passage of the Proclamation. Likewise Lyndon Johnson was powerfully transformational in his passion for civil rights legislation. But he too had to be his most cunning transactional self to get the bill through Congress. Goodwin has shown that both modes of behavior are required for a viable society. Thus in an early anticipation of Godwin's thesis, our Psalms committee clearly understood that Israel could not choose between the Psalms; Israel had to have both at the very outset of the Psalter.

I can, moreover, imagine yet another dramatic moment in the life of the canonizing committee. It was the occasion when both parties—of Torah and of king—became staggeringly aware that their most treasured faith claims were not fully reliable. The Torah-party had to conclude that rigorous Torah obedience did not fully guarantee good outcomes, so that the wonderment of Job rang true for them:

> Why do the wicked live on,
>> reach old age, and grow mighty in power? (Job 21:7; see Jer 12:1)

These passionate Torah advocates finally had to assert:

> We have not forgotten you,
>> or been false to your covenant.
> Our heart has not turned back,
>> nor have our steps departed from your way,
> yet you have broken us in the haunt of jackals,
>> and covered us with deep darkness. (Ps 44:17–19)

In the same moment, I imagine, the king-party had to recognize that the unconditional divine promise to the king would not hold, even

---

9. Goodwin, *Leadership in Turbulent Times*.

though Psalm 89, a favorite royal hymn, had boasted of divine "steadfast love" toward the king. They had to groan out:

> Lord, where is your steadfast love of old,
>   which by your faithfulness you swore to David? (Ps 89:49)

In that moment of honesty and disillusionment, the committee, with all of its several advocacies, was required to make a leap into new psalms they had not expected to need. As a result, the canonical committee added to its hymnal as many as fifty psalms of lament, protest, and complaint that honesty required of them.[10] In this fresh genre of psalms, Israel (and the committee) did not turn away from YHWH. But they knew, from that moment foreword, that honest faith required more than *determined transactionalism* (as in Ps 1) and more than *buoyant expectation* (as in Ps 2). The outcome is a collection of songs and hymns that explore the full range of human emotion, the full spectrum of historical emergences, and the full repertoire of ways in which the God of all truth can be addressed. In our reading of the Psalms, it is crucial to begin with Pss 1 and 2 and observe our predecessors in faith in their several advocacies. But having done that, it is then essential to ask, what new songs do our context and circumstance require of us now, songs that heretofore we never knew we would need? The challenge is to mobilize the entire repertoire of human emotions, historical emergences, and ways of addressing the God of all truth. This is a much thicker repertoire than timid contemporary lectionary committees have in mind. The old psalm committee was more prescient than most of our present practice; we may benefit from their venturesome psalm-making.

April 19, 2019

---

10. The fullest exposition of the lament psalms we have is by Fredrik Lindstrom, *Suffering and Sin: Interpretations of Illness in the Individual Complaint Psalms.*

6

In the "Thou" Business
The Travail of Biblical Language ... Again

IN WHAT FOLLOWS I will consider the vexed and long-standing contestation between the *covenantal-dialogical rhetoric* of the Bible and the alternative of *Cartesian-modernist rhetoric* that is everywhere around us. That contestation, so it seems to me, now has peculiar urgency among us. My current interest in this subject is triggered, most immediately and quite practically, by the bewildered comment of a "progressive" Protestant layperson who said, in innocence, "Since none of us believe all this YHWH-stuff, what are we to do with the Bible?" My interest, consequently, is a quite practical one as well, because there can hardly be any doubt that the rhetoric we employ yields the world in which we live. Or as Paul Ricoeur has programmatically stated, "Symbol gives rise to thought."[1] Or to paraphrase, the way we imagine (and so utter) is the way we will live. While the problem of what someone who is shaped by Cartesian-modernist rhetoric is to do with covenantal-dialogic rhetoric may be peculiarly and currently acute in progressive (liberal) Protestantism, I submit that it is a deep issue finally for Jewish and Christian faith and more broadly for our society, precisely because the rhetoric we utilize will generate the world that is available and compelling to us.

I will develop my argument in four moves. First, in an extended section I will consider how the language of "Thou" permeates the text

---

1. Ricoeur, *The Conflict of Interpretations*, 288, 296–303.

of Israel, without which Israel cannot say what it wants to say. Second, I will consider the interruption of that rhetoric by the alternative rhetoric of modern Enlightenment reason. I will consider the ways in which that modern reason and rhetoric have bequeathed to us a certain kind of anxiety-ridden world; finally I will reflect on the task of the recovery of "Thou" language and what is at stake in that recovery.

I.

There is no doubt that the Bible is deeply and resolutely committed to personal/interpersonal language that Martin Buber has characterized as "I–Thou."[2]

1. Thus YHWH, the creator of heaven and earth and the deliverer of Israel, is addressed as "Thou" and is credited with being as lively character who has the undoubted capacity for decisive agency.

On the one hand, YHWH is the "You" of Israel's hymns of praise and songs of thanksgiving. As Claus Westermann has shown, many such songs are "descriptive" of God in the third person and speak of God's actions and attributes.[3] But more visceral are the "declarative" songs that address God directly:

> I love you, O LORD, my strength. (Ps 18:1)

> I will extol you, O LORD, for you have drawn me up,
>   and did not let my foes rejoice over me.
> O LORD my God, I cried to you for help,
>   and you healed me.
> O LORD, you brought up my soul from Sheol,
>   restored me to life from among those who had gone down
>   to the Pit . . .
> You have turned my mourning into dancing;
>   you have taken off my sackcloth and clothed me with joy.
>   (Ps 30:1–3, 11)

---

[2]. Buber's work is defining for the topic of the dialogical. See *Between Man & Man*, and *I and Thou*.

[3]. Westermann, *Praise and Lament in the Psalms*, 116–35. His analysis has been greatly supplemented by the extended discussion of Miller, *They Cried to the Lord*, 178–232.

> For you, O God, have tested us;
> > you have tried us as silver is tried.
> You have brought us into the net;
> > you have laid burdens on our backs;
> you let people ride over our heads;
> > we went through fire and through water;
> yet you have brought us out to a spacious place. (Ps 66:10–12)

> But you, O Lord, are enthroned forever;
> > your name endures to all generations.
> You will rise up and have compassion for Zion,
> > for it is time to favor it.
> > the appointed time has come. (Ps 102:12–13)

And even descriptive Psalms that speak of YHWH in the third person credit YHWH with decisive agency:

> The Lord upholds all who are falling,
> > and raises up all who are bowed down.
> The eyes of all look to you,
> > and you give them their food in due season.
> You open your hand,
> > satisfying the desire of every living thing.
> The Lord is just in all his ways,
> > and kind in all his doings.
> The Lord is near to all who call on him,
> > to all who call on him in truth.
> He fulfills the desire of all who fear him;
> > he also hears their cry, and saves them.
> The Lord watches over all who love him.
> > But all the wicked he will destroy. (Ps 145:14–20; see 146:7–9)

Thanks tends to be more specific than praise, and therefore the intimate addresses of "you" seems natural and appropriate:

> See, I have not restrained my lips,
> > as you know, O Lord.

> I have not hidden your saving help within my heart,
>> I have spoken of your faithfulness and your salvation;
> I have not concealed your steadfast love and your faithfulness
>> from the great congregation. (Ps 40:9–10)

> I give thanks to you, O Lord, with my whole heart;
>> before the gods I sing your praise;
> I bow down toward your holy temple
>> and give thanks to your name for your steadfast love
>> and your faithfulness,
>> for you have exalted your name and your word above everything.
> On the day I called, you answered me,
>> You increased my strength of soul.
> All the kings of the earth shall praise you, O Lord,
>> for they have heard the words of your mouth. (Ps 138:1–4)

The praise and thanks of Israel constitute speech acts whereby Israel gladly cedes itself over to God in wonder (as in praise) and in gratitude (as in thanks). These self-transcending and self-yielding acts are clearly evoked by and aimed toward a remarkable character who has both a narrative past and a promised future with Israel.

On the other hand, the "Thou" language of Israel is even more direct and intense in Israel's poetry of lament, complaint, and protest. The second person pronoun figures large in Israel's accusations against God; for the simple language of prayer dos not linger over secondary causes, but readily attributes trouble to God as the primary cause. Perhaps most familiar and famous is the "unredeemed" speech of Psalm 88:

> You have put me in the depths of the Pit,
>> in the regions dark and deep.
> Your wrath lies heavy upon me,
>> and you overwhelm me with all our waves.
> You have caused my companions to shun me;
>> You have made me a thing of horror to them.
> I am shut in so that I cannot escape . . .
> O Lord, why do you cast me off?
>> Why do you hide your face from me?

> Wretched and close to death from my youth up,
> > I suffer your terrors; I am desperate.
> Your wrath has swept over me;
> > your dread assaults destroy me.
> They surround me like a flood all day long;
> > all sides they close in on me.
> You have caused friend and neighbor to shun me;
> > my companions are in darkness (Ps 88:6–8, 14–18)

And of course the petitionary summons to God that God should respond and intervene are in the imperative of the second person. Israel exhibits stunning courage in addressing God in imperatives, a mode of speech that I characterize as provisional role reversal in which Israel seeks to command YHWH, a role reversal in urgency that is commensurate with the speaker's dire straits:

> Rise up, O Lord!
> > Deliver me, O my God! (Ps 3:7)

> O Lord, do not rebuke me in your anger,
> > or discipline me in your wrath.
> Be gracious to me, O Lord,
> > for I am languishing;
> O Lord, heal me,
> > for my bones are shaking with terror.
> My soul is also struck with terror,
> > while you, O Lord—how long?
> Turn, O Lord, save my life;
> > deliver me for the sake of your steadfast love.
> For in death there is no remembrance of you;
> > In Sheol who can give you praise? (Ps 6:1–5).

> O Lord, my God, in you I take refuge;
> > save me form all my pursuers,
> > and deliver me . . .

> Rise up, O LORD, in your anger;
>> lift yourself up against the fury of my enemies;
> awake, O my God;
>> you have appointed a judgment (Ps 7:1, 6)
>
> For you have maintained my just cause;
>> you have sat on the throne giving righteous judgment.
> You have rebuked the nations,
>> you have destroyed the wicked;
>> you have blotted out their names forever and ever.
> The enemies have vanished in everlasting ruins;
>> their cities you have rooted out;
> the very memory of them has perished ...
> Rise up, O LORD! Do not let mortals prevail;
>> let the nations be judged before you. (Ps 9:4–6, 19)
>
> Rise up, O LORD; O God, lift up your hand;
>> do not forget the oppressed. (Ps 10:12)
>
> Contend, O LORD, with those who contend with me;
>> fight against those who fight against me!
> Take hold of shield and buckler,
>> and rise up to help me!
> Draw the spear and javelin against my pursuers;
>> say to my soul, "I am your salvation." (Ps 35:1–3)

The examples of this mode of prayer are nearly limitless. They voice an intensity, a connectedness, and a leverage that are possible only in the direct address of dialogic speech. Thus all the way from exuberant praise through aggressive imperative to energetic gratitude, all the way from praise through lament to thanks, Israel addressed God in intensely personal terms and could do so in no other terms.

2. More than that, the "Thou" of God can speak as an "I," a practice of self-announcement, self-resolve, and agency. While such divine articulation is, perforce, mediated through human rendering, the rhetoric itself is recurringly direct and without any footnotes that qualify by

acknowledging human mediation. YHWH is a robust, defining character in the rhetoric and imagination of Israel.

God is self-affirming and self-celebrating in self-praise. God unembarrassedly offers self-doxology in which YHWH struts before the nations and before the other gods.

> When the poor and needy seek water,
>   and there is none,
>   and their tongue is parched with thirst,
> I the Lord will answer them,
>   I the God of Israel will not forsake them.
> I will open rivers in the bare heights,
>   and fountains in the midst of the valleys;
> I will make the wilderness a pool of water
>   and the dry land springs of water.
> I will put in the wilderness the cedar,
>   the acacia, the myrtle, and the olive;
> I will set in the desert the cypress,
>   the plane and the pine together,
> so that all may see and know,
>   all may consider and understand,
> that the hand of the Lord has done this,
>   the Holy One of Israel has created it. (Isa 41:17–20)

> I, I am the Lord,
>   and besides me there is no savior.
> I declared and saved and proclaimed,
>   when there was no strange god among you;
>   and you are my witnesses, says the Lord.
> I am God, and also henceforth I am He;
>   there is no one who can deliver from my hand;
>   I work and who can hinder it? (Isa 43:11–13)

> I am the Lord, who made all things,
>   who alone stretched out the heavens,

>   who by myself spread out the earth …
> who says of Jerusalem, "It shall be inhabited,"
>   and of the cities of Judah, "They shall be rebuilt …" (Isa 44:24–26)

> My purpose shall stand
>   and I will fulfill my intention,
> calling a bird of prey from the east,
>   the man for my purpose from a far country.
> I have spoken, and I will bring it to pass;
>   I have planned it, and I will do it. (Isa 46:10–11)

This is indeed a "Magnificat" through which God magnifies God's own self. The "I" utterances are not only world-defining; they are also world-disrupting. The divine utterance dramatically changes everything for Israel who hears the doxology.

God's capacity for self-praise has a counterpoint in God's impatience and irritation with all that does not conform to YHWH's self-celebrating governance. Thus the "I" of YHWH resounds in oracles of judgment wherein God resolves to take action to reclaim governance where it has been diminished or disregarded. Thus in the exodus narrative, "I will gain glory for myself over Pharaoh and his army, and the Egyptians will know that I am the Lord" (Exod 14:4, 17). The niph'al form of the verb *kbd* ("glory") serves well that the God who self-declares effectively acts. Prophetic utterance exhibits YHWH in direct intervention:

> Therefore I will take back my grain in its time,
>   and my wine in its season;
> and I will take away my wool and my flax,
>   which were to cover her nakedness.
> Now I will cover her shame in the sight of her lovers,
>   none shall rescue her out of my hand.
> I will put an end to all her mirth,
>   her festivals, her new moons, her sabbaths,
>   and all her appointed festivals.
> I will lay waste her vines and her fig trees,
>   of which she said,

> "These are my pay
> > which my lovers have given me."
> I will make a forest,
> > and the wild animals shall devour them.
> I will punish her for the festival days of the Baals . . . (Hos 2:9–13)

Or in the catalogue of curses in Amos:

> I gave cleanness of teeth . . .
> > and I also withheld the rain from you . . .
> I struck you with blight and mildew;
> > I laid waste your gardens and your vineyards . . .
> I sent among you a pestilence after the manner of Egypt
> > I killed your young men with the sword;
> I carried away your horses;
> > and I made the stench of your camp go up into your nostrils . . .
> I overthrew some of you as when God overthrew Sodom and
> > Gomorrah. (Amos 4:6–11; see 8:9–10; Jer 5:14–17)

In the cadences of Jer 51:20–23, the "with you" suggests a mediating agency, but the rhetoric is dominated by the divine "I":

> with you I smash nations,
> > with you I destroy kingdoms,
> with you I smash the horse and its rider;
> > with you I smash the chariot and the charioteer;
> with you I smash man and woman;
> > with you I smash the old man and the boy;
> with you I smash the young man and the girl;
> > with you I smash shepherds and their flocks;
> with you I smash farmers and their teams;
> > you I smash governors and deputies. (vv. 20–23)

And perhaps the most extreme self-resolve:

> I will stop you from playing the whore, and you shall also make no more payments. So I will satisfy my fury on you, and my jealousy shall turn away from you; I will be calm, and will be angry no longer. (Ezek 16:41b–42)

Remarkably the divine "I" of self-praise and of judgment is capable of reversal of field, to pledge one's self to a promise-filled future wrought only by the generosity of divine resolve through the processing of divine pathos:

> How can I give you up; Ephraim?
> > How can I hand you over, O Israel? ...
> My heart recoils within me;
> > my compassion grows warm and tender.
> I will not execute my fierce anger;
> > I will not again destroy Ephraim;
> for I am God and no mortal,
> > the Holy One in your midst,
> > and I will not come in wrath. (Hos 11:8–9)

> Is Ephraim my dear son?
> > Is he the child I delight in?
> As often as I speak against him,
> > I still remember him.
> Therefore I am deeply moved for him;
> > I will surely have mercy on him,
> > > says the Lord. (Jer 31:20)

On such a basis of a complex interior life that the divine I resolves to restore Israel fully and to revivify creation that has been defeated and lost through divine anger:

> I will seek the lost, and I will bring back the strayed, and I will bind up the injured, and I will strengthen the weak, but the fat and the strong I will destroy. I will feed them with justice. (Ezek 34:16)

> I will save you from all your uncleannesses, and I will summon the grain and make it abundant and lay no famine on you. I will make the fruit of the tree and the produce of the field abundant, so that you may never again suffer the disgrace of famine among the nations. (Ezek 36:29)

> I am going to open your graves, O my people; and I will bring you back to the land of Israel ... I will place you on your own soil; then you shall know that I the Lord have spoken and will act, says the Lord. (Ezek 37:12–14)

In every dimension, the self-declaration of YHWH in a first person pronoun matches the second person address of Israel who does not doubt the reality of the connection. Thus Israel can discern in its life the making, the unmaking, and the remaking of all reality by the agency of YHWH. Its rhetoric exhibits an awareness that every facet of this drama of death and life is wrought through an agency other than its own. It is, perhaps, not so difficult to acknowledge the limited capacity of human agency; but it is an act of immense chutzpah of the highest order to dare to give name and voice to the character of freedom and fidelity on which everything depends. There are, to be sure as Fretheim observes, many cautions and qualifications in the text to such voicing of divine agency; but the sum of the rhetoric is clear on the point.

The outcome of such sustained rhetoric is that the world is rendered in a dialogic way in which the self-announcement of Israel is matched and overmatched by the self-announcement of God. Faith is the capacity and readiness to participate fully and confidently in that on-going exchange, an exchange that has become the substance of memory and of hope, and of buoyancy in the present. That ongoing exchange, moreover, is a bilateral practice of fidelity, and of freedom that can take the form of infidelity. Both parties are, in such rhetoric, pledged in fidelity; and amid the vagaries of history both parties become subject to critique for fidelity violated. On the one hand, Israel can, in its nadir of displacement, rally in this way:

> The steadfast love of the LORD never ceases,
>   his mercies never come to an end;
> they are new every morning;
>   great is your faithfulness. (Lam 3:22–23)

In that same crisis, on the other hand however, Israel can in bewilderment wonder:

> Lord, where is your steadfast love of old,
>   which by your faithfulness you swore to David? (Ps 89:49)

The I of Israel addresses the Thou of YHWH and the I of YHWH addresses the Thou of Israel; that mutual address yields risk and gift and loss and always lively engagement. In the depth of the crisis of fidelity, YHWH can both admit and reassure. The divine admission consists in the first two lines of the double verse:

> For a brief moment I abandoned you ...
> In overflowing wrath for a moment
> > I hid my face from you. (Isa 54:7a, 8a)

The reassurance comes in the two lines that follow those two lines:

> But with great compassion I will gather you ...
> But with everlasting love I will have compassion on you,
> > says the LORD, your Redeemer. (Isa 54:7b, 8b)

Even though divine wrath "overflows," the steadfast love outruns it in its everlasting durability. To be a faithful participant in the covenantal-dialogical relationship each party must be willing to subject the other and to be subject themselves to charges of fidelity and infidelity. A faithfulness that is inherently open to infidelity is necessary not only because each party has the freedom to violate the terms that define fidelity, but also because the terms that define fidelity remain open to transformation, either by the vagaries of history or the freedom of each party. When Israel calls on God to show God's faithfulness once again to them in exile, their petition is undoubtedly for a different faithful act than it was when they petitioned God for faithfulness during the monarchic period. This dialogic engagement is the primary speech of Israel and of the God of Israel. It has become, in due course, the primary speech of the church, divine speech that the church says came to be "enfleshed."

II.

There is no doubt, moreover, that what is modeled as divine "Thou" language in the Psalms and as divine "I" speech in prophetic oracles persists in Israel's narratives and historiography. Consequently YHWH is portrayed in Israel as a lively character and effective agent in the historical process, capable of emancipation and emancipatory action, and not subject to the rulers or the rules of the day. In the rhetoric of Israel, this is a God who acts in transformative ways.

I have taken so much time with so many texts in order to underscore the way in which this dialogic rhetoric is characteristic and defining for the imagination of Israel and so for the practice of its life.[4] I have taken

---

4. It is now fashionable in scholarship to bash the "urban elites" who, in the later period assembled the Old Testament. No doubt there is such an influence that helped to shape the text. And no doubt the religious practice of ancient Israel was pluralistic.

so long with so many text in order to focus on the fact that in the modern Western world, the credibility and effectiveness of this dialogic rhetoric has been seriously interrupted and disrupted. That interruption/disruption has occurred with the rise of modern rationality that was, in some sense perhaps, a response to the sectarian failure of European Christian theology in the seventeenth century with its quest for an alternative rhetoric and an alternative practice of faith and reason.[5] In that axial moment in Western history, the explorations of Descartes and the genius of Newton converged to produce a world that was mathematically exacting, that was universal in its credibility, and that made the world ordered and predictable in a mechanical way.[6] That ordering, functioning to produce manageable knowledge of the world, served the expansionist propensity of the European powers in the pursuit of economic domination through exploration and colonialization.

One consequence of such a rationality that carried all before it was that the dialogic logic of faith, Jewish and/or Christian, was judged to be primitive and pre-rational, a logic that could yield only a world of superstition.[7] Thus modern rationality produced, instead of such superstition, a generic mode of "religion" in its quest for universal truth and, as James Buckley has shown, out of such generic universal categories Christian faith was to be defended in the early modern period in distinctly non-Christian categories, that is, according to the closest reasoning that conformed to the mathematical requirements of Cartesian, Newtonian reason. Seen from that perspective, the practice of dialogic language seemed irrelevant and foolish. Such speech constitutes rhetoric freedom and fidelity. Clearly modernist categories cannot not allow for such daring freedom that is seen to violate what passes for symmetrical inviolate "universal order." That perspective has no patience for fidelity and the risk of infidelity, when everything can be safely reduced to reasonableness that could yield certitude. I deliberately interface and contrast fidelity and certitude. Because of a confusion of categories, the hunger for fidelity is often mistaken to be a quest for certitude. That confusion leads

---

But insofar as ancient Israel was understood as the people of YHWH, such a defining imagination may well have been broad and deep across the spectrum of subcommunities that constituted Israel. There is nothing narrowly elite in such an act of theological imagination.

5. On the impetus of such cultural anxiety, see Bordo, *The Flight to Objectivity*.
6. See Buckley, *At the Origins of Modern Atheism*.
7. Buckley, *At the Origins of Modern Atheism*, 207–8.

to the seeking for a relational reality by reducing it to a cognitive claim, a reduction that misleads and distorts, and fails to satisfy.[8]

The result of this disruption as concerns Scripture study was deep and all-inclusive. It resulted in a history-of-religions approach, so that all faith articulations, including that of dialogic practice, came to be seen as nothing more than human imagination and human projection. Resistance to such *historical relativism* in turn evoked *absolutist propositional language* that eventually became fundamentalist. Such scholastic absolutism was cast in the same rationalistic categories, so that both the relativists and the absolutists confirmed and adhered to the requirements of modern reason. The outcome was and continues to be antagonism between *eighteenth century absolutists* and *nineteenth century relativists* that we now label as *fundamentalism* and *liberalism*.

That crisis in Scripture study was acknowledged only belatedly, notably in the remarkable, brief article of Langdon Gilkey in 1961 in which he spoke of "The Travail of Biblical Language."[9] Gilkey argued that biblical rhetoric about "the God who acts" struggles mightily to be intelligible. In his attempt to locate language that would adequately express universal and immanent meaning, Gilkey concluded that the language of "God who acts" is unintelligible. It is impossible to overstate the influence of Gilkey's article and his line of reasoning in the wake of the so-called Biblical Theology Movement, with particular reference to the work of Gerhard von Rad and G. Ernest Wright.

It was not much noticed that Gilkey's argument, without acknowledgment or self-awareness on his part, simply took for granted that "intelligibility" meant and had to mean conformity to the Enlightenment rationality rooted in Descartes and Newton. That is, such mathematical predictability precluded any thought or speech about divine agency that could violate such order. Consequently, the dialogic rhetoric of biblical faith turns out to be nonsense, that is, nonsense from the angle of modernity. Since the demise of the so-called Biblical Theology Movement, interpreters have worked overtime to find other ways of making credible the biblical rhetoric of I–Thou that offers YHWH as agent and character.

I suggest two extrapolations from this wholesale disruption. On the one hand, the "character of God" has been transposed from an active subject to a harmless object that is no more than an image, or an icon

---

8. On the relational risks of fidelity, as contrasted with the flat offer of certitude, see Moltmann, *Theology of Hope*.

9. Gilkey, "Cosmology, Ontology, and the Travail of Biblical Language."

or an idol that is completely without capacity for agency. The disposal of YHWH as agent echoes the cynical verdict reported by Zephaniah:

> The Lord will not do good,
>> nor will he do harm. (Zeph 1:12)

This articulation of the irrelevance of God as object is echoed in the Psalmic characterization of idols who cannot make any impact on their environment:

> Their idols are silver and gold,
>> the work of human hands.
> They have mouths, but do not speak;
>> eyes, but do not see.
> They have ears, but do not hear;
>> noses, but do not smell.
> They have hands, but do not feel;
>> feet, but do not walk;
>> they make no sound in their throats. (Ps 115:4–7)

And then in a move that would move from a Marxist heaven to a Marxist earth:

> Those who make them are like them;
>> so are all who trust in them. (v. 8)

That is, we become like that which we worship (see Jer 2:4; Hos 9:10). And if we worship a flat object, we become objects and not subjects in our own history. And of course, power "from above," divine or human, prefers us not to be subjects of our own history. The reference to "silver and gold," moreover, suggests the reduction of agency to commodity (Ps 115:5). In the modern world, that reduction that makes God impotent causes God to be banished from the public domain and public relevance and consigned to the safety of interpersonal interactions, thus a major abandonment of the claims of biblical faith.

On the other hand, the vacuum left by the loss of dialogic rhetoric, and consequently the loss of a "significant Other," has been occupied by the "turn to the subject." As a result, the "I" of human agency takes up all the space and energy and yields an unfettered human freedom, unfettered in its exploitation of the environment (now no longer "creation") and the exploitation of human persons (now no longer "neighbor"). The loss of dialogic articulation, rendered impossible modernist rationality, has led to complete abdication of dialogic capacity, either before the coldness of absolute reality that is unbending, unengaging, and unresponsive, or before a complete conquest of reality by human ingenuity without answerability to anyone for anything. Either cold absoluteness or totalizing subjectivity leaves no possibility of mutual engagement of the kind that belongs to dialogic speech and life.[10]

III.

This disruption of dialogic speech and faith has two practical outcomes that we may consider. On the one hand, the outcome of unfettered human freedom has led to an unrestrained and undisciplined human control and exploitation of all visible reality. If knowledge is power, as Bacon averred, then the pursuit of power is advanced by the remarkable capacity for knowledge appropriated in unfettered freedom, a knowledge enacted through limitless scientific imagination that is, in turn, generative of unlimited technological administration. The immediate and visible outcome of the loss of the dialogical is a technological rampage in the interest of control and an effort at self-sufficiency and self-security. Thus the continuing threat of nuclear damage (now not from bombs but from power plants), the endless thirst for energy that produces such crises as the Gulf oil spill, and the onslaught of global warming that jeopardizes the health of creatureliness are not aberrations but are the playing out of the extremity of the human eagerness for technological control.[11]

---

10. The misconstrual of biblical testimony in the modern period has led to the exploitation of the earth, on which see Wybrow, *The Bible, Baconism, and Mastery over Nature*. Wybrow's argument is important because in recent time the Bible has been credited with the invitation to "have dominion" over the earth. Wybrow shows in a clear way that it is the objectification of nature in the modern period that has provided the impetus for such an abuse of the earth.

11. Goodchild, *Theology of Money*, 48, 57, 81, 84, has seen the intimate connection between the instability of the environment and the end of modernity, a connection he sees because modernity depends above all on stability:

> The end of modernity will be met by climatic instability, fuel poverty, food shortages, disease, social unrest, conflict, and war ... Once nature is no longer stable it cannot be effectively represented and mastered; once concepts are no longer stable, political decisions can no longer be taken according to principles or pragmatic considerations ... *Economy and ecology are mathematically incompatible* ... The problem of the

Zygmunt Bauman, moreover, has been able to argue, credibly, that even the Shoah in Germany with its amazing technological capacity and organizational finesse was not an aberration of evil in a civilized world, but was in fact a part of the end-game of modernism.[12] Thus the capacity for human brutality now on such visible, large scale is a counterpoint to unbridled technology that can mobilize power for control at the cost of all things human. That mobilization, moreover, depends on an economic practice that is void of covenantal, dialogical restraint. The concentration of large wealth can manage the political process and render social, covenantal control over technology null and void.

I should add an important qualifier to this broadside against technological aggression. Clearly this is not to critique much of the current scientific enterprise, especially in the Neurosciences and the Life Sciences that are alert to the plasticity of the natural world and that ponder the ways in which the that world is wired and re-wired. An important distinction must be made between thin technological positivism that lacks self-criticism and scientific ventures that are open to the surprise and wonder of the natural world in which new gifts emerge beyond our flattened expectations. My impression is that such flat positivism more likely grips those who quest for certitude than those who attend to the complex and generative reality of the world that is in front of us.

On the other hand, the crisis of technological reductionism is matched by a theological obtuseness that has in concrete ways reduced faith to modernist rationality. That reductionism is evident, of course, in fundamentalist circles that blithely sign on for the technological-capitalist engine of totalism. But more important, in my judgment, is the fact that theological "progressives" shiver in aversion to "an interventionist God" who may speak and act freely to upset the carefully arranged orderliness of a world under safe management. Such "progressives" cannot entertain the thought that of a God who is free or faithful or sovereign enough to assert purpose in the real world. It is impossible in such a purview to imagine a dialogical, covenantal exchange in which there really is a voice and agent on the other side that is other than our own. The practical outcome of such theological reductionism is to "down-size" the mystery of God to modernist proportion so that there is no meaningful

---

clash between economic growth and ecological finitude derives from a capitalist system that is based on perpetual growth.

12. This judgment was made by Horkheimer and Adorno, *The Dialectic of Enlightenment*, and more recently by Bauman, *Modernity and Holocaust*.

theological dimension to human discernment or practice. There is then in fact nothing left to say that might critique, restrain, or summon the self-serving system of control that is beyond criticism or alteration. The God "approved" in such context "will not do good or do evil"!

IV.

Given such a disruption of dialogic rhetoric and the human crisis that arises with that disruption, the hard work of theological interpretation amid the closed system of modernism leaves us with two tasks, the critical and the constructive.

The critical task, I suggest, is to think clearly about the cost and consequences of the anti-dialogical legacy that is indispensable for the world of knowing human control. Gilkey was preoccupied with "The Travail of Biblical Language." It may now be time to reverse his proposition to consider the "Travail of Modernist Language." That is, the work is to consider the deficits of such modernist rhetoric and the impossibly hard work such rhetoric has to do in order to carry more than it is able to carry. Specifically the transposition of our rhetoric from dialogue to rational control has meant the loss of the categories of freedom, fidelity, and responsibility, and inevitably the loss of the notion of neighbor or neighborhood, that is, nothing less than the disappearance of "the common good."[13] The "turn to the subject," that is, the preoccupation with self, or more specifically "the possessive self," as the only agent, has yielded an autonomous agent who is not organically connected to any other.[14] The ultimate loss in such rhetoric of the autonomous self is the loss of the "holy Other" who eagerly engages the world and its creatureliness or, as Israel puts it, "The Holy One in your midst" (Hos 11:9).[15] The loss and the gap left by the loss are perhaps signaled by the recognition of Fukuyama that "trust" is indispensable for the viable working of society.[16] To be sure, Fukuyama, in good Enlightenment fashion, tries to quantify the requirement of "trust," an ironic juxtaposition of the dialogic (trust) and

---

13. See my exploration of the theme of "the common good" in biblical perspective, *Journey to the Common Good*.
14. See Macpherson, *The Political Theory of Possessive Individualism*.
15. See Eichrodt, "The Holy One in Your Midst."
16. Fukuyama, *Truth: The Social Virtues and the Creation of Prosperity*.

monologic (quantified) modes of reality, an effort that misunderstands trust, but at least it is an acknowledgment of that requirement.

But the more important work in the emergency is the recovery of dialogic rhetoric that at bottom can generate a very different practice of humanness in the world. The recovery of dialogic reality is the fundamental burden of Karl Barth in his explosive commentary on Romans. In that commentary Barth saw that the only ultimate and genuine dialogue depends on the presence and participation of the Holy One of Israel.[17] Without that voice from the other side, Barth saw that there can be no dialogue of an ultimate and defining kind. Barth witnessed, after the witness of Paul, to the shape and quality and order of reality that refused and violated all the reductions of monologue. The legacy of Barth has most recently been brought to terse expression by Robert Jenson:

> It is time and past time for the church to say without hedging that modernity has it backward. Few would want to eschew modernity's many material and political blessings, but the way in which modernity related truth and tradition is now manifest as the great error that it was, and indeed, as culturally and even demographically suicidal error . . . We must summon the audacity to say that modernity's scientific/metaphysical metanarrative . . . is not the encompassing story within which all other accounts of reality must establish their places, or be discredited by failing to find one. It is instead a rather brutal abstraction from reality . . . As pop scientists urge over and over, the tale told by Scripture and creed finds no comfortable place within modernity's metanarrative. It is time for the church simply to reply: this is certainly the case, and the reason it is the case is that the tale told by Scripture is too comprehensive to find place within so drastically curtailed a version of the facts. Indeed, the gospel story cannot fit with *any* other would-be metanarrative because it is itself the only true metanarrative—or it is altogether false.[18]

Philosophical underpinnings for this work of recovery have been available to us through important long-standing probes of which I will mention two. Susanne K. Langer, already in 1942 in her book *Philosophy in a New Key*, proposed an alternative to the rationality of modernity.[19] She did so by accenting the way in which language, symbol, art, music,

---

17. Barth, *Commentary on the Epistle to the Romans*.
18. Jenson, *Canon and Creed*, 119–20.
19. Langer, *Philosophy in a New Key*.

and sacrament make meaning that does not depend upon the mathematically certitude of modern rationality. She builds from the programmatic statement of Edward Sapir who writes:

> Language is heuristic ... in that its forms predetermine for us certain modes of observation and interpretation ... While it may be looked on as a symbolic system which reports or refers or otherwise substitutes for direct experience, it does not as a matter of actual behavior stand apart from or run parallel to direct experience but completely interpenetrates with it.[20]

Langer comments:

> The fact is that our primary world of reality *is* a verbal one. Without words our imagination cannot retain distinct objects and their relations but out of sight is out of mind ... The transformation of experience into concepts, not the elaboration of signals as symbols, is the motive of language. Speech is through and through symbolic; and only sometimes signific.[21]

Second, Michael Polanyi, in his book of 1958 *Personal Knowledge*, protested against the reductionism of scientism and argued that serious knowledge is inescapably personal and interpretive.

> Having made a discovery, I shall never see the world again as before. My eyes have become different; I have made myself into a person seeing and thinking differently. I have crossed a gap, the heuristic gap that lies between problem and discovery. Major discoveries change our interpretive framework.[22]

It strikes me as crucial that both Langer (building on Sapir) and Polanyi focus on the *heuristic* function of language. That is, language is generative and forward leaning—leaning toward possibility that is not available before utterance.[23] While neither Langer nor Polanyi has an explicit interest in theology, clearly their work creates a philosophic environment amenable to resistance to the totalism of modernity.

This alternative to the Enlightenment rationality of modernity is an affirmation that linguistic, rhetorical, artistic, interpretive imagination

20. Langer, *Philosophy in a New Key*, 126. Langer cites Sapir, "Language," 157.
21. Langer, *Philosophy in a New Key*, 126.
22. Polanyi, *Personal Knowledge*, 143.
23. Kearney, *The God Who May Be*, ponders the generative future of God, based on Exod 3:14, in a way that takes the self-disclosing utterance of God as generative of new possibilities.

generates futures. And clearly such work of utterance requires *an utterer* and leads us to dialogic practice with a person and the personal that is outside and beyond us. This accent on the active personal as we ponder faith is recently probed by Marilyn McCord Adams as she thinks through the problem of evil:

> My philosophical instinct to make human personality fundamental is matched by a drive . . . to join the mainstream of Christian theological tradition in regarding divine agency as personal—that is, at bottom, agency that acts by thought and will . . . Once freed from this down-sizing disadvantage, Divine personhood offers systemic advantages where the problem of horrendous evils is concerned. For horror-defeating power is meaning-restoring power, and meaning-making is personal activity par excellence![24]

In a world beset by limitless exploitation of "nature" and unrestrained savagery against neighbor, Adams's phrasing seems particularly pertinent. What is surely required now among us is power that is capable of "horror-defeating," "meaning-restoring," and "meaning-making." Such work is surely personal. And while human agents can address these dreadful issues in modest ways, faith attests a larger, more compelling, more effective personal agency, surely "the holy one in your midst." Of course for the "progressives" who continue to have confidence in the modern world that "has been so good to us," the horror is not seen to be so deep, and the loss of meaning not so acute when present manageable meanings continue to be available. But such an "innocent" view of social, worldly reality is possible only among those privileged and protected.

Such innocent claims, moreover, are indispensable when this rationality is given concreteness in the economic claims of capitalism.[25] Such "innocent" faith, incapable of thinking or imagining outside the promise and possibilities of capitalism, reduces everything to commodity, and more than that, to measurable, manageable commodity that

---

24. Adams, *Horrendous Evils and the Goodness of God*, 81.
25. Goodchild, *Theology of Money*, 257–58, connects the dots:

> Modern reason, modern politics, and modern economics have been founded on the ideal of autonomy . . . The modern rejection of political theology consists in the ideal of autonomy: instead of asking how one may serve nature, society or God, one asks how nature and society may be made to serve oneself. The disavowed spiritual energy that gives authority to such an autonomous subject is embodied in money. Money has replaced God.

does not allow for the immeasurability of the Holy One who can and does make all things new. Such innocence is a practice of totalism in which the narrative of sufficiency and control screens out and denies the real world of life and death, of estrangement and reconciliation, of enslavement and emancipation, of wealth and poverty, of despair and hope, of denial and truth.[26] These elemental facets of real life that refuse to go away require us to host dialogic rhetoric that inevitably disrupts the disruptions of modernity.

V.

In the end the crisis is a practical one and not a theoretical one. The practical issue is to disrupt the totalizing capacity of modernity-cum-capitalism by a rhetoric and by a life of freedom and fidelity. Such a rhetoric and such a life entail regard and respect for the God who engages in dialogic discourse with those who pay attention, who are, like Moses, able to "turn aside" (Exod 3:3). We may not, in the first instant, anticipate that such an alternative life will be visible in the corridors of modernity that are pledged to a different narrative of reality, a narrative that leaves variously in hubris or in despair, but always in anxiety.

But then, the faith community, Jewish and Christian, is not pledged to that narrative or that rationality. The language and imagination of the faith community is of another kind, pledged to love God and to love neighbor, that is, to acknowledge *Another* who summons and compels us, to regard *the other as neighbor* and not as threat or competitor. That mandate, rooted in Sinai, is a practical one that implies a different construal of social and economic power. But that concrete and practical alternative construal depends upon imagination that is carried and evoked by rhetoric.

For that reason, surely, the faith community cannot afford the "innocent" rhetoric of "progressives" that expect or welcome no initiative other than their own. For that matter, it also cannot afford the triumphal rhetoric of conservatives who traffic in absolutes. Neither such "innocence" nor such triumphalism can produce a viable world. Such a world depends on discourse that concerns freedom and fidelity and responsibility, all the language of dialogue.

26. On the violent potential of totalism, see Lifton, *Witness to an Extreme Century*. On pp. 67–68, 381, Lifton details the "eight deadly sins" of totalism. One can see such elements in the force and control of late capitalism among us.

Thus the most immediate and practical work of faith communities, I propose, is the recovery of the language of I and Thou and the nerve to trust it. Such rhetoric, deep in the tradition, attests an "I" who can self-announce and a "Thou" who is present in tradition and in contemporary liturgical performance, the Thou who gives and commands and emancipates and summons and promises.

I am moved by the proposal of Terry Eagleton that the ground of faith from which to refute the "new atheists" is not theoretical but it is practical. It is the deep valuing of "the scum of the earth."[27] The story of faith, Jewish and Christian, concerns the way in which the Holy One engages with "the scum of the earth." In ancient Israel it is "rabble" (*aspesuph*; Num 11:4) or the "mixed multitude" (*erev rav*; Exod 12:28; see Neh 13:3), an undifferentiated mish-mash of unidentified people. In the early church it is "tax-collectors and sinners," folk who do not belong to or qualify for the successful world of propriety (Luke 5:30; 7:34). It is with these that the Holy One engages. It is to these that the Holy One speaks. It is among these that the Holy One creates a community of those who will pray imperatives of hope and sing doxologies that bespeak the "Thou" of the holy one. It is in that entourage that the juices of life are unleashed. And where that rhetoric is not practiced and those juices are not released, we are consigned, by our innocence or by our triumphalism, to a world of control and threat and anxiety and loneliness and despair. The news that arises in dialogic exchange is that it need not be so. And because the "Thou" of the holy one has been found to be reliable, it will not be so.

The several monologues of modernity shrivel the human spirit and the human possibility. Israel's dialogic language refuses such shriveling. Thus I return to my beginning point:

—*Doxology* is the glad yielding of self while the modern self never yields:

> I will extol you, O LORD . . . (Ps 30:1)

—*Thanks* is the voice of gratitude for gifts generously given:

---

27. Eagleton, *Reason, Faith, and Revolution*.

> I give thanks to you, O Lord, with my whole heart;
>> before the gods I sing your praise;
> I bow down toward your holy temple
>> and give thanks to your name
>> for your steadfast love and your faithfulness. (Ps 138:1–2)

The modern self has no reason to be grateful or to give thanks or to hope.

—*Petition* is the insistent voice of expectation:

> Rise up, O Lord!
>> Do not let mortals prevail. (Ps 9:19)

> Rise up, O Lord;
>> O God, lift up your hand. (Ps 10:12)

The modern self does not expect or hope or ask.

Faithfulness listens; faith waits; faith hears. The Thou addresses and sometimes speaks a newness that authorizes a new world that can be given only in such utterance.

—It is *the speaking Thou* who rejects hubris:

> Therefore I will take back my grain in its time,
>> and my wine in its season. (Hos 2:9)

—It is *the speaking Thou* who undertakes possibility:
> I will open rivers on the bare heights,
>> and fountains in the midst of the valleys. (Isa 41:18)

—It is this *speaking Thou* who imposes the pain of alienation and then reaches into that pain to embrace:

> How can I give you up, Ephraim,
>> how can I hand you over? (Hos 11:8)

—It is *this speaking Thou* who inhabits and convenes alternative worlds of fidelity and freedom.

The faith communities, Jewish and Christian, even in a world of monologue, are in the Thou business. And that in a culture of conformist capitalism and illusionary freedom that begins with no "Thou" and ends with a feeble "I" that is soon dismissed. When the faith community refuses its proper rhetoric and opts for either innocence or triumph, the world is left in bottomless anxiety—a complete disruption of our humanness. It is in such a world, marked by innocence, triumphalism, and anxiety, that this Thou sometimes surprises, evoking new possibility.[28]

Columbia Theological Seminary
September 19, 2011
Hebrew Union College, Cincinnati OH

---

28. Kearney, *The God Who May Be*, 80–100, on the "Possibilizing God." His argument would be easier and more compelling were there reliance on the dialogical rhetoric of the Bible.

7

Reaping the Whirlwind

Our little systems have their day;
They have their day and cease to be;
They are but broken lights of thee,
And Thou, O Lord, art more than they.
—Tennyson "In Memoriam"

I don't see it as an act of God; I see it as something no one saw coming.
—Donald J. Trump, March 19, 2020

THE LINGERING IMPACT OF the virus has summoned our best science to respond to human emergency. That lingering impact has also invited fresh theological consideration. In what follows I will explore some complex interpretive options in the Old Testament concerning the coming of the "plague" that in some way or another, in biblical horizon, is inflected by the reality of God. It is possible to trace out in the Old Testament at least three (maybe more!) interpretive options for such a God-linked reality of the plague.

I.

The first and most obvious interpretive possibility is *the transactional mode of covenant*. That transactional mode is based on the simple premise that in a tightly ordered world "good people prosper" and "evil people suffer." Covenant requires obedience to commandments. Obedience is rewarded; disobedience is punished. This calculus is readily articulated in Psalm 1:

> for the LORD watches over the way of the righteous,
>   but the way of the wicked will perish. (Ps 1:6)

We can trace that reasoning in the two great recitals of blessing and curse in the Torah:

> If in spite of these punishments you have not turned back to me, but continue hostile to me, then I too will continue hostile to you. I myself will strike you sevenfold for your sins. I will bring the sword against you, executing vengeance for the covenant; and if you withdraw within your cities, I will send pestilence among you, and you shall be delivered into enemy hands. When I break your staff of bread, ten women shall bake your bread in a single oven, and they shall dole out your bread by weight; and though you eat, you shall not be satisfied. (Lev 26:23–26)

The phrasing is exactly symmetrical: you are hostile: I will be hostile! Divine hostility takes the form of a *sword* of vengeance; upon retreat from battle there comes *pestilence*; and the result of pestilence is *famine*. Thus we get the great triad of divine response. That triad, moreover, is readily seen in sequence. From war there may come pestilence and from pestilence there may come famine. This is the outcome, described in advance, for violation of Torah. There is no uncertainty. These curses are not a natural threat. They are simply statement of the future Israel may choose by the way it orders its life.

We are able to see this same triad in play in the narrative of David in the divine response to the royal census (2 Sam 24:12–13). It is noteworthy that David chooses pestilence in order to submit to direct divine action rather than suffer from the "human hands" of the sword. David trusts that even in this divine response, he may find "mercy" that he will not find in human interaction. In 2 Chr 20:9, moreover, prayer in the temple is offered as the one and only antidote to this triad of divine judgment. The same triad shows up as "the horsemen of the Apocalypse" (Rev 6:8). The matter is tightly transactional with no slippage: a pure quid pro quo.

The same reasoning is voiced in the second recital of curses, though with expansive exposition:

> The LORD will make the pestilence cling to you until it has consumed you off the land that you are entering to possess. The LORD will afflict you with consumption, fever, inflammation, with fiery heat, and drought, and with blight and mildew . . .
>
> The LORD will cause you to be defeated before your enemies . . . A people whom you do not know will eat up the fruit of your ground and of all your labors; you shall be continually abused and crushed, and driven mad by the sight that your eyes shall see. (Deut 28:21–34)

The cause of such trouble is that "You have forsaken me" (v. 20). After pestilence in v. 21, the sword is signaled in v. 25, and in vv. 30–33 there will be famine because of the seizure of all food by the enemy. This is the same as Leviticus 26; again, there is no slippage in the transaction.

In a general way the prophetic "lawsuits" share the premise of *obedience/disobedience* and *blessing/curse*. In prophetic rhetoric covenantal *commandment* issues in *indictment* for disobedience and *curse* becomes *prophetic judgment*. The logic is the same. That logic is pervasive in prophetic discourse. It is most intense and acute in Jeremiah and Ezekiel, likely because these particular traditions are closest to the final demise of contrary Israel. Thus Jeremiah's concern for false prophets, surely informed and shaped by the tradition of Deuteronomy:

> Here are the prophets saying to them, "You shall not see the sword, nor shall you see famine, but I will give you true peace in this place. (Jer 14:13)

In 15:3 Jeremiah reiterates the triad and adds a fourth element, captivity; but the pattern is the same:

> Those destined for pestilence, to *pestilence,*
>   and those destined for the sword, to the *sword;*
> those destined for famine, to *famine,*
>   and those destined for captivity, to *captivity.* (Jer 15:3)

The prophetic tradition regularly and frequently reiterates the triad of coming trouble for the city (Jer 21:9; 24:10; 29:18; 32:36; 34:17; 38:2; 42:17, 22; 44:13). (It will be noted that most of these uses are in prose that no doubt reflect subsequent editing). It is clear that in this important covenantal trajectory of interpretation, the transactional assumptions of covenant are in full play. The same reiteration is evident in the nearest contemporary of Jeremiah, namely, Ezekiel (Ezek 6:11; 7:15; 12:16).

This quid pro quo calculus in the Deuteronomy-covenantal tradition employed by the prophets becomes the ground for the judgment that Jerusalem was destroyed by YHWH for covenantal violation. Thus "the plague" (along with sword and famine) is an instrument of divine punishment against those who violate the covenantal order of creation willed by God.

Such reasoning may indeed strike us as brutalizing and repulsive, given what we would regard as more "reasonable" interpretive categories. We may, however, linger over this reasoning for two reasons. First this calculus is grounded in the conviction that God's creation is ordered according to a reliable moral intention that is non-negotiable. This most elemental conviction about reliability is not, in my judgment, to be dismissed lightly, because such reliability does not yield to relativity or situational nuance. It leaves for us a chance for wonderment: Is there indeed a line in the sand? A second reason for attending to this calculus is that it is the uncritical assumption of many very well-intended serious people. It is that same "base line" into which we inculcate our children from early on. We do believe and trust that there are non-negotiable givens of moral coherence in the world, even though their exact content is not clear or readily agreed upon. Indeed it is the critical work of science to continue to probe such matters.

II.

A second interpretive trajectory exhibits YHWH's *purposeful enactment of force* in order to implement the *specific purpose of YHWH*. This trajectory is different from that of the transactive mode traced above because there is in this exhibit of force no explicit quid pro quo. A quid pro quo may sometimes be tacit and inferred, but is not expressed. The accent is on the purposeful resolve of YHWH's force.

The normative exhibit of this trajectory, of course, is the sequence of "plagues" (smitings) in the Exodus narrative. This sequence of ten episodes features destructive actions against Pharaoh's Egypt in order that the slave community of Hebrews may be liberated from the brutality of Pharaoh. That sequence of ten episodes constitutes ten mighty exhibits of power in order that Pharaoh may discern the power and wonder of YHWH. It is proper to term these dramatic narrative encounters "miracles" as long as the term is understood (not as "a violation of natural order") as an exhibit of holy, divine power. (Attempts have been made to "explain" the sequence of plagues as a chain of natural cause-and-effect events whereby one natural event triggers the next. That, however, is to miss the point of the narrative. The aim is to exhibit the capacity of the creator God to mobilize the various elements creation in the service of divine intentionality.

That divine intentionality in the Exodus narrative is precisely that the community of Hebrew slaves may be emancipated:

> I will free you from the burdens of the Egyptians and deliver you from slavery to them. I will redeem you with an outstretched arm and with mighty acts of judgment. (Exod 6:6)

The outcome of the deliverance is the making of a covenant bond with the emancipated community:

> I will take you as my people, and I will be your God. You shall know that I am the LORD your God, who has freed you from the burdens of the Egyptians. (6:7)

The concluding formula of Exod 14:30 echoes the same intentionality.

Alternatively the Priestly tradition sees the Exodus as a means whereby YHWH is enhanced:

> I will harden Pharaoh's heart, and he will pursue them, so that I will gain glory for myself over Pharaoh and all his army; and the Egyptians shall know that I am the LORD. (Exod 14:4, 17)

Taken together these two accents assert that YHWH's *enhancement* is accomplished by acts of *emancipation* that require purposeful action against Pharaoh. The two aims cannot be separated. On the one hand, this exhibit of YHWH's force is in order that Israel may know that YHWH is God (Exod 6:7; 7:17; 10:2; 11:7). On the other hand, it is in order that Egypt may know that YHWH is God (Exod 7:5; 8:10, 22; 9:29–30; 14:18). *Israel and Egypt* together are instructed through this exhibit of divine power that takes violent form.

The purposefulness of YHWH's mobilization of destructive power set loose in Pharaoh's domain, moreover, is honed with precision. This is evident in the affirmation that YHWH makes a distinction between Egypt and Israel, so that the utilization of destructive power has a specific identifiable historical target:

> But the LORD will make a distinction between the livestock of Israel and the livestock of Egypt, so that nothing shall die of all that belongs to the Israelites. (9:4)
>
> And the LORD rained hail on the land of Egypt; there was hail with fire flashing continually in the midst of it, such heavy hail as had never fallen in all the land of Egypt since it became a nation. The hail struck down everything that was in the open field throughout all the land of Egypt, both human and animal; the hail also struck down all the plants of the field, and shattered every tree in the field. Only in the land of Goshen, where the Israelites were, there was no hail. (9:23–26)
>
> Every firstborn in the land of Egypt shall die, from the firstborn of Pharaoh who sits on his throne to the firstborn of the female slave who is behind the handmill, and all the firstborn of the livestock. Then there will be a loud cry throughout all the land of Egypt, such as has never been or will ever be again. But not a dog shall growl at any of the Israelites—not at people, not at animals—so that you may know that the LORD makes a distinction between Egypt and Israel. (11:5–7)

The narrative is at pains to assert that this wild destructive "force of nature" is not random or indifferent to historical distinction. This claim of intention in the exhibit of force goes with the awareness that the destructive action is not any "natural event"; it is the accomplishment of an intentional agent who has a specific historical intent. This historical intentionality is further elucidated in the doxological rendition of the plagues in Ps 105:26–36. The destruction is portrayed as wholesale in Egypt. The adversative conjunction of v. 37 marks the contrast between devastated Egypt and emancipated Israel:

> *Then* he brought Israel out with silver and gold,
>   and there was no one among their tribes who stumbled. (v. 37)

Amid the devastation Israel is unscathed! It is impossible to read the Exodus narrative without recognition that the destructive plagues are purposeful, propelled by intentional agency and aimed at a particular historical circumstance, namely, the emergence of a new historical people Israel (see Exod 4:22).

A second such show of destructive force is articulated in the remarkable poem of Isa 2:12–17, a poem that is dominated by the word "against" that YHWH executes. These verses are framed in vv. 10 and

19 by a warning to flee into hiding before the terror of YHWH. That warning, moreover, is laden with the further awareness that there will be nowhere to hide from the divine terror.

The target of the terror of YHWH is identified only by poetic allusion: "proud, lofty, lifted up, high, cedars of Lebanon, oaks of Bashan, high mountains, lofty hills, high tower, fortified wall, ships of Tarshish, beautiful craft, haughtiness." The imagery tumbles out! None of it is precise, until we refer to the context of Isaiah. Then we can notice that the allusions are to commercial and military matters. In context, of course, the poetry refers to the royal-temple establishment in Jerusalem that the prophet takes as a visible, historical, political enactment of God-defying hubris. The mode of assault and attack against that establishment is left unnamed. The imagery could suggest a mighty wind—a force of nature—that will blow down the great trees. In context, however, it is likely that the threat is the mobilization of Assyria (and later the threat of Babylon). The prophet is here not concerned with secondary causes. It is not "the day of the wind or of Assyria or of Babylon. It is "the day of YHWH"! YHWH will mobilize force that will terrorize the commercial, military establishment the prophet has in purview. Chapter 2 ends with an imperative to turn away from "The Man" (v. 22) "The Man" has only breath that is the gift of the creator and merits no regard. "The Man" in context surely refers to the "royal man" who presides in Jerusalem but who turns out to be quite penultimate. He is incapable of withstanding the mighty force of the creator God who decisively impinges upon the security system of "The Man."

These verses themselves suggest no quid pro quo that would evoke the devastation. It is enough to see that the terror of YHWH is mobilized in order to preserve and enhance the rule of YHWH against usurpatious pride. It is evident that earlier verses in the chapter provide ground for a quid pro quo as Jerusalem is:

> Full of diviners and soothsayers;
>
> Full of silver and gold,
>
> Full of horses and chariots,
>
> Full of idols. (Isa 2:6–8)

The idols will not save; Israel will throw them away in order to travel lightly into the caves. The security system of "The Man" is impotent and irrelevant before the terror of YHWH!

These two texts taken together, from Exodus and Isaiah, bespeak the capacity and resolve of YHWH to act in massively destructive ways against any historical ordering that contradicts the intent of YHWH. YHWH, it turns out, has many tools of sovereignty beyond the force of love. We may refer to David's conviction in 2 Samuel 24 that even the "pestilence" of YHWH may have a dimension of mercy to it. That dimension, however, was not made available to Pharaoh or to the targets of the poem of Isaiah. Only belatedly, long after the Exodus memory, it is allowed that even Egypt may be heard and healed:

> The LORD will strike Egypt, striking and healing; they will return to the LORD, and he will listen to their supplication and heal them. (Isa 19:22)

That however will happen only after much smiting, and after an abrupt "turn to the LORD."

III.

Beyond any *tight quid pro quo* and beyond *the purposeful mobilization of violent force in the service of sovereignty*, we may identify a third interpretive possibility concerning the destructive action of God. This third possibility concerns the sheer holiness of God that God can enact in utter freedom without reason, explanation, or accountability, seemingly beyond any purpose at all. The classic textual example is in the whirlwind speeches in the book of Job where God declares that God's forceful creative actions are beyond any capacity of Job to master, explain, or comprehend. God, moreover, intends that God's actions should expose Job's anemic capacity for understanding. One can cite almost any text from those speeches:

> Where were you when I laid the foundation of the earth?
>   Tell me, if you have understanding.
> Who determined its measurements—surely you know!
>   Or who stretched the line upon it?
> On what were its bases sunk,
>   or who laid its cornerstone
> when the morning stars sang together
>   and all the heavenly beings shouted for joy?

> Or who shut in the sea with doors when it burst out from the womb?—
>> when I made the clouds its garment,
> and thick darkness its swaddling band,
>> and prescribed bounds for it,
>>> and set bars and doors,
> and said, "Thus far shall you come, and no farther;
> and here shall your proud waves be stopped"?
> (Job 38:4–11 see vv. 31–33; 39:1–2, 9–12; 41:1–7)

God addresses Job with questions. God probes Job to see how far Job is able to engage the wonder of God's performance. Thus the questions posed by God to Job are acts of defiance and put down; Job cannot answer. God knows very well that God's own wondrous work is fully beyond the ken of Job. God appeals to Job's competence and then arrives at a triumphant "then" asserting that Job can never replicate the lordly action of God. Job will have no victory over the bottomless capacity of God!

> *Then* I will also acknowledge to you
>> that your own right hand can give you victory. (40:14)

Job cannot answer because Job has no capacity for answer. YHWH's defiant questions have put Job in his proper place as a dependent creature with clear limitations that he is wont to deny. He cannot ever catch up to God's glorious sovereignty that is cast in holiness. In the rhetoric of dismissive questions, God is exhibited as "wholly other," as completely unlike Job and not at all subject to Job's mode of knowledge or categories of explanation. Job is brought to an awareness that he stands before a sovereignty he cannot penetrate:

> See, I am of small account;
>> what shall I answer you? (40:4)

Job's final response is an acknowledgment of God's capacity for freedom that need not answer to Job's small insistent probes:

> I know that you can do all things,
>> and that no purpose of yours can be thwarted. (42:2)

Job's final utterance in 42:6 is inescapably ambiguous. That ambiguity, however, can only follow Job's admission of his own limit.

It was Tod Linafelt who first suggested to me that *The Idea of the Holy* by Rudolf Otto is a useful reference point for reading the poetry of Job. It will be remembered from Otto that the *tremendum* of God's holiness is both *fascinating and threatening*. That is how God is presented in the book of Job. There is a compelling freshness about God who is offered with artistic style in Job. At the same time, however, there is a dangerousness that the God before whom Job must stand does not offer closeness, intimacy, or fidelity. This God has no obligation for such availability. Otto's "sublime" concerns greatness that is beyond calculation that evokes awe but at the same time off-putting distance. It is no wonder that the Priestly interpreters in ancient Israel and in the ancient world generally attempted to corral holiness into manageable administratable categories (see for example Deut 14:1–21). The early narratives of 1 Sam 6:19–20 and 2 Sam 6:6–11 concerning the ark, however, attest an awareness that the holiness of God cannot be presumed upon. That dangerous holiness of God defies the domesticating efforts of the ancient priests even as it escapes the efforts modern science.

The outcome of this trajectory concerning God' holiness is the recognition that God will not be entrapped in our best efforts. God may and will do wild things beyond our hopes or expectations. Thus the "wonders" that God performs in creation and in history are beyond expectation or administration. Both Job and his friends sought to reduce God to their quid pro quo explanations. But the God who emerges in the whirlwind will do otherwise and their reasoning is ineffective before God.

We can identify subsequent echoes of this strange outcome of the poem of Job. While the poem of Job remains in the sphere of creation, Israel's tradition boldly carries the same affirmation into the sphere of history. Thus concerning God's demolition of Assyria, there is nothing Assyria can do against such divine resolve. The prophetic poem ends in this defiant declaration:

> For the LORD of hosts has planned, and who can annul it?
> His hand is stretched out, and who will turn it back. (Isa 14:27)

The answer is, "No one will annul; no one will turn it back!" No one can annul or turn it back because the holy one of Israel has declared that purpose. Such a claim renders penultimate all of our best management of the historical process. In like manner concerning YHWH's dealing with and through Babylon, the prophet dismisses those in Israel who question God's intent:

> Woe to you who strive with your Maker,
>> earthen vessels with the potter!
> Does the clay say to the one who fashions it, "What are you making?"
>> "Your work has no handles"?
> Woe to anyone who says to a father, ""What are you begetting?"
>> or to a woman, "With what are you in labor?" (Isa 45:9–10)

Israel has no warrant to question YHWH; YHWH acts freely and need not give account. Belatedly even Nebuchadnezzar learned the hard way:

> All the inhabitants of the earth are accounted as nothing,
>> and he does what he wills with the host of heaven and the inhabitants of the earth.
> There is no one who can stay his hand
>> or say to him, "What are you doing?" (Dan 4:35)

No one! No one can question. And even such an innocent looking text as the book of Proverbs allows, as Gerhard von Rad has seen, that in the end, God acts inscrutably, human intent notwithstanding:

> The human mind may devise many plans,
>> but it is the purpose of the Lord that will be established.
>> (Prov 19:21; see 16:2, 9; 20:24; 21:2, 30–31)

YHWH does not offer explanation, as both Israel and Nebuchadnezzar learned. Life lived in God's world requires coming to terms with the inscrutability of God that defies all limitation and all efforts at domestication.

In light of this exposition we may recognize in biblical testimony three angles of vision for our interpretive work concerning the onslaught of a plague:

—A *transactional quid pro quo* that issues in punishment for violators;

—A *purposeful mobilization of negative force* in order to effect God's own intent, and

—A *raw holiness* that refuses and defies our best explanations, so that God's force is an irreducible reality in the world.

IV.

None of these interpretive options is of much use or interest in the midst of the virus. We do not have energy or inclination for such matters when more closely we are preoccupied with germs, infections, contagion, pandemic, and a general sense of jeopardy. In a word we want science that can be effectively administered through responsible political channels. We want experts who can be trusted and who will provide relief from both threat and anxiety. And we want political administrators who have the courage and honesty to make effective antidotes available to us without deception or denial.

That is what we want and must have, and nothing more. And, of course, biblical faith is not in any way inimical to such science that probes into what seems ahead of time as the inscrutability of creation. Sometimes the church has been fearful of science (Galileo!); that, however, is not the case for the Bible. (We can recognize that the Bible is indeed *inimical* to scientism of the kind fostered by some of the neo-atheists. Such scientism seeks to make the work of science into the master-narrative of worldly reality, a claim that it cannot sustain.)

But while being fully appreciative of responsible scientific work, the Bible at the same time is fully cognizant of the limitation of such work. In the singular poem of Job 28, the poem endorses human exploration of the earth and gladly affirms gains made by such probes:

> The sources of the rivers they [miners] probe;
>> hidden things they bring to light. (Job 28:11)

But then the poem reverses field to ask:

> But where shall wisdom be found?
>> And where is the place of understanding? (vv. 12, 20)

And then comes answer:

> God understands the way to it,
>> and he knows its place.
> For he looks to the end of the earth,
>> and sees everything under the heavens.
> When he gave to the wind its weight,
>> and apportioned out the waters by measure;

> when he made a decree for the rain,
>> and a way for the thunderbolt;
> then he saw it, and declared it;
>> he established it, and searched it out. (vv. 23–27)

God knows! And then the poet draws a conclusion concerning human engagement with the mystery of creation:

> Truly, the fear of the Lord, that is wisdom;
>> and to depart from evil is understanding. (v. 28)

True knowledge is finally not in scientific exploration but in the fear of YHWH and the shunning of evil. Important as it surely is, scientific exploration has its limits.

More directly, a proverb makes a categoric distinction between the inscrutability of the creator God and the work of human investigation:

> It is the glory of God to conceal things,
>> but the glory of kings to search things out. (Prov 25:2)

Human investigation (characteristically funded by governments, often in the service of the military), seeks to "search things out." That is the proper work of human curiosity and, as with the virus, an urgent human need. The second line in the proverb, however, is matched by the first line concerning God's proper work. Thus *human searching* out and *God's concealment* are the endless riddling process concerning the wonder of creation. There are limits to seeking things out, not in the form of prohibition, but in the endless capacity of God to conceal. The claim of the proverb, however, is that divine concealment will always run beyond human searching out, so that science will always have more work to do, but will not finally, according to the proverb, master the mystery of creation. The enterprise is an on-going cat and mouse game. The cat will prevail; but the game requires energetic and brave mice as well. Sometimes a wily mouse may outwit the cat for an instant! The human scientific enterprise is indeed to search things out; that enterprise does not and need not linger too much over the three trajectories of faith that I have exposited. And in the midst of a pandemic, we surely will not linger there.

V.

So why bother with the interpretive categories of biblical faith when in fact our energy and interest are focused on more immediate matters? The answer is simple and obvious. We linger because in the midst of our immediate preoccupation with our felt jeopardy and our hope for relief, our imagination does indeed range beyond the immediate to larger, deeper wonderments. Our free-ranging imagination is not finally or fully contained in the immediacy of our stress, anxiety, and jeopardy. Beyond these demanding immediacies, we have a deep sense that our life is not fully contained in the cause-and effect reasoning of the Enlightenment that seeks to explain and control. There is *more than that* and *other than that* to our life in God's world!

I became acutely aware of that "more and other" when my friend Peter Block commented on the virus. Peter is a Jewish secular guy not prone to meta-commentary. Nonetheless he said, "The virus is God's way of ending consumerism; it is the end of the narrative of globalism." Peter's utterance was likely not a sober, critical, theological judgment. But he said it knowingly, and in his cunning way he meant exactly that. He meant, I take it, that the narrative of globalism and its conceit that we may master and use up the resources of the earth in our indifferent indulgence will fail. They will fail because such practices contradict the given reality of creation and the will of the creator.

To speak of such limit does not make it necessary to render God as a character or an agent. But Peter did! And we do! We do so partly out of tradition, piety, and force of habit. But we also move to name God because we are confronted with mystery that goes deeper than our "searching out." It turns out that such God-talk does not situate God at the edge of our life or as "God of the gaps," but attests God in, with, and under the several processes of creation. This God who will not be mocked, not by Pharaoh or by Assyria or by Babylon or by any contemporary embodiment of hubris. Tennyson does not insist that God causes our "little system" to cease, only that they cease to be. That is what my friend Peter noticed, that our "little system" is ceasing to be. It is a cessation caused by a will that exceeds our categories. It does not matter if we name such an assault as an "act of God" or, with Trump, name it otherwise. Both Tennyson and Trump recognize, in different idioms, that such an assault is undoubtedly beyond our management or explanation. The reason none saw it coming is because it has come from beyond our world of knowledge or control, from an elsewhere that is laden with inscrutability. We arrive, in our honesty and fear, at the unspeakable for which our faith tradition has provided proximate language.

Thus it is possible, when pressed beyond our explanation, to speak according to our faith tradition about the virus:

- It is possible to think about *a transactional quid pro quo*; we reap what we sow in a world governed by the creator God. Some practice and policies may evoke wrath. So Job and his friends!

- It is possible to think about *the purposeful mobilization of the negative forces of creation* to perform the intention of the creator God, plagues that defy every "high tower" and every "fortified wall."

- It is possible to pause before God's *raw holiness* in a world that is not tamed by our best knowledge.

None of this is possible in the world of modern Enlightenment rationality. The church, however, has long understood that that modernist narrative is not adequate for the mystery of creation. In times of emergency, it is possible (and necessary?) to step outside that modern narrative and to take a peek into the vast claim of creator and creation. It will be only a peek, not a permanent habitation. But the peek might be revelatory and transformative.

The preacher has amazing interpretive resources available for such a season of wonderment. The wonderment does come, perhaps at night, perhaps in the midst of quarantine. It comes upon us because we are gifted with imagination that will not settle for explanation. We are often, soon or late, pressed to ask about "the fear of the Lord" and "the shunning of evil." In our imagined autonomy we have, in the global narrative, been on a spree of self-indulgence and self-actualization that has exercised little regard for the neighbor. And now we are required to wonder more deeply. It is the work of the preacher to authorize and guide such wonderment. The *end* of such wonder may happily come in the form of a vaccine. But its *beginning* is in the fear of the Lord. This is a lesson learned always too late—too late for Pharaoh, too late for Nebuchadnezzar . . . always too late . . . or just in time!

Finally this, dear preachers: We preachers are not mandated to live within the confines of modern rationality; we are, rather, called to bear witness to another realm, the vast governance (kingdom!) of God that encompasses our modernist logic. That vast governance, on our lips, may outflank the fearful logic of the Enlightenment, will surely judge it, and may in mercy redeem it.

3/21/2020

8

The Poem: Subversion and Summons
Second Sunday of Advent

ISAIAH 11:1–9; MATTHEW 3:1–12

ADULTS HAVE ALWAYS KNOWN that critical thinking is the best way to manage our life. Adults, since Plato, have learned to trust reason and proceed reasonably with their lives. Adults, since Aristotle, have preferred syllogistic logic that makes things certain. Adults, since the ancient Greeks have, by reason, logic, and critical thinking, been able to reduce reality to a memo, a syllogism, a syllabus, a brief. The Romans took over this Greek way to adulthood, and combined it with ruthless power to accomplish control and wealth and security.

In latter days, we in the United States have replicated Rome with our practice of memo, syllogism, syllabus, and brief . . . together with raw power. We have found our way to wealth, security, and control. And to sustain that way in the world, we have founded great universities to champion critical thinking, reason, and logic. How is that for a quick summary of Western civilization?!

I.

Except this! Mostly unnoticed and not taken seriously, mostly under the radar in this adult world of control and order, there have been Jews. For the most part Jews have not committed to reason and logic and memo and syllogism and brief. Because the Jews came with their peculiar stories of odd moments of transformation, all about emancipation and healing and feeding and newness, all under the rubric of "miracle." And behind the stories there were poems . . . lyrical, elusive, eruptive, defiant. Jews have known from the outset that a commitment to memo and syllogism will not make things new. Jews have known all along that in poetry we can do things not permitted by logic or reason, because poems never try to sound like memos. Poetry will break the claims of the memo. Poetry will open the world beyond reason. Poetry will give access to contradictions and tensions that logic must deny. Poetry will not only remember; it will propose and conjure and wonder and imagine and foretell.

So Jews, in their covenantal fidelity, did poems. Miriam did poetry when they crossed out of Egyptian slavery. Deborah did poetry when it dawned on them that the Canaanites were not so formidable. Hannah did poetry when little Samuel was born. Eventually Mary did poetry when she found out she was pregnant. All these mothers in Israel celebrated the impossible that was right before their eyes, even though they could explain none of it. They did poetry while the hard men were still parsing logic, and writing memos to each other, and drafting briefs. I propose that Advent is a time of struggle between the poem that opens the future that God will work and the memo that keeps control. Advent is a time for relinquishing some of the control in order to receive the impossible from God.

II.

Well, not just any poem. After the mothers in Israel there came the other poets, the ones we call "prophets." They turned the poetry toward the future, never doubting that God would give new futures out beyond our memos. The book of Isaiah, complex as it is, is framed by poetry. The poems of Isaiah are about the future God will yet give. At the beginning of Isaiah, in chapter 2, there is this poem:

> In days to come . . .
> They shall beat their swords into plowshares,
>   and their spears into pruning hooks;

> nation shall not lift up sword against nation,
>> neither shall they learn war any more. (Isa 2:4)

It is an imaging out beyond our posturing in power through which we will never prevail. At the end of Isaiah, in chapter 65, there is this poem:

> For I am about to create new heavens
>> and a new earth;
> the former things shall not be remembered
>> or come to mind.
> But be glad and rejoice forever
>> in what I am creating;
> for I am about to create Jerusalem as a joy,
>> and its people as a delight (Isa 65:17–18).

The poet anticipates, against all the data, that there will be no more infant mortality and no more economic displacement:

> No more shall there be in it
>> an infant that lives but a few days . . .
> They shall not build and another inhabit;
>> they shall not plant and another eat . . . (vv. 20a, 22a)

And finally, a peaceable creation with no oil spills:

> The wolf and the lamb shall feed together,
>> the lion shall eat straw like the ox . . .
> They shall not hurt or destroy
>> on all my holy mountain,
>>> says the Lord. (v. 25)

It is promised! It is imagined! It is proposed! Surely the memo writers did not pause; but the poem lingered. The book of Isaiah moves from "not learn war any more" in chapter 2 to "not hurt or destroy" in chapter 65, a sweep of well-being that contradicts the facts on the ground.

III.

And right in the middle of this poetry, in chapter 11, is the poem entrusted to us on this Advent Sunday. It is a poem that refuses the facts on the ground, and invites us listeners to watch for newness outside our constricted, frightened logic. It begins with this that takes our breath away: "Out of the stump of Jesse . . . ," Jesse being David's father. David's family and dynasty run out in failure, no king, no future, no royal possibility, only a stump. But, says the poet, the stump will produce a shoot, a shoot of new life that was not expected. The memo writers no doubt were at work thinking how to honor the stump and close down that history. But the poet said, "Watch for the shoot," the new David, the new possibility of shalom. The poem that follows is about that shoot that cannot be explained by our reason.

What a shoot it will be, conjured by the poet! This new ruler to come, only imagined here, will have qualifications like you have never seen, wisdom (not mere knowledge), understanding (not just data), wisdom and understanding from the Lord, fear of the Lord, recognition of the holy mystery that is at the core of the power process. This new shoot will be glad to sign on for God's promises. Like every ruler, he must sort things out and make economic decisions. He will decide with righteousness on behalf of the poor. He will break the monopoly of the power elite and will notice that other neglected public. He will rule for the meek, the ones who have no voice and no political clout and no smart lawyers. He will be all dressed up in robes of covenantal fidelity, and he will not forget what his vocation is.

The poem requires us to take a deep breath, because it is reality defining. What we usually have is authority with knowledge but no wisdom, with data but no understanding, the kind of power that governs on behalf of the billionaire club, so that the rich get richer. And now comes a poem of the new incursion of God's spirit that will break open the cabal of the critical control.

But there is more. The poet takes a long pause. Since we are already into God's impossibilities, the big impossibility is lined out:

> The wolf shall live with the lamb,
>   the leopard shall lie down with the kid,
> the calf and the lion and the fatling together,
>   and a little child shall lead them.
> The cow and the bear shall graze,
>   their young shall lie down together;
> and the lion shall eat straw like the ox. (11:6–7)

The old enmities, the old appetites of the food chain, the old assumptions of the survival of the meanest, all of that is subverted. The wild will not stay vicious, because the coming one, marked by righteousness and justice, will overrule raw power in the interest of new possibility. Finally, the young child will toy with the asp and the adder; nobody will get hurt, because the poison will be removed from the world. The poison will be gone because the shoot will override all business as usual. All will be well, and all manner of things will be well:

> They will not hurt or destroy
>> on all my holy mountain;
> for the earth will be full of the knowledge of the LORD
>> as the waters cover the sea. (v. 9)

The poem is about advent, about the coming one. And we dare to say, we confessing Christians, that the poem concerns the Christmas baby who refuses Rome's rule of force and religion's rule of code, opening the world to healing, freedom, forgiveness, and joy. So try this in advent. Depart from logic and memo and syllogism, and host the poem.

IV.

But there is an important caveat about the poem. Those who listened to John the Baptist, the big advent guy, loved the poem. They thought they owned the poem. They thought they had the poem as a special promise just to them. It is the temptation of entitled people to think we have privilege about the poem. So John addresses them, calls them seething, slippery, creepy reptiles, low-lifes. And he says to them: Don't just enjoy the poem. Do the poem. Sign on!

> Bear fruit worthy of repentance . . . every tree therefore that does not bear good fruit is cut down and thrown into the fire. (Matt 3:8, 10)

This is the bite of advent. It is not just marveling at newness God will give. It is not about cozy, comfortable hope. It turns out, as always among Jews, that the poem is a summons to action. In these days of advent, then, imagine if the poem is true. Imagine if the poem is the true text of our life. What then?

Well, be a carrier of wisdom and not just knowledge;
be an agent of understanding, and not just data.

Take on "the fear of the Lord," a sense that there is an out beyond us who finally governs.

Watch for the poor and make a difference with them;
watch for the meek and be a voice for the voiceless.

Embrace the lamb and summon the wolf to newness;
enfold the kid and deal with the leopard;
watch for the hissing snake and notices the end of the poison.

And watch for the child:

> The little child will lead them . . .
>> wolf and lamb,
>> leopard and kid,
>> calf and lion,
>> cow and bear,
>> lion and ox.
>
> The nursing child will play over the hole of the asp.

The poem anticipates the child. And when he is born, we should not be preoccupied with memos and logic and brief and critical thought. Because the child . . . and the poem . . . evoke a leap beyond our control. It is a leap to another world that requires daily obedience. And it ends . . . the poem ends . . . this way:

> They will not hurt or destroy
>> on all my holy mountain;
> For the earth will be full of the knowledge of the LORD
>> as the waters cover the sea. (v. 9)

That end of the poem is our beginning—beginning beyond memo and brief and syllogism. It is a world that began in the Jerusalem temple, ran through Bethlehem, and breaks open among us. Watch for the little child!

December 5, 2010

9

The Impossible Possibility of Forgiveness

HERE ARE THREE QUESTIONS a preacher might ponder concerning the opportunity to preach the good news of forgiveness. They are, I submit, not simply questions for preachers; they are questions that can be articulated for and pondered by church folks, for the proclamation and experience of forgiveness do not amount to an instantaneous happening for most of us, but belong in the flow of the narrative life of each of us. For that reason forgiveness as a theological possibility needs to be framed in intelligible and critical ways. In what follows I will suggest how each of these questions is processed and resolved in Old Testament texts.

WHAT MAKES FORGIVENESS IMPOSSIBLE?

"Sometime the hating has to stop" (*The Railway Man*)[1]

Forgiveness remains impossible when life is parsed in the mode of "deeds–consequences," when it is thought and experienced that deeds have an unbreakable, tight, predictable connection to consequences that arise from them. While this mode of thinking can be imagined positively, that good deeds evoke blessings, most often this assumption is understood and accented negatively, that bad deeds inevitably and inescapably produce negative consequences, whether by automatic results (smoking

---

1. The phrase is from the film; I have not read the book, Lomax, *The Railway Man*.

causes cancer) or by punishing authorities that guarantee moral order (three strikes and you are out). Because the calculus of deeds and consequences cannot be broken or violated, forgiveness is impossible. One must live with the consequences of one's deeds . . . to perpetuity!

This notion of "deeds–consequences" is pervasive in the Old Testament (and reflected is the probe of John 9:2):[2]

1. It is the theological assumption of the theology of Deuteronomy, the dominant theology of the Old Testament. Obedience to the commandments yields well-being, disobedience yields covenant curses (see Deut 28:1–68):

> See I have set before you today life and prosperity, death and adversity. If you obey the commandments of the LORD our God that I am commanding you today, by loving the LORD your God, walking in his ways and observing his commandments, decrees, and ordinances, then you shall live and become numerous, and the LORD your God will bless you in the land that you are entering to possess. But if your hearts turn away and you do not hear (obey), but are led astray to bow down to other gods an serve them, I declare to you today that you shall perish; you shall not live in the land that you are crossing the Jordan to enter and possess. (Deut 30:15–18)

The disproportionate accent on curses in chapter 28 indicates that the force of this double "if-then" arrangement is on the negative.

2. This same "deeds–consequences" construct is the structural assumption of the recurring prophetic speeches of judgment that regularly consist in an *indictment* of Torah disobedience and a *sentence* that follows from old covenant curses.[3] The two are characteristically connected by a "therefore" that allows for both for automatic outcomes and divine agency:

> Hear the word of the LORD, O people of Israel;
>
> for the LORD has an indictment against the inhabitants of the land.
>
> There is no faithfulness or loyalty,
>
> and no knowledge of God in the land.

---

2. The classic statement is in Koch, "Is There a Doctrine of Retribution in the Old Testament?"

3. See Miller, *Sin and Judgment in the Prophets.*

> Swearing, lying, and murder,
>> and stealing and adultery break out;
>> bloodshed follows bloodshed.
> Therefore the land mourns,
>> and all who live in it languish;
> together with the wild animals,
>> and the birds of the air,
>> even the fish of the sea are perishing. (Hos 4:1–3)

> Its rulers give judgment for a bribe,
>> its priests teach for a price,
>> its prophets give oracles for money;
> Yet they lean on the LORD and say,
>> "Surely the LORD is with us!
>> No harm shall come on us."
> Therefore because of you
>> Zion shall be plowed as a field;
> Jerusalem shall become a heap of ruins,
>> And the mountain of the house a wooded height. (Mic 3:11–12)

The prophets, reflective of the tradition of Deuteronomy, assume a close connection between deeds and consequences, between covenantal disobedience and covenantal curse. The "divine therefore" permits connections to be made that might otherwise elude us.

3. The same connection of deeds and consequences is the tacit assumption of the wisdom teaching in the book of Proverbs:[4]

> A slack hand causes poverty,
>> but the hand of the diligent makes rich. (Prov 10:4)

> The wage of the righteous leads to life,
>> the gain of the wicked to sin. (v. 16)

> The fear of the LORD prolongs life,
>> but the years of the wicked will be short. (v. 27)

---

4. See von Rad, *Wisdom in Israel*, 124–37.

> The righteous will never be moved,
>> but the wicked will not remain in the land. (v. 30)

It is, moreover, the assumption of both Job and his friends, and the governing subject of the dispute between them. The God of the whirlwind is not interested in such a calculus, but it nonetheless dominates the book of Job as an heir to the book of Proverbs.

Thus the *Deuteronomic, prophetic,* and *sapiential* traditions all agree on this basic assumption. That assumption, on the one hand, operates as *social control* to motivate people to "get it right." On the other hand, it serves to assure a *moral coherence* to reality, so that one's actions are important and are significant in shaping the future: "What you sow, you reap!"

This same assumption is pervasive in popular religion and in civic life among us:

1. It is the basis of much *right-wing religion* that preaches "hell, fire, and damnation" that frightens people into a "moral life." Wrong living will evoke long-term punishment that is inescapable. It is astonishing to notice that many who have long since left such religion continue to host such assumptions.

2. That same assumption has been transposed in powerful ways from religion to *market ideology,* so that obedience to the mandates of the market brings economic preference; those who do not produce endlessly may be left behind unforgivable, intractable debt. Those who do not shop and consume continually, moreover, are "letting down our side." The pressure of getting kids into the right preschool and building kids' "dossiers" with soccer and dance lessons is all a part of the "deeds–consequences" pressure of the market. If one does not "perform" adequately one will surely "suffer the consequences."

3. I dare imagine that the same pressure, less closely articulated, permeates good citizenship among *good liberals* who perform their duty in generous engaged civic ways, because some liberals are quite like Job; we do not "serve God for naught" (Job 1:9). Indeed I could imagine that the same unspoken assumption operates with some duty-propelled liberal pastors who must endlessly "prove themselves," and even seminary teachers who must endlessly produce one more published article!

The assumption behind these performance-based forms of faith is that God's world is organized in an inexorable way that yields rewards and punishments. It is this assumption that interpreted the major crisis of the Old Testament, the destruction of Jerusalem as divine punishment for long-term disobedience to Torah. The long telling of royal history in the books of Kings concerns the demise and failure of Jerusalem, its monarchy and temple, that effectively ended the history of Israel in the exile with its shame, deportation, and displacement (see 2 Kgs 24:13—25:21; Jer 52:12–30). The long prayer of Ezra (Neh 9:6–37) and the long recital of Ps 106 attest to this long term failure.

4. I suggest that in contemporary popular culture the defining anthem of this theology is "Santa Claus is Coming to Town":

> He's gonna find out
>
> Who's naughty and nice . . .
>
> He knows if you've been bad or good
>
> So be good for goodness sake!

In teasing good humor the song is in fact a form of social control with the prospect of "coal" for poor performances that are never forgiven. This applies not only to "our kids" but to many adults as well!

WHAT MAKES FORGIVENESS POSSIBLE?

> Without sundering, there is no reconciliation (James Joyce)[5]

According to the theology of "deeds–consequences," the history of Israel would properly have come to an end in the destruction of Jerusalem. That "end" is voiced in the grief of the book of Lamentations:

> The roads to Zion mourn,
>
>   for no one comes to the festivals;
>
> all her gates are desolate,
>
>   her priests groan;
>
> her young girls grieve,
>
>   and her lot is bitter.
>
> . . .
>
> because the LORD has made her suffer
>
>   for the multitude of her transgressions . . .

---

5. Joyce is quoted by Kearney, *Anatheism*, 108; Kearny provides no specific citation.

> so I say, "Gone is my glory,
>> and all that I had hoped for from the LORD." (Lam 1:4–5; 3:18)

Hope is gone! Deeds have received consequences. Disobedience has evoked covenant curses. *Fini*! No forgiveness! No possible future!

The wonder of the Old Testament, of Judaism, and consequently of Christian faith is that this turns out not to be the end. There is a continuation that is grounded in forgiveness. So the poet in Lamentations can continue:

> But this I call to mind,
>> and therefore I have hope:
>
> The steadfast love of the LORD never ceases,
>> his mercies never come to an end;
>
> they are new every morning,
>> great is your faithfulness. (3:21–23)

Continuation is grounded in divine steadfast love, faithfulness, and mercy, the "big three" of covenantal possibility.

What makes forgiveness possible is the astonishing readiness of God to reach beyond deeds–consequences, to restore and sustain the relationship that had by all proper measure been terminated in disobedience. It is this inexplicable reach of God beyond "deeds–consequences" that makes forgiveness possible. We may see this in two texts that are likely pre-exilic. In Exodus 34, after the Golden Calf incident and the hard negotiations on the part of Moses, Moses utters a final, desperate petition to YHWH:

> Although this is a stiff-necked people pardon our iniquity and our sin, and take us for your inheritance. (34:9)

The answer to the prayer is not certain, which is why the prayer is an act of risky hope. The divine answer, however, opens the future:

> I hereby make a covenant. Before all your people I will perform marvels, such as have not been performed in all the earth or in any nation; and all the people among whom you live shall see the work of the LORD; for it is an awesome thing that I will do with you. (v. 10)

God has moved beyond the indignation over the golden calf to generate a new future based in forgiveness.

In Hos 11:5–7, YHWH is in a rant against recalcitrant Israel. But then, in mid-rant, YHWH interrupts YHWH's own speech with self-questioning wonderment:

> How can I give you up, Ephraim?
> > How can I hand you over, O Israel?
> How can I make you like Admah?
> > How can I treat you like Zeboiim? (Hos 11:8)

YHWH comes in that instant to realize that YHWH has no inclination to enact fierce anger, but turns the rant of anger into a reach of compassion:

> My heart recoils within me;
> > my compassion grows warm and tender.
> I will not execute my fierce anger;
> > I will not again destroy Ephraim;
> for I am God and no mortal,
> > the Holy One in your midst,
> and I will not come in wrath. (vv. 8b–9)

That divine reach is inexplicable, but it is the indispensable act of God that makes new life possible for Israel.

It is in the exile, when "deeds–consequences" reached its completion in punishment and all hope is lost, that there is a surge of divine forgiveness for Israel grounded in God's reach to generate newness.

1. In the tradition of Isaiah, we have had a long condemnation of society in a series of "woes" (Isa 5:8–24). But now, at the end of Second Isaiah, the poet has God make a bid for restoration:

> Seek the LORD while he may be found,
> > call upon him while he is near . . .
> Let him return to the LORD,
> > that he may have mercy on them,
> and to our God,
> > for he will abundantly pardon. (Isa 55:6–7)

The operational word is "pardon." That God's ways are "higher" may mean, in context, that they supersede "deeds–consequences" in order to make new life possible. What follows in vv. 12–13 is an imagined, unexpected glorious procession home, made possible by the God who has broken the tired, killing grip of deeds–consequences.

2. The tradition of Jeremiah has at length castigated Jerusalem and arrived in 19:11 at the harsh ultimate judgment:

> So I will break this people and this city, as one breaks a potter's vessel, so that it can never be mended.

The phrase "cannot be mended," "cannot be healed" puts Jerusalem beyond restitution. And yet, when we reach "The Book of Comfort " in Jer 30–31 there is "grace in the wilderness" (31:2), an "everlasting love" (31:3) that culminates in new covenant (31:31–34). That famous passage ends:

> I will forgive their iniquity,
>> and remember their sin on more. (31:34)

"Deeds–consequences" causes us to remember our failure longer than God remembers. Newness in Israel is grounded in YHWH's readiness to break the cycle of disobedience–punishment with a generous act of forgiveness whereby old calculations about consequences are removed from reckoning. The assertion of forgiveness is reiterated by the prophet in Jer 33:7–8:

> I will restore the fortunes of Judah, and the fortunes of Israel, and rebuild them as they were at first. I will cleanse them of all the guilt of their sin against me, and I will forgive all the guilt of their sin and rebellion against me. (33:7–8)

3. The prophet Ezekiel, in one of his best-known passages hews to the line of deeds–consequences:

> If a man is righteous and does what is lawful and right . . . follows my statutes and is careful to observe my ordinances, acting faithfully—such a one is righteous; he shall surely live, says the Lord God . . . But if the wicked turn away from all their sins that they have committed and keep all my statutes and do what is lawful and right, they shall surely live, they shall not die. (Ezek 18:5, 9, 21)

Later on, however, Ezekiel must have concluded that such a "turn" is not possible. In 36:24–27, in a torrent of unconditional divine promises, Israel will be transformed by YHWH's reach for new beginnings:

> I will take you from the nations, and gather you from all the countries, and bring you into your own land. I will sprinkle clean water on you, and you shall be clean from all your uncleannesses, and from all your idols I will cleanse you. A new heart I will give you, and a new spirit I will put within you. And I will remove from your body the heart of stone and give you a heart of flesh. I will put my spirit within you, and make you follow my statutes and be careful to observe my ordinances.

It is spectacularly the case that all three "major prophets" have God moved from "deeds–consequences" that issues in punishment to a fresh reach beyond to new possibility. That of course is the point of possibility. I do not think, however, that point has force unless and until we are clear about the weight of "deeds–consequences" in our lives. It is precisely in the hopeless outcome of "deeds–consequences" that generates fear, self-hated, and endless pressure that the divine reach of compassion and forgetfulness has transformative power as it did for ancient Israel. This means that God,

—reaches beyond hell, fire and damnation to create new life;

—reaches beyond self-hatred and shame with tender mercy that vetoes such hatred;

—reaches beyond the defeats and hopeless pressures to "catch-up" in the market economy to validate those "left behind."

—reaches to the pressure of liberals with their endless commitments to enter into an unbelievable sabbath rest.

It is not easy for those of us inured to "deeds–consequences" to accept such a reach. I think, however, that the preachable point is that such a reach is not easy for God either. God, so the tradition attests is, like us, inured to "deeds–consequences" and to acute self-regard that will not be mocked by casual defiance or prideful recalcitrance. Forgiveness, as we may imagine, requires nothing less than God's capacity to resituate God's own life outside the orbit of deeds–consequences. It is for that reason, I judge, that it is exactly in the exile that we begin to get new maternal images for God. God must move in new ways if the lethal cycle of deeds–consequences is to be nullified. As a result, the congregation might be led to consider how forgiveness has been experienced, and who it has been who has been able to step outside "deeds–consequences" to allow for the slippage that make new life possible.

Since we pray, "forgive us our sins as we forgive those who sin against us," we might be invited to consider how we ourselves might step outside "deeds–consequences" for the sake of forgiveness. If as James Joyce asserts, "There is no reconciliation without sundering," we may ask, "What must be sundered? And the answer is that God's way of governing needed to sundered. And so with us, what must be sundered is our self-concept, our self-presentation, our old habits of holding grudges and keeping score and harboring long term resentments.

After the phrasing of the prayer, it is likely that we cannot *receive* forgiveness unless we are in something of a posture of *enacting* forgiveness. That is, we cannot entertain God's reach beyond "deeds–consequences" unless we ourselves are alive to the possibility of such a reach beyond. All of our conventional habits of grudge preservation are called to account. Such a sundering may variously pertain to:

—long held familial alienations,

—old habits of quarreling in the congregation,

—old party conversations that regularly excommunicate "red" or "blue" folks in the community.

—old stereotypes of race, gender, class,

—old resentment of the "undeserving poor,"

—old caricatures of those "not like us," for example Jews or Muslims.

The history of life beyond "cannot be mended" is the story of the reach that requires sundering.

WHAT DOES FORGIVENESS MAKE POSSIBLE?

When I develop a mindset of forgiveness, rather than a mindset of grievance, I don't just forgive a particular act; I become a more forgiving person. With a grievance mindset, I look at the world and see what is wrong. When I have a forgiveness mindset, I start to see the world not through grievance but through gratitude. (Desmond Tutu and Mpho Tutu)[6]

The ancient "assurance of pardon" anticipated that one forgiven would be able to lead a "godly, righteous, and sober life," that is, a life in sync

---

6. Tutu and Tutu, *The Book of Forgiving*, 218.

with the God who forgives. I suggest that the text, beyond such rhetoric, affirms that one forgiven can do anything that one might want to do that is congruent with the reality of forgiveness and with the one who forgives. Forgiveness is an emancipation from the fear, shame, guilt, and self-hatred to a new freedom:

—It is a break beyond hell, fire, and damnation to be one's true self;

—It is a break beyond the claims of market productivity to be rather than to do;

—It is a break beyond liberal "duty" to bask in a truly accepted, acceptable life.

Forgiveness is an emancipation that lifts all the weight of "deed–consequences" and invites to "lightness of being." A genuinely forgiven person is one who is deeply and gladly attached to the forgiver—not "indebted" but grateful.

In the Old Testament prophets, what comes from forgiveness is the capacity to imagine, host, and perform concrete and specific newnesses that are impossible, except for forgiveness. The preacher thus may ponder that what follows from forgiveness is "that all things are possible."

1. In the book of Isaiah, Second Isaiah ends, as noted, with promised pardon (Isa 55:6–9) and joyous homecoming (vv. 12–13). After that, what follows in the book of Isaiah is a reimagined society that is now possible. In chapter 56 we have imagined inclusiveness for those most eagerly excluded, eunuchs and foreigners. The new prospect is that,

> My house shall be called a house of prayer for all peoples. (56:7)

In chapter 58, a new social fabric is proposed that will make possible a common good shared between haves and have-nots:

> Is not this the fast that I choose:
>   to loose the bonds of injustice,
>   to undo the thongs of the yoke,
>   to let the oppressed go free,
>   and break every yoke?
> Is it not to share your bread with the hungry,
>   and bring the homeless poor into your house;
>   when you see then naked, to cover them,
>   and not to hide yourselves from your own kin? (Isa 58:6–7)

Most especially, in anticipation of "I Have a Dream," 65:17–25 can hold in purview a new Jerusalem, new urban ordering of social power in which they "will not hurt or destroy in all my holy mountain," i.e., in Jerusalem. An unforgiven urban economy will systematically hurt and will programmatically destroy. But not now! Because urban newness is possible!

2. The book of Jeremiah is rooted in the old Torah memory of Sinai via the tradition of Deuteronomy. When Jeremiah comes to imagine what is possible via forgiveness, he imagines a new covenant in which there will be glad acceptance of Torah commandments—not as coercion, but as a body of teaching that will bring life. The anticipation of a new covenant is a marvel because Jeremiah can recall broken covenant, a brokenness that recurs but that reaches back all the way to broken covenant caused by the Golden Calf (Jer 11:10). But because of forgiveness, restored covenant is possible and with it a covenantal community and a covenantal ordering of social power. Implicit in "new covenant" is a new neighborly economy that specializes in forgiveness of debts, not a bad thing to think about as public policy in a society that leaves students with unbearable debts and that generates and accepts as normal a permanent underclass.

3. Ezekiel by contrast is rooted in the priestly tradition reflected in the book of Leviticus that is preoccupied with holiness. He has earlier imagined the departure of God's glory from Jerusalem and its temple because God could not remain in a place of profanation (Ezek 9–10). In time, Ezekiel imagines that in time to come there will be a new temple (Ezek 40–48). YHWH will return in glory to reside permanently in the new temple. This act of prophetic imagination is counter to all the facts on the ground of Israel's failed holiness. Ezekiel's temple is not primarily about architecture. It is about the readiness of God to be with God's people and to invest their common life with holiness. It is forgiveness that makes the divine presence possible in Israel. This God who will come in glory will, in time to come, be shepherd of Israel:

> I myself will be the shepherd of my sheep, and I will make them lie down, says the Lord God. I will seek the lost, and I will bring back the strayed, and I will bind up the injured, and I will strengthen the weak, but the fat and the strong I will destroy. I will feed them with justice. (Ezek 34:15–16)

It is worth considering this vision of a new temple and a new sense of divine presence in a society like ours. It is remarkable to think that that glory has indeed departed from among us (thus the collapse of US exceptionalism), precisely because profanation is emphatic in our society... the trivializing of common life and the reduction of everything and everyone to a commodity. But now, forgiven, new temple and new presence!

IV.

It is useful, I think, to give narrative body to the crisis of forgiveness. Thus the sequence I propose in the Old Testament is,

1. The symmetry of "deeds–consequences";

2. The reach beyond "deed–consequences" symmetry in generosity that sunders old patterns and old assumptions; and

3. Lightness of being that makes all things possible.

It will occur to some readers familiar with my work that this sequence is yet another articulation of my typology in the book of Psalms of "orientation, disorientation, and new orientation."[7] Of course, the "old orientation of "deeds–consequences" is on all counts powerful among us and will continue to be so. It is, I propose, a disorientation in God's own life with the emergence of pathos-filled solidarity that causes a genuine break in old patterns of governance. The performance that that solidarity makes all things new, a possibility never possible under the aegis of "deeds–consequences."

I am, of course, aware that this dramatic sequence is acted out many times in the narratives that cluster around Jesus. It is reflected, moreover, in the most normative "three point sermon" of sin–salvation–new life, the original classic form of the three point sermon, always the same three points. Except that in the sequence that I have traced, the first accent is not explicitly on "sin." It concerns, rather, the theological-moral assumption of "deeds–consequences" that produce a graceless world. This dramatic sequence is not only definitional for the narrative of Jesus and in the faith of ancient Israel for the destiny of Jerusalem. The same drama is many times performed in the life of a congregation. I hazard that many people come to church along with the assumptions of "deed–consequences." The best hope (and fear!) is that the claim of "deeds–consequences" will be broken, hope because we yearn for reconciliation, fear because such a

---

7. Brueggemann, "The Psalms and the Life of Faith."

break signifies the eclipse of an old order of certitude. The reach beyond such certitude feels to some like a plunge into unbearable relativism.

Thus three questions arise:

1. *What makes forgiveness impossible?*
   It is the grip of "deed–consequences" that allows no "out."
2. *What makes forgiveness possible?*
   It is the inexplicable reach of generous graciousness beyond "deeds–consequences."
3. *What does forgiveness make possible?*
   Everything congruent with the forgiver.

These are questions that belong primarily (not exclusively) to the Gospel community. What a way to imagine the church, a community that is preoccupied with these questions (and answers) that eventually concern both our personal destiny and our social, communal possibility! I suggest that preaching forgiveness is not simply a declaration of God's love, but it is a close attentiveness to costly sundering that makes new life possible. It is a wonder to imagine God's readiness to be sundered for the sake of newness. It is an equal wonder to consider our readiness for such a break in our way of being present in the world.

My title, "impossible possibility" is a play on the phrasing of Kierkegaard. The phrase is exactly to the point. We know in our habitual practices about the stubborn impossibility of forgiveness. We only rarely experience the way in which the impossibility of forgiveness becomes possible. But that is the primal truth of our faith. God turns that impossibility to possibility, and from that possibility all other things become possible. This is a truth that our society little suspects. But we know better. We constitute a body that is resolved to receive and embrace this truth, along with the freedom and courage for the "reach beyond" that comes with sundering.

July 21, 2014

10

On Appearing before the Authorities

JEREMIAH 5:14–17; 20:7–13; 23:29–32;
LUKE 21:9–19

I WANT TO THINK with you, dear sisters and brothers who preach, about the words you dare not speak from the pulpit and what that "not daring" does to our hearts. Because when you preach, every time you do it, it is done as you "appear before the authorities."

I.

As some of you will know, George Carlin has a list of seven words you cannot say on television. He is as hilarious about the list as he is obscene. All of his prohibited words refer to bodily or sexual functions, the kind that cause Junior High boys to giggle and blush. Carlin has a debate with himself about his list, because some of the words are hyphenated and so reiterate others on the list. But when he gets the list set, he can recite it in two nano-seconds.

The reason Carlin cannot say these words on television is because the censors will not allow it, the censors being the guardians of establishment power to keep things nice and therefore safe. He cannot say these words because they remind us of bodily functions that we cannot control. We do not speak them because they remind us that we are bodies, and therefore frail and therefore mortal and therefore about to die. Arnold Toynbee has said that death is "un-American," an affront to everyone's right to life, liberty, and the pursuit of happiness. The censors prefer matters nice and safe. They prefer that people like us talk of spiritual matters and not such topics as the body or the body politic or the economics of the body politic. The list censored and disapproved concerns the smelly and unsavory, so that we do better to deny the body.

II.

Well, George Carlin is not the first to have such a list of things that could not be said in public. Already Jeremiah, in his frightened, jeopardized world, knew such a list of things not to be uttered in public in Jerusalem:

- he could not say that the divine promise to David was sheer ideology;
- he could not say that God's perpetual presence in the Jerusalem temple was a priestly hoax;
- he could not say that being chosen did not give Israel a pass on moral responsibility;
- he could not say that Nebuchadnezzar, the hated superpower, was a tool of God to bring it all down;
- he could not say that the Jerusalem network was under judgment and would not be spared or sustained;
- he could not say that God's eternity did not extend to the little human accomplishments that they loved too much with all their hearts. (Is that seven?)

He could not say these things, because he knew that saying them was inflammatory:

> I am now making my words in your mouth a fire,
>   and this people wood, and the fire shall devour them.
> I am going to bring upon you a nation from far away,
>   O house of Israel, says the Lord. (Jer 5:14b–15a)

He knew he had to say these words because there were so many false words that needed to be countered in Jerusalem:

> Is not my word like fire, says the Lord, and like a hammer that breaks a rock in pieces? See, therefore, I am against the prophets, says the Lord, who steal my words from one another [more than plagiarism!]. See, I am against the prophets, says the Lord, who use their own tongues and say, "Says the Lord." See, I am against those who prophesy lying dreams, says the Lord, and who tell them, and who lead my people astray by their lies and their recklessness, when I did not send them or appoint them; so they do not profit this people at all, says the Lord. (Jer 23:29–32)

It was too dangerous to say what had to be said. And he did not say it. And it tore his guts apart. He risked saying it, but at the last minute he did not. And then he gets sick for not saying it:

> For whenever I speak, I must cry out,
>   I must shout, "Violence and destruction!"
> For the word of the Lord has become for me
>   a reproach and derision all day long.
> If I say, "I will not mention him,
>   or speak anymore in his name,"
> then within me there is something like a burning fire
>   shut up in my bones;
> I am weary with holding it in,
>   and I cannot. (Jer 20:8–9)

So finally he said it! He said it over and over! He was brought to trial for his words, because the "spiritual leaders," the priests, wanted him silenced for saying the prohibited words on television, uttering the unutterable. In that trial he escaped by the skin of his teeth, because of some tough old witnesses who supported him and who stood by him (26:17–19, 24). But he was regarded as a traitor who "weakened the hand of the soldiers," that is, who "undermined the war effort" (38:4). It is no wonder that he cries out to God in pain and anguish: "You have seduced me." You have given me an impossible assignment. He prays in honesty for vengeance against his adversaries. Because he had to say what he dared not say. And all hell came upon him.

III.

Well, George Carlin is not the last one to have such a list of the unsayable. There is, for example, you, you preachers who pray and brood and study and know. And then mostly must retreat to the "nice" of denial. Or you preach your heart out; and the vestry or the session doubles the pain like a hammer, or a major donor stomps out in indignation. Or worse, you preach your heart out and the most you get is that someone reminds you that you forgot the Lord's Prayer . . . for God's sake!

I am led to this thought by the many preachers who have told me, almost in passing as though it were normal, that they could not speak about the Iraq war in their church, or about immigration or about global warming. And I am, moreover, a member of a theological faculty that was not permitted to say something at the outset about the war because the institutional risks were too great! And my own daring preacher, on the Fourth of July Sunday, had a person walk out in a huff because he said something about US arrogance and privilege.

I have been thinking about a list of things, give or take, that a preacher cannot say. Or if said, is dismissed as one who never met a payroll:

- Some could not say that the war is stupid and we are expending our precious young on the folly of the National Security State;
- Some could not say that present-day capitalism has failed in its excessive greed that devours the poor and now reaches into the middle class;
- Some could not say that the oil-spill is simply the token of Western technological hubris at its extreme;
- Some could not say that we have forfeited our democracy to a secret government that runs over the Constitution and shreds civil rights in order to defend the intemperate wealth of the few;
- Some could not say that the frantic rush to get a child to the next soccer practice and the next dance class is membership in the rat race that cannot be won;
- Some cannot say that the technological fixes violate the neighborly fruitfulness of the creation;
- Some cannot say that the immigrants are indeed sisters and brothers who come under the welcome sign;

- Some cannot say that our penchant for violence is toxic for the heart of our common life;
- Some cannot say that the experiment in greedy entitlement has failed, and we will have to find other ways to maintain our Hummers. (Is that seven?)

Some cannot say things because the cocoon of denial claims us all, and we would rather not risk so much. Well, maybe this is not quite your list. You can adjust. All I know is that there is a lot not being said; and we all know why.

This is not a sermon about being prophetic or taking on the world or blowing the lid off the church in one loud binge. This is a pastoral reflection on what it does for us, alongside Jeremiah and George Carlin, to be silenced in ways that shrink and cramp our humanness. Such coerced silence is not benign. It makes us inordinately weary. It drives us to despair . . . or cynicism. It compels us to denial. It reduces us to managers and therapists and cheerleaders and entertainers and program directors. And all the while the word grinds at our guts because we know better. What we cannot say is that the body is fragile and smelly and cannot be made otherwise. What we cannot say is that the body politic now has a smell of death about it. What we cannot say is that evangelical faith is about bodily existence in the neighborhood, bodily since the creator called it "good," bodily since God freed the slaves from their pained bodily bondage, bodily since, as we say in the creed:

> For us and for our salvation
>
> he came down from heaven,
>
> was incarnate of the Holy Spirit and the Virgin Mary,
>
> and became truly human.

Or as we know it more anciently, "and was made man!" Became human, fragile, vulnerable, smelly, about to die. Became man! When about to die, as "man" or as body politic or as us, then Carlin's "piss" or "fart" are not really objectionable or interesting, because such smelly regularity beyond our control belongs inescapably to our short-term creatureliness.

IV.

Well, I thought it was worth reflecting on the fix we are in. The preacher in our society is given words that cannot be uttered. And if not uttered, the preacher grows cold, plays it safe, and perhaps needs to be loved more. And as I pondered this, I am aware that not once in my life, in my tenured life, have I been in the dangerous place that many of you occupy every week. You are like the apostles in the book of Acts, sure to be called before the authorities and examined for your testimony, to see whether your words are safe and acceptable, or as dangerous and inflammatory as those of George Carlin or Jeremiah. The authorities sit before you and conduct your trial.

But then I came to this other text given me by C. S. Song, the great Korean theologian, who has indeed been before the authorities. In Luke 21, Jesus anticipates the coming debacle. You wonder how he knew about our coming debacle: "Not one stone will be left on another." It sounds like an oil spill or an economic melt-down. They asked him, "When?" He said, "I do not know." But then he says, before whatever time line in which it will occur:

> But before all this occurs, they will arrest you and persecute you; they will hand you over to synagogues and prisons, and you will be brought before kings and governors because of my name. This will give you an opportunity to testify. (Luke 21:12–13)

They will ask you to speak up. They will expect you to utter your truth. They will watch your words to see if any of your words are like those of George's list or the list of Jeremiah. Then I thought, even if Luke is anticipating the Roman destruction of the Jerusalem temple, he is making connections to our time and place and danger. Now like then, the authorities are bewildered. They want some guidance or assurance for a dangerous time; but they do not want to do to the bedrock faith of these witnesses. So what do you have to tell us, Ms. Apostle, of the truth and nothing but? What have you got for us, Reverend?

And then Jesus says—or Luke says, or the Jesus Seminar says—these most stunning words:

> So make up your minds not to prepare your defense in advance; for I will give you words and a wisdom that none of your opponents will be able to withstand or contradict. (vv. 14–15)

Don't work it out logically and carefully or anxiously or with too much calculated caution, because that venue presses you beyond that. Trust the spirit of Jesus, he says, and receive wisdom that will admit you to new freedom. Imagine, on hard issues of the day before the Roman authorities, Jesus will be close at hand with a word. What he says is, "I will give you mouth."

And then he says two things to his followers:

- First, this truth-telling will get you into a lot of trouble: "You will be betrayed even by parents and brothers, by relatives and friends; and they will put some of you to death. You will be hate by all because of my name" (vv. 16–17).
- Second, you will be safe: "But not a hair of your head will perish. By your endurance you will gain your souls" (vv. 18–19).

Big trouble . . . and you will gain your soul, your identifiable center of vitality. You will get yourself back in the process of telling the truth before the authorities. You likely will find allies among tough old witnesses. But for sure, you will have yourself in all your vocational freedom.

I do not give you advice. I give you only a text. I do know about the risk of the church budget, and about the risk to one's family (I am a PK!), and about being without tenure, and the danger to one's pension and medical coverage. Of course!

But I also know about the diminishment of self through coerced silence and the loss of freedom and courage and vitality and energy and joy. I crave for you an edge of freedom that will let you witness to the full truth that has entrusted to you. Jeremiah discovered, through his much anguish, that he had allies as he ran risks, that he was kept safe in ways he could not have imagined. He could not know that before he bore witness. I have thought about what it means for us to walk close to the gospel. There is no doubt that greater freedom for the word is needed among us. It is needed by those who need to hear. But it is also needed by those who are called to speak. This is a gospel time. This is a time when the old reliances have failed, when autonomous, arrogant ways of life, in many manifestations, have been shown to be empty. This is a moment to line out an alternative. We have that alternative and it must be uttered for the sake of the body politic.

The utterance is not only for the sake of the body politic. It is also for the sake of our souls. Imagine what it will be like to break out of fatigue and despair and resignation and gentle denial to be one's self with the truth of the gospel. You do not need to be Jim Forbes, and I do not need to be Tony Campollo with their bravado. We need only be ourselves with the word entrusted to us, with God's word given us, with news that sets us free from heart burn or ulcers or anger with Jeremiah.

The word we will be given in gospel freedom is not a nice word about a nice world. It is rather a true word about our bodies and our body politic, the bodies infused with God's truth, but nonetheless temporary, passing, fragile, mortal.

All of us in his gathering are in it together. So I thought, let us together hold this moment precious. Let us think about the truth entrusted to us, the truth of God, God from God, true God from true God, the word that "was made man," suffered and died, and was indeed raised to new life and new freedom.

It is not a wonder that Jeremiah, at the end of his struggle with speech and silence, finally, in v. 13, breaks out in doxology:

> Sing to the LORD;
> > praise the LORD!
> For he has delivered the life of the needy
> > from the hands of evildoers. (20:13)

He comes to joy by breaking his silence. I do not urge you to say more than you can say. I do not urge you to run risks in dangerous places that you cannot run. I do not lay a guilt trip on you. Rather I invite you to take stock of the truth you have been given, and to ponder what it would be like for you to move to greater freedom. Finger your head; check your hairs. Imagine them all counted and guarded and kept safe. Imagine the way the hairs on your head are safe and the way in which *the freedom for your mouth* is connected to *the safety of our hairs*. And then imagine, as your silence is broken, "Free at last, free at last, thank God almighty, free at last!"

Columbia Theological Seminary
Festival of Homiletics
May, 2011

11

Getting Your Sibilants Right
The Evangelical Shibboleth

JUDGES 12:1–6; I CORINTHIANS 1:10–31

"Sibilant" is an "s" sound; the word comes from the Latin that means "hiss." The Hebrew alphabet has four sibilants: *samek, tsade, sin*, and *shin*. A "sin" looks like a three-pronged candle stick with a dot over one corner. A "shin" looks the same, except that the dot is over the other corner. Say these four sibilants: *samek, tsade, sin, shin*.

I.

I tell you this so that we can read the text from Judges knowingly. The narrative concerns a conflict and eventually war between the Israelite tribe of Ephraim and the tribe of Gilead led by Jephthah. Over time fugitives from Ephraim fled east across the Jordan and proposed to sign on with the enemy Gilead led by Jephthah. While the Gilead army needed recruits, it was highly suspicious of these fugitives, fearing that they could not be trusted. In order to trust their identity and their loyalty, the Gileadites devised a linguistic test, asking the fugitives to say the word "Shibboleth" with a *shin*, the three candle letter with a dot over it. When the fugitives tried to pass the test of dialect, they were in fact Ephraimites and so enemies; they mispronounced the test word because they had the wrong sibilant and said, "Sibboleth." They used the wrong sibilant, *sin*, the three-pronged candle with a dot over the other corner. The narrative reports, "They could not say it right." And so they were identified as outsiders who did not know the tribal mantra, and they were executed. The text says 42,000 were killed. It was unacceptable and dangerous not to know the right sibilant and not to know the tribe-identifying dialect. The narrative ends with the report that Jephthah governed and died, a conclusion that sounds affirmative. To be successful he had to identify those who had the wrong sibilant.

II.

Then I got to thinking: I wondered if the church might have a dialect that we expect people to get right, as with the correct sibilant. After that I concluded, well yes, we have such a shibboleth that is known to insiders and that can easily identify outsiders who do not know the language, practice, or the wonder of the gospel.

Paul begins his First Letter to the Corinthians with an honest recognition that there is a division in the congregation there. Its members have chosen up sides, following different leaders, variously Paul, or Apollos, or Cephas, or Christ. They have divided up the gospel, championing their own clichés, ideologies, and party lines, none of which had the right sibilant or the right tribe-identifying mantra. Paul condemns those who have false dialects and are ignorant of gospel truth. He scolds those who do not know enough to get it right.

And then Paul, with a deep breath, gives us what is surely the most eloquent and authoritative presentation of our tribal code as his summation of the gospel. Here it is in three parallels:

First, the membership identifying-mark is this: The *foolishness of God* is *wiser* than human wisdom. What a mouth full! Paul knew about human wisdom. He was a learned Jew. He had engaged with the worldly wisdom of the Greek philosophers. He knew about the organizational genius of Rome. Were he alive now, he would have mastered the electronic arts of computer, iPad, Facebook, and Twitter. He knew his way around the world!

But he understood that the foolishness of the cross contradicted all of that capacity for mastery. For the cross, emblematic of Jesus' entire life, is a totem of risk-taking self-abandonment. Against his erstwhile stringent orthodoxy, Paul understood that God is self-giving and self-risking, and self-emptying, and that Jesus is an agent of such self-giving, self-risking, self-emptying foolishness who could not possibly cut any ice in the real world. It is so foolish to give one's life away for the world. It is so stupid to give one's self away for the neighbor.

And so the church, from the outset, was tempted already at Corinth to be wise, shrewd, and effective, to imitate the way of the world, to package the mystery of the gospel in human reasoning that can yield certitude and compelling conclusions that will withstand the reasoning of the world. It has turned out however, that when the church imitates the wisdom of the world, it forgets its summons to evangelical foolishness; it becomes prudent and calculating in a way that mocks the foolishness of its own gospel truth.

Second, the membership identifying mark is this: The *weakness of God* is *stronger* than human strength. What a mouth full! Paul knows about human strength. He was quite familiar with the Roman legions and sometimes appealed to Rome for his own safety and security. In the book of Acts he is often in communication with Roman authorities, and he surely knew the gospel narrative of the Roman governor, the Roman centurion, and the Roman execution on a Friday afternoon. He knew that such power would prevail.

But for less than forty-eight hours! Only from Friday afternoon until Sunday at dawn. He knew the Easter recital of the earliest church. At the end of this epistle, moreover, he well report that "Last of all, the risen Christ also appeared to me." He was fully aware of the power of the world but is fully convinced that the weakness of Christ had prevailed in the face of the empire. The authorities who manage such mastery were regularly bamboozled by this weak, vulnerable Jesus, so that his cross has become a totem for the truth of God's self-emptying vulnerability.

That effective vulnerability, however, is a great embarrassment in the church. It is an embarrassing scandal to imagine that such self-emptying weakness could prevail over real power. It is an intellectual impossibility, so that we make every interpretive maneuver we can imagine; it is a myth; it is a metaphor. We can easily see that the earliest evangelists were bamboozled by the prevailing of Easter vulnerability; it did not fit their explanatory categories any more than it does ours. So they tried to say it in many ways, and it nearly cannot be said. It defies our intellect. But more than that, it defies our pragmatic common sense. We appeal to a business model for his church. We reduce the mystery to program and budget and building and membership rolls; they all turn out to be empty of transformative potential, because they have been too much grounded in an alien sibilant. Thus we learn, over and over many times, that the true sibilant of the weakness of God has transformative power. We appeal to Mother Teresa and Martin Luther King Jr. and the all-stars in vulnerability that have made such a difference. We do not need, however, to look so far. The weak ones are active among us everywhere; they are those who are naive and innocent and vulnerable and self-giving, who never make the vestry or the session, but who persist in self-giving generosity . . . because they know the correct sibilant.

Third, the membership identifying mark is this: The *poverty of God* is *richer* than human wealth. What a mouthful! I did indeed transport this third element to our text from 2 Cor 8, because it completes the evangelical triad. In that chapter Paul is busy making a fund appeal to help the needy church in Jerusalem. In a most stunning statement in which Paul asks for money, he makes a Christological appeal. Here is his formulation that contradicts our assumed supply-side economics:

> For you know the generous act of our Lord Jesus Christ, though he was rich, yet for our sakes he became poor, so that by his poverty you might become rich. (v. 9)

This lyrical formulation is a monetized version of the Philippian hymn:

> He was in the form of God . . . though he was rich;
>
> He emptied himself . . . for our sake he became poor;
>
> God has highly exalted him . . . That by his poverty he might make many rich.

Who knew that self-giving could enrich others? Who knew that instead of fear of contamination from touching a leper, touching a leper with gospel flesh would heal? Who knew that by taking no thought what you would eat or where you would live that it turns out that your heavenly Father knows what you need and all these things will be added to you? There is an urgent reason that so many of the parables of Jesus are cast in economic matters . . . the rich fool, workers who came late, the banquet for all, Lazarus and the rich man, and so on and on. Jesus is effecting a transformation of the economy away from the wealth of the world that of itself has no life-giving capacity.

But, of course, that evangelical poverty that makes others rich is very hard for us. It is hard for us who are depression babies. It is hard for those us who are young and want it all now. It is hard for Boomers who expect well-being to keep growing to maximum share. It is hard for all of us now who need to "update" all the old luxuries that have become indispensable necessities. So we devise excuses that justify our parsimonious wealth. And then Pope Francis shows up in a Fiat to remind us that we know better.

What an evangelical shibboleth!

- the foolishness of God is wiser than human wisdom;
- the weakness of God is stronger than human strength;
- the poverty of God is richer than human wealth.

And we, to the contrary, do not have our sibilant right! We imagine our better way:

- do not be foolish; be prudent;
- do not be weak; work from strength;
- do not be poor; because nice guys finish last.

> But we proclaim Christ crucified, a stumbling block to Jews and foolishness to Gentiles, but to those who are the called, both Jews and Greeks, Christ the power of God and the wisdom of God. For God's foolishness is wiser than human wisdom and God's weakness is stronger than human strength. (vv. 23–25)

III.

We know enough about this true evangelical shibboleth to know that this sibilant is too dangerous, too costly, and too demanding; it contradicts everything we know:

- It contradicts the need to be smart in the ways of the world;
- It contradicts the need to be powerful in the ways of the world.
- It contradicts the need to be rich and masterful in the ways of the world.

As a result, we tone down, we compromise, we explain away by a rule of *prudence, privilege,* and *parsimony*:

Prudence as wisdom;

Privilege based in power;

Parsimony that lets us pretend generosity.

We have, moreover, done this rendering with the wrong sibilant long enough that it seems proper and faithful and persuasive to us. For that reason it sounds ok to us to say "sibboleth" when the right tribal identity marker in our own dialect is "shibboleth."

IV.

The truth, however, is that people like us—we preachers—are designated to lead communities that know and trust and believe and practice the faithful evangelical shibboleth. We are called to live right in the midst of that contradiction that we know so well in our own lives. We are called to stand by and with folk who walk, often inadvertently, into that contradiction and are bamboozled by it.

I do not need to tell you that the dominant way of wisdom, power, and wealth has not kept its promise and is not able to keep its promise. It is a credible argument that the mess we are in . . . about race, environment, violence, and poverty . . . has come from our uncritical reliance upon worldly wisdom that knows too much, upon worldly power that controls too much, and upon worldly wealth that owns too much. So this could be our time, when we embrace a metric other than that imposed upon us by the world. That evangelical metric is not about members or dollars or program or pensions. It is about the neighborhood. Thus Paul can write in this same chapter:

> Consider your own call, brothers and sisters; not many of you were wise by human standards, not many were powerful, not many were of noble birth. But God chose what is foolish in the world to shame the wise; God chose what is weak in the world to shame the strong.; God chose what is low and despised in the world, things that are not, to reduce to nothing things that are, so that no one might boast in the presence of God. (vv. 26–29)

God chose what is foolish . . . people like us in the church. *God chose what is weak* in the world, people like us in the church. *God chose what is poor* in the world . . . people like us in the church.

God chose us with the true shibboleth of foolishness, weakness, and poverty to offer an alternative to the deathly way of the world. Paul concludes:

> He (God) is the source of our life in Christ Jesus, who became for us wisdom from God, and righteousness and sanctification and redemption, in order that, as it is written, "Let the one who boasts, boast in the Lord." (vv. 30–31)

God is the source of our life in Christ, not our wisdom, not our strength, not our wealth. Paul, in these verses alludes to Jeremiah who said it this way:

> Do not let the wise boast in their wisdom, do not let the mighty boast in their might, do not let the wealthy boast in their wealth, but let those who boast in this, that they understand and know me, that I am the Lord; I act with steadfast love, justice, and righteousness in the earth, for in these things I delight. (Jer 9:23–24)

Sisters and brothers, take a deep breath and give thanks. Our assignment is not for the sake of wisdom, strength, or wealth. Our ministry depends upon the things of God . . . righteousness, justice, and steadfast love. The fugitives in the book of Judges could not pronounce it correctly. But we can . . . and we do! This table is precisely for the foolish, the weak, and the poor; those are the marks of new life and we bear them gladly.

April, 2017
Festival of Homiletics

12

Do the Numbers!

MEET AMOS WILDER (1895–1993). Wilder was a pastor, a poet, and a long-time New Testament scholar at Harvard. He was also the brother of Thornton Wilder, author of *Our Town*. I introduce him to you, dear reader, in order that you may, along with me, savor his wonderful enigmatic dictum:

> The zero breeds new algebras.[1]

Every element in this sentence evokes careful attentiveness as each element is thick with intent.

The zero is the moment when we reach the nadir of possibility and have no reason to anticipate any good prospect. The zero hour is devoid of capacity and brings us into the depth of despair. In ancient Israel the zero hour was the exile of defeat, destruction, and displacement when the holy city and its temple were destroyed and God's promises had run out. Israel had no possible future:

> My way is hidden from the LORD,
>   and my right is disregarded by my God. (Isa 40:27)

> But Zion has said, "The LORD has forsaken me,
>   My Lord has forgotten me. (Isa 49:14)

---

1. Wilder, "A Hard Death."

> They say, "Our bones are dried up, and our hope is lost; we are cut off completely. (Ezek 37:11)

That moment of despairing resignation is reiterated in the New Testament narrative in the execution of Jesus. In the wake of that Friday, the disciples could assert:

> But we had hoped that he was the one to redeem Israel. (Luke 24:21)

The verb "hope" is in the past tense. Now hope is gone. That same moment of hopelessness arises for us personally and publicly when our lives are broken beyond repair. Just now, of course, amid economic meltdown and the virus we are, in our society, at something of a zero hour. Our leaders continue to assure, "We will get through this," or "We will get through this together." But there is for now no light at the end of the tunnel. To be sure, none of these moments of failure is comparable to the depth of the cosmic shut-down of that crucifixion Friday (see Matt 27:51–54; Luke 23:44–45), but we do imagine by analogue. The work of faith is the embrace of that zero hour.

Wilder has chosen the rich and suggestive verb, "*breed.*" He does not say "make" or produce," or "evoke." "Breed" suggests something organic to the zero hour that is itself generative of the possible we have taken to be impossible. The Bible does not use the verb "breed," but in Num 11:12 Moses suggests that YHWH has "conceived" Israel; see Isa 49:15 as well)." Thus the notion of "breed" is not far from the way in which the Bible speaks of the emergence of the inexplicably new. For the male party in the birth process the verb is "beget," and for the female we get "birth." In the pairing of "beget" and "birth" we get something like "breed," a hidden, inscrutable, inexplicable emergence of new life that is impelled we know not how. The Bible is perforce reticent about the process, but clearly understands that hidden emergence of new life is within the governance of God's holiness. It is for that reason that Isaiah can have God voiced in the specificity of the quotidian process of birthing:

> For a long time I have held my peace,
>   I have kept still and restrained myself;
> now I will cry out like a woman in labor,
>   I will gasp and pant. (Isa 42:14)

The Bible does not and cannot explain the breeding process, but marvels at it:

> By faith he received power of procreation, even though he was too old—and Sarah herself was barren—because he considered him faithful who had promised. Therefore from one person, and him as good as dead, descendants were born, as many as the stars of heaven and as the innumerable grains of sand by the seashore (Heb 11:11–12)

The capacity of God to deliver newness is given more grand doxological articulation by Paul:

> ... who gives life to the dead and calls into existence the things that do not exist. (Rom 4:17)

The capacity for newness from the zero hour is peculiarly in the gift of God.

What emerges in this hidden process, according to Wilder, is *new algebra*. The newness does not accommodate any of our old calculations or our usual explanations. What we get is a new world of reality that does not answer to our old certitudes. In the zero hour what is "bred" is a wonder that defies our old controls. The over-used word for such a wonder is "miracle." That word works, however, only when we refuse the notion that it is a "violation of the natural order." No, "miracle" is a disclosure of the holiness of God, an event, says Martin Buber, that is laden with "abiding astonishment."

So consider Wilder's formulation:

—*Zero hour*: a moment without possibility;

—*Breed*: a hidden process of newness laden with holiness;

—*New algebra*: a way of configuring reality beyond all of our old certitudes.

I could think of three instances in Scripture when the new algebra arrives as a surprise. (You may think of others).

In the book of Judges Israel reaches a very low point of helplessness before the incursive power of the Midianites who violently seize their life resources. This is indeed a zero hour for ancient Israel:

> They would encamp against them and destroy the produce of the land, as far as the neighborhood of Gaza, and leave no sustenance in Israel, and no sheep or ox or donkey. For they and

> their livestock would come up, and they would even bring their tents, as thick as locusts; neither they nor their camels could be counted; so they wasted the land as they came in. Thus Israel was greatly impoverished because of Midian. (Judg 6:4–6)

After some extended negotiation, Gideon is dispatched by YHWH to rescue Israel from the Midianite threat:

> Then the LORD turned to him and said, "Go in this might of yours and deliver Israel from the hand of Midian; I hereby commission you." (v. 14)

Gideon can do the numbers quite well. He knows that Israel is outnumbered and outmanned for any challenge to the Midianites:

> But sir, how can I deliver Israel? My clan is the weakest in Manasseh, and I am the least in my family. (v. 15)

But after he is given assurance of YHWH's backing, he issues a general order of mobilization to all the tribes. The call to recruit was effective, in all, 32,000 men. Gideon adheres to Colin Powell's doctrine of "massive force." The number could be overwhelming for the coming confrontation. There is, however, a catch:

> Then the LORD said to Gideon, "The troops with you are too many for me to give the Midianites into their hand. Israel will only take the credit away from me, saying, 'My own hand has delivered me.'" (7:2)

Such huge numbers would remove any hint of vulnerability and detract credit from YHWH who has pledged to save Israel. Consequently, Gideon, in response to YHWH's insistence, pares down his number of troops. He sent away the fearful:

> Thus Gideon sifted them out; twenty-two thousand returned, and ten thousand remained. (7:3)

He is very good at numbers! That, however, does not yet satisfy YHWH:

> The troops are still too many. (7:4)

Gideon is acting by the old calculus. But this zero hour with the Midianites evokes from YHWH a new algebra that Gideon must finally embrace. By the use of the wisdom of guerilla war the number of troops is cut to 300. That new algebra in which Gideon is instructed turns out well in the end with only 300 warriors:

> They seized the waters as far as Bethbarah, and also the Jordan. They captured the two captains of Midian, Oreb and Zeeb; they killed Oreb at the rock of Oreb, and Zeeb they killed at the wine press of Zeeb, as they pursued the Midianites. They brought the heads of Oreb and Zeeb to Gideon beyond the Jordan. (7:24–25)

No one could have foreseen the outcome of the zero hour; the new algebra has prevailed!

An even more spectacular case of the new algebra is narrated in 2 Kgs 6:8–23. In this zero hour for Samaria, the threat of Aram (Syria) is acute. The king of Syria regards Elisha as an intelligence "leaker" and so surrounds his home with his threatening troops. As Elisha's attendant is alert to the danger of this threat, he cries out in fear, "Alas, master, what shall we do?" v. 16). The guy can count: Two of us, a host of them! Elisha, however, is a master of the new algebra:

> Do not be afraid, for there are more with us than there are with them. (v. 16)

His servant is quite bewildered because he lives by the old math. He knows that "two" is a very small number. He wonders about "more with us." How could that be? But then the servant has his eyes wondrously opened to what could be seen only when YHWH gives vision. He was able to "do the numbers" in a fresh, very different way:

> So the LORD opened the eyes of the servant, and he saw: the mountain was full of horses and chariots of fire all around Elisha. (v. 17)

The hidden resources of God were decisive in moving Israel beyond the zero hour of threat to a new algebra. That new algebra, for Elisha, ended in a "great feast" that for an instant turned an enemy into a neighbor (v. 24).

Among the most spectacular instances of the new algebra on the horizon of Christians is the twice reiterated narrative of food. The zero hour was that a great crowd was in the wilderness that was "like sheep without a shepherd" (Mark 6:34), "without anything to eat" (8:1). The "breeding" of the new algebra, for Jesus, was that he was "moved with compassion" (6:34; 8:2). That is, his innards were in turmoil with the urgent need he saw. In response to that desperate need, he took from the crowd "five loaves and two fish" (6:38), "some bread" and "a few small fish" (8:5–7). He performed his dominical act in four steps:

He took,
> he blest,
>> he broke,
>>> he gave.

The outcome of that "breeding" moment was variously twelve baskets of surplus bread for the twelve tribes of Israel (6:43) or seven loaves of bread for the stereotypical "seven nations" (8:8), that is, in both cases, ample for all! The disciples had, of course, not understood: "How can one feed these people with bread here in the desert?" (8:4). How could such a small amount of food feed so many? What they then glimpsed, well beyond their expectation or explanation, was the new algebra of abundance. And when the church reperforms that "breeding moment" of his four transformative verbs, we are led to the new algebra. Every time we remember and participate, moreover, we are recruited into the new algebra that supersedes and defies the old math of parsimony.

And now, we are heirs of Gideon, Elisha, and Jesus—always again learning the new algebra while we remain stuck in the old math. The old math is informed by fear, scarcity, greed, and hostility. The old rule is a practice of "doing the numbers" according to shortage and surplus, predation and vulnerability. We have had, twice, glimpses of the new algebra in ample bread, and every once in a while we observe its transformative practice among us.

Just now, surely, in the midst of the virus we are at a defining zero hour in our society and in the world. That zero hour evokes fear, anger, and even hoarding. In that moment of fear, anger, and hoarding, however, when we have eyes to see, we see the new algebra working the numbers in fresh ways. In the new algebra, the silenced and the invisible among us count. In the new algebra, there is no parsimony in the face of deep bodily need. Through the new algebra we may notice the emergence of new neighborly policies that treat others like neighbors. The old rule continues to have a deep grasp on our imagination. As a result, we are fearful that someone somewhere will get something for nothing. In the old math, we regard "mine" as "mine," not ever to be shared. In the old math, we protect privilege and advantage. But the new breeding goes on in spite of us! And then, from time to time, we are amazed as was Gideon, as was the servant of Elisha, as were the disciples and the crowds around Jesus. Amos Wilder would have us do the numbers. But the numbers, in the new algebra:

—let 300 with Gideon prevail against a large military host;

—let Elisha and his servant, these two, host a transformative feast;

—let the 5000 and the 4000 feast on five loaves and a few small fish.

Those numbers get our attention and cause us to marvel: 300, two, and five loaves with two fish that eventuate in victory, feast, and surplus bread! The numbers evoke in us wonder. It is a wonder that the holy generosity of God is not contained in our conventional arithmetic. It is, moreover, a wonder when we are so inured in the old math and yet are invited beyond our calculations.

Jesus conducts a review session with his disciples so that they can engage the new algebra:

> When I broke the five loaves for the five thousand, how many baskets full of broken pieces did you collect?" They said to him, "Twelve." And the seven for the four thousand, how many baskets full of broken pieces did you collect?" And they said to him, "Seven." Then he said to them, "Do you not understand?" (Mark 6:52)

I suspect that if Amos Wilder had narrated this exchange he would have had Jesus ask, "Do you not yet understand about the new algebra?"

26 August 2020

13

Awaiting the Verdict
Good Friday

ISAIAH 52:13—53:12; PSALM 22;
JOHN 18:1—19:42

We are, on this night, at the pivot point of the Jesus story. And it turns out that on this night we are at the pivot point of the story of the world. Everything depends on the outcome of the trial of Jesus before Pilate.

It is a trial we get to remember tonight.

It is a trial we get to observe as it is performed.

It is a trial in which we get to participate.

It turns out that this trial, like every serious trial, is a contest to determine who is telling the truth and who is offering fake truth.

I.

On the one side is Pontius Pilate, the one we mention in the creed. He is the Roman governor who presides over the occupied territory of Galilee. He is a stand-in for Caesar and for Roman power. He appears at "headquarters" in all the pageantry of the empire; likely he wore a sash of Roman authority; maybe he entered the courtroom with drums and bugles, and imperial flags flying. It is impressive drama. He is a perfect icon of great power.

He is, moreover, a stand-in for the gods of the Roman Empire. These are the gods of force who did not mind violence when it is necessary. More than that,

> He stands in for raw male power;
>
> He stands in for money power and the legitimacy of greed;
>
> He stands in, among us, for white power in its supremacy.

He assumes, with all this "god-backing," that everyone can see and accept his authority. So he says to Jesus:

> Do you not know that I have power to release you, and power to crucify you? (John 19:10)

There is no doubt who is in charge in the courtroom. There is no doubt who is in charge in the world!

II.

On the other side is Jesus; just Jesus! He has no credentials. He has no pedigree. He has neither a phalanx of lawyers nor any visible support. He is all alone in the courtroom, arraigned because his dangerous teaching was seen as subversive of imperial authority. Jesus, however, is not intimidated by the Roman governor. He says to the governor: "My kingdom is not from this world . . . My kingdom is not from here" (John 18:36).

This does not mean that Jesus' "kingdom" is in the never-never land of the afterlife. Nor does it mean that his "kingdom" is simply an internal, psychological matter of being right with God. He means, rather, that his authority is not derived from Rome. He does not depend on the governor's validation because his authority is not "from here." He owes Rome nothing. He did not depend on the imperial power of greed and violence, the imperial force of money, or the imperial claim of male power or white power.

That is because he is a stand-in for the God of the covenant:

- This is the God who showed up as the emancipator in the slave camps of Egypt.

- This is the God who came to the displaced exiles in Babylon.

- This is the God of widows who have no other advocate.
- This is the God of orphans who have no family.
- This is the God of immigrants who have no homeland.

This is what they saw in this rabbi from Galilee:

- He carried no purse and had no money.
- He paid attention to women and valued them;
- He welcomed those of every tribe, tongue, and nation;
- He was like an advocate for widows,
  — like a guard for orphans,
  — like an attorney for immigrants.

When they looked at him, they saw the God of Israel who specializes in justice, righteousness, mercy, faithfulness, and steadfast love.

Jesus stands in the courtroom before the imperial governor. In every way he contradicts the claims of the governor. There he stands in the court of public opinion:

> Wounded for our transgressions,
>
> Bruised for our iniquities.

Jesus confused the governor. Finally the governor must ask, "What is truth?" (John 18:38). The governor has lived so long with fake news that he did not know what to make of Jesus who did not fit any of his categories. He has the sense that Jesus is the truth right in front of him, but he lacks the courage to recognize that truth lies outside the claims of empire in the drama of mercy, compassion, and restorative justice. So the issue is joined at the trial!

III.

There are two other parts in the drama. A third player is the crowd that is eagerly waiting outside the courtroom. The crowd is like a mob . . . boisterous, blood-thirsty, and thoughtless. The mob uncritically supports imperial authority. They did not wait for evidence, but shouted "Crucify him, crucify him." I suppose for us the like mantra, for either party, is "Lock him up, lock him up." Because he does not fit the impressive world of imperial Rome.

We do not need to linger long over the crowd. The crowd is predictable. It is impressed by money, power, greed, and it readily trusts in promises that cannot be kept. Pilate has tentatively labeled Jesus, "King of the Jews." The crowd rejects that: "He is not the king of the Jews!" But Pilate wants to allow, in a grudging way, that this may be the Jewish Messiah. But he has no courage, so he gives in to the mob that shouts, "Crucify him, crucify him!"

IV.

The fourth part is played by his disciples who represented by the fearful Simon Peter who refused to acknowledge him because it was too dangerous. You can imagine that the several disciples were scattered in the crowd watching the execution. It was not safe to be seen together.

But they watched. And they wondered:

Is this what he meant when he said that "The last shall be first"?

Did he mean that this odd teacher from Galilee would be first and the Roman governor would be last?

Did he mean that the generous would be first and the greedy would be last?

Did he mean that the vulnerable would be first and the violent would be last?

Did he mean that women would be first and men would be last?

Did he mean that Blacks would be first and whites would be last?

Did he mean that immigrants would be first and that home grown citizens would be last?

His statements are enigmatic and we have to decide.

He said,

> All who exalt themselves will be humbled,
> and all who humble themselves will be exalted. (Matt 23:12)

He said,

> Everyone who wants to save one's life must lose it. (Mark 8:36)

No wonder we have this poem that witnesses to him:

> He had no form or majesty that should look at him,
>   nothing in his appearance that we should desire him.
> He was despised and rejected by others,
>   a man of suffering and acquainted with infirmity
> as one from whom others hide their faces
>   he was despised and we held him of no account. (Isa 53:2–3)

So his disciples watched and wondered. Not until now, on Friday, did they understand who he was or what he was doing. Late in the day, I imagine, one of them said, "Even in our sadness we have to eat something." Then they remembered that they had some leftovers from his final meal with them on Thursday night. Do you know what they ate that night? They ate *broken bread* and they drank *poured out wine*. It was food unlike that of Pilate. The Roman governor never wanted broken bread, but would eat the whole loaf in one bite. He never wanted poured out wine, but swallowed the whole cup in one gulp. That, however, is what the disciples had late on Friday night, and it tasted to them like new life.

> We know how the trial ended then.
>
> But the trial is being reenacted again in our midst,
> a context for truth.
>
> We wait for a verdict this time.
>
> Or if you like, we get to decide the verdict.

There is nothing easy about Friday. It is the pivot point of the history of the world. We are left, like the old governor, with the haunting question, "What is truth?" And there he stands, like he did before the governor, before us. The verdict will not be long in coming.

St. Timothy Church
Good Friday, March 30, 2018

14

At the Death of Peter Knauert
Peter amid Remembering and Hoping

THERE ARE NO WORDS to match Peter's death. The depth of loss, sadness, and anger is beyond all of our words. But my assignment is to find words for the loss, sadness, and anger of Leigh and Harrison and Lily and David, and all of us. Maybe I have found some adequate words for this moment . . . maybe not. The best words may be in the old book of Lamentations. It is a long poem of grief about the loss of Jerusalem when Jerusalem was destroyed. The city was so loved and treasured, and then it was gone in a flash . . . lost in destruction and devastation. The city is so beloved that it had to be grieved for a very long time. I think that poetry is our poetry today. All we have to do is to shift the grief of that old beloved city to this well beloved Peter, beloved son, beloved brother, beloved grandson and nephew. We can only speak of our love for Peter the way they loved the city. And now we sink in free fall in grief and loss and anger. So listen to these old words that might be our words:

> She weeps bitterly in the night,
> > with tears on her cheeks . . .
> she has none to comfort her. (1:2)

In its death the city weeps, abandoned, with none to comfort. The poet watches the people who pass by and are too busy. They do not even notice, even when we want them to stop and pay attention to this unbearable loss:

> Is it nothing to you, all of you who pass by?
> > Look and see
> if there is any sorrow like my sorrow,
> > which was brought upon me
>
> . . .
>
> in the day of fierce anger. (1:12)

The poet knows that our sorrow on this day is like no other sorrow that has ever been. No one has grieved with us in the loss of the city, or in the loss of beloved Peter. And even God could not escape the loss, so we ask about God's failure and implication in our loss.

The poet's grief touches our bodies in anguish:

> From on high he sent fire;
> > it went deep into my bones;
> he spread a net for my feet;
> > he turned me back;
> he has left me stunned, faint all day long. (1:13)

The loss moves into our bones, so that we can hardly stand it. It leaves us stunned. We are left with only tears of sadness or of anger.

> For these things I weep;
> > my eyes flow with tears;
> for a comforter is far from me,
> > one to revive my courage;
> my children are desolate,
> > for the enemy has prevailed. (1:16)

There is no consolation, any possible comfort is remote from us, and we refuse to be comforted in his death. Nobody can receive our anger and our children, these children, are left in their own abandonment. The poet gives us words for the anguish of our bodies, without much sleep, with no appetite, only the food of salty tears:

> See, O Lord, how distressed I am;
> > my stomach churns,

> my heart is wrung within me…
> In the street it is like a sword cuts to the heart,
>> in the house it is like death.
> They heard how I was groaning,
>> with no one to comfort me. (1:20–21a)

The poetry dares to line out the way in which God has been absent to need:

> He has filled me with bitterness;
>> he has sated me with wormwood.
> He has made my teeth grind on gravel,
>> and made me cower in ashes;
> my soul is bereft of peace;
>> I have forgotten what happiness is;
> so I say, "Gone is my glory,
>> and all that I had hoped for from the Lord."
> The thought of my affliction and my homelessness
>> is wormwood and gall!
> My soul continually thinks of it
>> and is bowed down within me. (3:15–20)

Gone is all we had hoped for. We had such hope for Peter. We had hoped for him, such a bright, alert, agile young man. We hoped for him the man in the family, and he has stepped up to the plate to fill that role as best he could. But he could not help it that it was too much. Nobody saw coming the rage he felt, not about that one moment of dispute, but about the way life had turned on him with a sense of abandonment. In that moment being possessed beyond himself, he could not bear the anger. And so gone is the wonder and the possibility and the giftedness … all vanished in an instant; all gone, beyond recall.

The poet repeats the themes of the day:

None to comfort;

No ground for hope.

Those surely are our words today.

But then there is a pause in the poem. It is like the pause after the Good Friday death of Jesus, before the in-breaking of Easter. The poet says:

> But . . . but in spite of that;
>
> But . . . but the loss notwithstanding,
>
> But . . . but this I call to mind.
>
> This I remember.
>
> This I have not forgotten, even in my loss.
>
> And therefore I have hope.

I remember and so I hope. And what I remember, says the poet, is this:

> The steadfast love of the Lord never ceases,
>
>> (not now, not in death; not even death can disrupt God's steadfastness).
>
> his mercies never come to an end.
>
> they are new every morning.
>
>> great is your faithfulness. (3:22–23)

The memory of God's people is saturated with God's action and steadfast love, mercy, and faithfulness. We never stop reciting the miracles of God's self-giving. It is like a mantra to us . . . steadfast love, mercy, faithfulness. All miracles:

> The miracle of life;
>
> The miracle of a new baby;
>
> So we remember Peter's birth;
>
> We remember his first talking that was tentative.
>
> We remember his first walking that was so precarious.
>
> We remember his first day of school, a mix of eagerness and timidity.
>
> We remember the moment when he fell I love with the Celtics.
>
> We remember the joy of his baptism.

All gifts, all gifts from God, followed by the miracles of Harrison and Lily and David. And we remember the gifts of father David, his strength and his power and faithfulness, gifts he has given to his children. And, says the poet, all these miracles in our lives are gifts of God's active steadfast love, mercy, and faithfulness.

God continues to do that. We remember such acts and we hope for them again. We know that Peter in this moment, for all our loss and bewilderment and anger and remorse, is located exactly in this steadfast love, mercy, and faithfulness from God. And so are we! That will carry him well beyond any anger he knew to a place of well-being with abiding mercy and faithfulness. And we ourselves, in our season of grief, are held by the same truth of God's steadfast love, mercy, and faithfulness that is not disrupted by his death or by our grief.

I do know, Leigh, Lily, Harrison, and David, that these are at the moment empty words for you and will not comfort. But we will hold to them for you. We will remember the old gifts and will continue to watch for the new gifts that are sure to be given. We will hold Peter's life and our lives to the truth of the Gospel of God's deep, reliable presence. Because God's absence is for a moment in the night, and joy comes only later, in the morning.

Here we are with our words and with many tears. But the reservoir of our faith is deep and resilient, and so we locate Peter's death in the midst of that faith that surpasses all of our anguish and pain. In the Heidelberg Catechism, a wondrous Reformation statement of our faith, the first question of the teaching is this:

> What is our only comfort, in life and in death?

This is an urgent question, given that the poet has said over and over, "There is none to comfort." And the answer in the catechism is this:

> My only comfort is that I belong—body and soul, in life and in death—not to myself, but to my faithful savior, Jesus Christ, who has completely freed me from the dominion of evil.

We belong to Christ in his faithfulness! Peter belongs to him! And so do we! The catechism answer goes on to say,

> He protects me so well that without the will of my Father in heaven not a hair can fall from my head; indeed, that everything must fit his purpose for my salvation.

This is the truth for us in this day of loss and death. All of our sadness and anger and bewilderment are held in the heart of God who knows the hair on our heads and the yearning of our hearts and the hunger for well-being that are among us. Peter is left to rest in that good assurance. And we, in our turn, can rest there as well. The God who birthed us and knows us and counts our hairs is the one we know in steadfast love, mercy, and faithfulness. That is our only comfort. We wait for that comfort to come among us. It is poised and will come for us in time to come.

December 15, 2012
At the death of Peter Knauert

15

Advantage McEnroe!

ISAIAH 45:1, 9–13; ACTS 10:34–43

Advantage McEnroe! It could have been "advantage Federer," or "advantage Williams." Or "advantage Nadal." It is usually "advantage" for the highest ranking players in the National Lawn Tennis Association. Because in tight tennis matches you cannot win a match without "advantage." Better than that, as long as you have "advantage" in tight tennis match, you cannot lose. You can do the numbers. So I want to think with you about having "advantage," the difference it makes and the problems it creates.

I.

History is the endless performance of the advantaged. The un-advantaged mostly do not leave a track in the sand. But the advantaged leave many tracks, many carefully recorded monuments, and rich carbon footprints on the earth.

The Bible is the memory and testimony of the advantaged. The Old Testament is the story of Hebrew-Israelite-Jewish advantage and was so from the beginning. The first word uttered to Abraham and to Sarah was about an advantage consisting in a name, a land, a great nation, a carrier of blessing. When that story impinged upon the slave camp of

Egypt, Israel is said to be "my first-born son," the one entitled to all the gifts and properties (Exod 4:22). It is anticipated that Israel will be for YHWH a priestly kingdom and a holy nation (Exod 19:6). By the time of Deuteronomy, it is declared:

> For you are a people holy to the LORD our God; the Lord our God has chosen you out of all the peoples on the earth to be his treasured possession. (Deut 7:6)

> For you are a people holy to the LORD our God; it is you the LORD has chosen out of all the peoples on earth to be his people, his treasured possession. (Deut 14:2)

That was not because Israel was big or righteous, but only because the Lord "set his heart on Israel," lusted after Israel, and gave Israel glorious gifts.

Likewise the New Testament is the story of God's chosen people:

> You did not choose me but I chose you. And I appointed you to go and bear fruit, fruit that will last, so that the Father will give you whatever you ask in my name. (John 15:16)

> But God chose what is foolish in the world to shame the wise; God chose what is weak in the world to shame the strong; God chose what is low and despised in the world, things that are not, to bring to nothing things that are (1 Cor 1:27–28)

> But you are a chosen race, a royal priesthood, a holy nation, God's own people, in order that you may proclaim the mighty acts of him who called you out darkness into his marvelous light.
>
> > Once you were not a people,
> >> but now you are God's people.
> >
> > Once you had not received mercy,
> >> but now you have received mercy. (1 Pet 2:9–10)

John, Paul, and Peter are all agreed on that.

As you know, we have parlayed that chosenness into economic authority and advantage, so that the Popes, the Popes for us Protestants for fifteen centuries, did not allow error the same right as truth. It is our pope who divided up the new world so that Spain and Portugal could split the income from the mineral deposits. Since then all kinds of profits and advantages have accrued to Jesus' well-beloved church, all the way to clergy discounts, and tax advantages, even baseball passes is such enlightened wise cities as St. Louis! All rooted in chosenness!

That Christian advantage for God's people has segued over into Western white advantage that Ta-Nehisi Coates has termed "The Dream" for those whom he characterizes as "the Masters of the Galaxy." Coates writes of white advantage:

> "White America" is a syndicate arrayed to protect its exclusive power to dominate and control our bodies. Sometimes that power is direct (lynching), and sometimes it is insidious (redlining). But however it appears, the power of domination and exclusion is central to the belief in being white, and without it "white people" would cease to exist for want of reason.[1]

The "advantaged"—whether Jewish or Christian or Western or white or even Black thugs who run dictatorships in Africa—control the press, the media, the courts, the church, the university . . . whatever; we are indeed "masters of the galaxy."[2] We have gladly performed such hegemony and mostly we do not even notice we are doing it. We simply assume it and expect others to acknowledge it as well. The Bible is a narrative of such wondrous divine advantage:

> From heaven he came and bought her to be his holy bride,
> With his own blood he bought her, and for her life he died.
> Elect from every nation, yet one o'er all the earth,
> her charter of salvation, one Lord, one faith, one birth.[3]

> Ye chosen seed of Israel's race, ye ransomed from the fall,
> . . . hail him who saved you by his grace, and crown him Lord of all![4]

II.

The Bible, however, is a narrative of *advantage negated*. Hard to believe! But the story concerns a God who extends advantage and then moves against the advantaged. Already among the Jews in exile; they waited

---

1. Coates, *Between the World and Me*, 42.
2. Coates, *Between the World and Me*, 92.
3. Stone, "The Church's One Foundation."
4. Perronet, "All Hail the Power of Jesus' Name."

for homecoming. In their grief they knew that God willed to bring them back home to Jerusalem. But God's intention for them was not so singularly Jewish. Isaiah has God declare that deliverance and homecoming will be accomplished by a Persian, by a *goy* whom God calls "my Messiah" (Isa 45:1). What a contradiction in terms! *Goy*-Messiah. The Jews had lost their assumed advantage in history and now must be saved, if at all, by the agency of a *goy*. God found it neither necessary nor possible to contain history in the confines of the advantaged. God's way lies beyond such tight assured advantage. Now it was a Persian who would tend to the advantaged in the world

Some among Isaiah's audience noticed the contradiction and did not like it. They must have protested. They wanted to be saved the way they we always were saved in the past, by the wonder of their Jewish advantage. Some said, "We will not be led home by a *goy*. We will wait for an advantaged Jewish Messiah." In response to such resistance, the poet chides his Jewish companions: How dare you question God's way of rescue, even of it is not the way of your old advantage! The advantaged Jews are like a clay pot that questions the potter. The advantaged Jews are like a fetus that questions the birth process, or like semen that does not want to follow the usual path of connection. The poet says:

> Woe to you who strive with your Maker . . .
>
> Woe to anyone who says to a father, "What are you begetting?"
>> or to a woman, "With what are you in labor?"
>
> . . .
>
> Will you question me about my children,
>> or command me concerning the work of my hands?
> I made the earth,
>> and created humankind upon it;
>
> . . .
>
> I have aroused Cyrus (the *goy*). (Isa 45:9–10, 12a)

It will be the way I say and not the way of your advantaged expectation. My ways are not your ways and my ways will not be squeezed into your advantage. The poet says "woe." Big trouble is coming to those who cling to their advantage when it collides with the purposes of God.

The resistance encountered by Isaiah is not unlike the resistance that Peter voices in the book of Acts. Peter knew the purity laws. He knew the guidelines of advantage. He knew that snakes are unclean and must not be eaten. When commanded to do so, he protested: "I have never eaten anything unclean" (Acts 10:14). I kept to the rules of advantage. He knew Gentiles are unclean and we should not eat with them because we reserve the right to refuse service to the unclean, to the colored, and mostly recently to gays.

Except that Peter's advantage is interrupted by a nightmare. The voice in the trance said, "What God has made clean you must not call profane" (Acts 10:15). It took some doing for the Spirit to bring Peter along. But when Peter gets ready to preach this new disclosure, he blurts it out: "I truly understand that God shows no partiality, but in every nation anyone who fears him and does what is right is acceptable to him" (10:34–35).

I truly understand that the old purity laws do not work. I truly understand that the old advantage is now completely compromised. In the opening section of his sermon, Jewish advantage is abruptly put to flight. In his homiletical thesis, the end comes dramatically to privilege, certitude, and control. The God who chose now shows no partiality.

And Paul will line it out, perhaps in baptismal formulation:

> There is no longer Jew or Greek,
>
> there is no longer slave or free,
>
> there is no longer male or female;
>
> for all of you are one in Christ.
>
> And. if you belong to Christ, then you are Abraham's offspring,
>
> heirs according the promise. (Gal 3:28–29)

Paul names the privileged ones: Jews . . . free . . . male. We transpose the list: free, male, Western, white, straight. We could imagine this new list of heirs is the equivalent to a *goy* Messiah, or like eating a snake or welcoming a Gentile who has come to emancipation, not unlike Jews, males, and free persons.

And now the protest against God's new arrangement is thick in our midst. Male advantage is disappearing. White advantage is being called into question. We know in our guts that advantage is evaporating all around us. American advantage is fading as China initiates its own IMF and controls bigger parts of the world and the economy. And straights are not, with their biblical advantage any longer privileged. And the church has no more advantage. In many churches it is said this way: a) "The world is going to the dogs," or b) "We must take back our country." When probed, this means taking back advantage, and "to the dogs" means the disadvantaged are asserting themselves. I say this to you because I have come to think that political health and economic wellbeing in our society now depend on the graceful and willing acknowledgment that ancient advantage has been taken from some of us by God. It is that loss of advantage that fuels the anger and anxiety and rage and violence among is. But that advantage is now over, as Isaiah taught his exiled companions and as Peter witnessed to the early church. It is by the mercy of God over. God has moved beyond old chosenness.

III.

We are inching by the mercy of God toward a new level playing field. Peter, in his post-trance sermon voices this hard truth as the Spirit had given it to him: "I truly understand that God shows no partiality" (Acts 10:34). The ground of that truth is the peace preached by Jesus Christ to Israel: "He is Lord of all" (10:36)! And the Peter, in his sermon, describes the inexplicable force of Jesus of Nazareth: "He went about doing good and healing all who were oppressed by the devil, for God was with him" (v. 38).

But the people who sought to maintain advantage killed him. They put him to death on a tree. And they will kill anyone who threatens their advantage . . . King, Romero, all the daring witnesses who attest the end of advantage. And then Peter, in his own testimony, reports on the instant in the sweep of human history when these ancient advantages came to an abrupt end: "God raised him up on the third day" (Acts 10:40).

The power of Easter does not let the old niceties of chosenness prevail. If Jesus had not been raised from the dead, the chief priests and the Roman governor and the entire male, straight white Western ownership class would have had partiality from God to perpetuity. But he has been raised! The world has new possibility because it is under new governance.

Peter concludes his sermon by declaring the nature of the new possibility beyond advantage and disadvantage: "All the prophets testify about him that everyone who believes in him receives forgiveness of sins through his name" (10:43). For believing in him means abandoning the kingdom of scarcity and entering the land of abundance with the neighbor. The new evangelical possibility is grounded in forgiveness, the cancelation of debts. People are held in disadvantage by unpayable debt. But the advantaged are also held in debt by the unending anxiety and the unforgiven guilt of exploitation and diminishment of brothers and sisters. We advantaged remain in a cocoon of denial and do not even know our guilt for such leverage that defiles the neighbor. But it is there. It is moreover, such a relief when all of that is forgiven. We become free, we males, we would-be free, we Jews, we chosen, we whites, we Americans, we so long in advantage.

It turns out that advantage is only a necessity (a desideratum) in the pre-Easter domain of death. That domain of death is a zone of a scarcity. There is not enough for all in the world, so holding advantage and keeping advantage and securing more than the neighbor is essential to well-being. Advantage protects us in a zone of scarcity where all are vulnerable.

But here is the news. Easter has dispelled the truth of scarcity. In the kingdom of the resurrection there is no more scarcity. There is an abundance. That is why debts are can be cancelled and sins can be forgiven, because post-Easter reality is the zone of generous abundance from God toward us and toward the neighbor. It is so abundant that in the next paragraph we are told that the gift of the Holy Spirit was poured out even on the Gentiles; dare say even on Greeks, even on slaves, even on females, even on non-Westerners, even on non-straights, even on non-whites, even on non-Christians. Because the Spirit is a flood and surge and a torrent of generosity for all.

IV.

We make the move, as we are led, from scarcity to abundance, from Friday scarcity to Sunday abundance, from fearful coercive leverage to glad emancipated wellbeing. I tell you this because many of you pastor among those who are losing their advantage and do not understand beyond their fearful anxiety. You pastor among those who have arrived at the edge of the new zone of abundant forgiveness and now must find new neighborly ways to exist, to share, and to love. Or at least this much; you and I live in a society that is stunned at the loss of advantage so long assumed that now must find a way to live in the alternative world of Easter abundance, in which no one is kept in hock to unpayable debt. All is forgiven.

I tell you this because you and I are a part of a great institutional advantage that is abruptly ending. We could be in despair, or in denial, or in disappointment. We could be, except that God raised him up on the third day. Here and there we have found in our loss of advantage that we are overwhelmed by the gift of the spirit who surges among us. This is the news:

- —there is no partiality;
- —the kingdom of death and scarcity has been defeated by this Sunday surprise; God raised him up!
- —the Spirit surges in forgiveness upon those who have no advantage.

We are then free for a different life, forgiven, empowered, free from fear, ready to turn the world right side up! McEnroe threw a tantrum every time he lost an advantage. So do most of the rest of us. It was never his best performance; neither is it our best performance.

Columbia Theological Seminary
Festival of Homiletics, Atlanta
May 16, 2016

16

What Does It Mean to Be Human?

IN THE CHRISTIAN BIBLICAL tradition, being "human" is being in the image of God. The kind of humanness we embrace depends on who God is and how God is. In this tradition (shared with Judaism) God is marked by five big terms: justice, righteousness, steadfast love, faithfulness, and compassion (*mišpaṭ, ṣedeqah, ḥesed, amunah,* and *raḥam*). All five terms refer to tenacious relatedness to the other who is unlike us. Being in the image of this God means we are most fully human when we are tenaciously related to others unlike us in terms of justice and righteousness.

There is, however, a fake god masquerading in Christian tradition whose actions contradict the gospel. This fake God yields a gospel that is fake news. The fake god is one of fear, greed, tribal exclusiveness, and ready violence. This is a god who is worshipped and obeyed by fake Christians who believe the fake news, and who advocate for fear, greed, tribal exclusiveness, and violence in their own lives. And when we are honest, we find that we ourselves, all of us, are susceptible and sometimes tempted to that fake news and that fake life.

As a result a Christian notion of being human is always one of contestation between the image of God and the false image that arises from fake news. That contestation needs always to be done in vigorous, intentional, and public ways around real issues of restorative justice at the sore points in our society. Thus Christian humanness is not a private parlor game or a head trip but an engagement with the reality of the world.

That contestation is well voiced by the prophet Jeremiah:

> Thus says the Lord: Do not let the wise boast in their wisdom, do not let the mighty boast in their might, do not let the wealthy boast in their wealth; but let those who boast boast in this, that they understand and know me, that I am the Lord; I act with steadfast love, justice, and righteousness in the earth, for in these things I delight, says the Lord. (Jer 9:23–24)

On the one side are might, wealth, and wisdom of a worldly kind. On the other side are those things in which God delights: justice, righteousness, and faithfulness. To be human means to be aligned with that in which God delights. Being human means to be at this work in a society that is smitten with wealth and might and that is enthralled by transactional wisdom. That humanness of a relational kind, in such a world, is risky inconvenience with practical costs. That contestation, we Christians say, is clearest in the life of Jesus who gave himself away for the sake of restorative justice in the face of the empire. Such humanness requires immense intentionality, because the alternative of a fake way sponsored by a fake god is compelling and convenient. This humanness consists in daily acts of resistance and subversion according to a truth that has come bodied among us in covenantal Israel and in the life of Jesus.

Columbia Theological Seminary
March 14, 2018

17

When the Music Starts Again

ANY FAMILY OR COMMUNAL festive occasion can become a "sign" or a marker. It could be a graduation, a birthday, a funeral, or a reunion. But let us consider a wedding . . . a wedding as a "sign" or a marker of social, historical significance. This is how it was for the ancient prophet Jeremiah as he watched his beloved Jerusalem sink into misery. He must have thought, "Let us consider a wedding as a significant social, historical marker and sign." As he thought that, he noticed that weddings in the city had stopped. There were no more weddings in Jerusalem! He took the cessation of weddings to be, on the one hand, a sign of *God's active sovereignty*, and on the other hand, *a measure of the dislocation* that the city must face in time to come.

The book of Jeremiah has the prophet comment on the matter of weddings three times (though it could be that the three citations are editorial reiteration). At the end of his "temple sermon" (Jeremiah 7) in which he anticipates the gruesome sight of many dead bodies piled up (7:32–33), Jeremiah concludes:

> And I will bring an end to the sound of mirth and gladness, the voice of the bride and bridegroom in the cities of Judah and in the streets of Jerusalem; for the land shall become a waste. (v. 34)

There will be no singing, or dancing, no laughter, no celebration. All weddings will be ended, a sign that the city will end in "waste." In that "sermon," it is anticipated that the end of weddings comes about, according to the prophet, because of a systemic violation of Torah, a contradiction of the purpose of God:

> Will you steal, murder, commit adultery, swear falsely, make offerings to Baal, and go after other gods that you have not known, and then come and stand before me in this house? (vv. 9–10)

The shame of such violation is compounded by the fact that after such systemic violation, the perpetrators come piously to the temple and imagine that they are "safe and secure from all alarms," hiding like a "den of robbers" (vv. 10–11).

The point is a second time articulated in Jeremiah 16. In that prose passage the prophet anticipates a wholesale devastation of the city. God declares:

> Do not enter the house of mourning, or go to lament or bemoan them; for I have taken away my *peace* from this people, says the LORD, my *steadfast love* and *mercy*. Both great and small shall die in this land. (vv. 5–6a)

The city cannot and will not prosper without the divine gift of peace, steadfast love, and mercy. After a devastating portrayal of massive death, the cessation of weddings is a measure of the trouble to come:

> I am going to ban from this place, in your days and before your eyes, the voice of mirth and the voice of gladness, the voice of the bridegroom and the voice of the bride. (v. 9)

In response to this verdict, the prophet has his people wonder why such trouble has come upon their city:

> They will say to you, "Why has the LORD pronounced all this great evil against us? What is our iniquity? What is the sin that we have committed against the LORD our God?" (v. 10)

And the prophetic response is:

> It is because your ancestors have forsaken me, says the LORD, and have gone after other gods and have served and worshipped them, and have forsaken me and have not kept my law; and because you have behaved worse than your ancestors, for here you are, every one of you, following your stubborn evil will, refusing to listen to me. (vv. 11–12)

The theme is reiterated a third time in Jeremiah 25. In this version the point is made more specific with reference to the coming of the

Babylonian army of Nebuchadnezzar who will utterly destroy the city and reduce it to shame and humiliation. The prohibition of weddings is linked to a climactic assertion of ruin and waste at the hand of the Babylonians:

> I am going to send all of the tribes of the north, says the LORD, even King Nebuchadnezzar of Babylon, my servant, and I will bring them against this land and its inhabitants, and against all the nations around; I will utterly destroy them, and make them an object of horror and hissing, and an everlasting disgrace. And I will banish from them the sound of mirth and the sound of gladness, the voice of the bridegroom and the voice of the bride, the sound of the millstones and the light of the lamp. This whole land shall become a ruin and a waste, and these nations shall serve the king of Babylon seventy years. (vv. 9–11)

It will be evident that this prophetic tirade does not hesitate or blink at the direct linkage between *historical eventuality* and *divine governance*. In all three usages, the cause of cessation of weddings is divine agency:

> I will bring an end. (7:34)
>
> I am going to banish. (16:9)
>
> I will banish. (25:10)

I call attention to this because this is a direct linkage that most of us would not make and almost none of us would want to make. We do not readily imagine God's governance to be so direct; nor do we consider that the God of covenant would so willfully cause the suffering and death of God's own people. (The reader may notice that in my little book, *Virus as Summons to Faith*, I have given careful nuance to this difficult matter.) It is nonetheless important for us to notice (and perhaps flinch) that the prophetic tradition has no such caution in making that direct claim for governance. This lack of reticence on the part of the tradition may give us some nerve and courage to imagine what it is like to live in a world where the purposes of God cannot be mocked with impunity. In the end God will not be mocked, not by our wealth, not by our wisdom, and not by our power. The weddings stopped. The music was silenced. The laughter ceased. Historical circumstance was too sobering. Social reality was too devastating. The songs stuck in our throats. Our feet were unmoving on the floor. Maybe there were weddings, but no glad sounds. Or maybe not at all, because lived reality had sunk deeply into an unmanageable pause.

Such poetic extremity as these verses of Jeremiah might give us an angle of vision on our social "shut down" amid the pandemic. Among us it is as though the celebration has stopped, that singing has silenced and the dancing paralyzed. Weddings delayed, family reunions postponed, churches vacated, schools hit and miss on-line and in person, and cinemas darkened, sports events without fans. Social life, social interaction, and social possibility all have come to a halt (except for some daring super-spreaders!) The pandemic is reason enough as an explanation for the silencing shut down. We do not need to look further for an explanation. The prophetic tradition, daring otherwise, pushes back further to the sovereignty of God who occupies active verbs like "banish" and "bring to an end." We would not push that far for an explanation; the silencing, nonetheless, is a stunning reminder of how unmistakably penultimate we are in managing the mysterious givens of our common life. Such an awareness of our penultimacy at least lets us resonate with the texts of Jeremiah. As we study the rising numbers of "cases" and "deaths" daily among us, we can draw close to the imagery of Jer 7:32–33 of corpses piled up for bird food; in our case, refrigerated trucks outside hospitals with many beloved bodies therein. As we stay safe in self-quarantine, we can weave into the urgency of Jeremiah 16:7–8 with no "cup of consolation" to drink and the avoidance of "the house of feasting." As we notice that our number of cases and deaths is even worse than that of Brazil, we can expect that the United States is something of an object of "horror and hissing" among the nations (see 25:9). And if Donald Trump would have his way, he would readily cast "China" in the role of Babylon who will "lay waste the whole land" (25:9–11).

Of course this is all an over-reading of Jeremiah. It nonetheless gives us pause as we read the old text that we claim to be "revelatory." What is "revealed" is that in and through the pandemic via this poetry is the truth that the world operates on a scale, at a pace, and in a texture other than one of our choosing. It is the singular work of poets, ancient and contemporary, to summon us into this mystery that is beyond our explanation or management. We begin with the obvious: the cessation of weddings. From that we work deeply into the mystery of our helplessness and our extensive efforts to "stay safe."

After these three instances of silenced weddings in Jeremiah, it may surprise and amaze us in a most welcome way that the prophet offers, eventually, a fourth usage of the imagery of a wedding in Jeremiah 33. That usage occurs in a chapter that is filled with the restorative promises of God. In vv. 1–9 we are offered a sweeping promise of recovery, healing, prosperity, security, and cleansing:

> I am going to bring it recovery and healing; I will heal them and reveal to them abundance of prosperity and security. I will restore the fortunes of Judah and the fortunes of Israel, and rebuild them as they were at first. I will cleanse them from all their guilt of their sin against me, and I will forgive all the guilt of their sin and rebellion against me. (vv. 6–7)

In vv. 12–13 we get a vision of a restored environment with viable agriculture in every part of the land:

> In the towns of the hill country, of the Shephelah, and of the Negev, in the land of Benjamin, the places around Jerusalem, and in the towns of Judah, flocks shall again pass under the hand of the one who counts them, says the Lord. (v. 13)

In vv. 14–22 it is promised that the Davidic line will be continued and restored, as certain as is God's covenant with day and night:

> If any of you could break my covenant with the day and my covenant with the night, so that day and night would not come at their appointed time, only then could my covenant with my servant David be broken, so that he would not have a son to reign on his throne. (vv. 20–21)

The chapter concludes with reassurance about God's most elemental promise, the one made to the offspring of Abraham:

> Only if I had not established my covenant with day and night and the ordinances of heaven and earth, would I reject the offspring of Jacob and my servant David and not choose any of his descendants as rulers over the offspring of Abraham, Isaac, and Jacob. For I will restore their fortunes, and will have mercy on them. (vv. 25–26)

This chapter mentions every possible dimension of God's commitment to Israel. It affirms that God is the keeper of every such promise.

And right in the midst of this overwhelming collage of promises is our theme:

> There shall once more be heard the voice of mirth and the voice of gladness, the voice of the bridegroom and the voice of the bride, the voices of those who sing, as they bring thank offerings to the house of the Lord. (33:11)

Weddings will begin again! Life will be resumed in all its joy. Churches will be opened. Sports will be on offer. Cinemas will be available. Social life and social possibility are at hand!

In response to this renewal and restoration grounded in God's goodness, Israel will bring thank offerings. These offerings consist in generous material returns to the God of all goodness. And like all good thank offerings, these offerings are accompanied by words of acknowledgment, explaining why the generous gratitude of Israel:

> Give thanks to the Lord of hosts,
>> for the Lord is good,
>> for his steadfast love endures forever. (v. 11)

For a time God's steadfast love had been absent in Israel (see 16:5). But not now! In the liturgic tradition of Israel, thank offerings are a glad recognition that God is good. Beyond that, God's abiding tenacious fidelity has persisted in and through the trouble, that is, in and through the pandemic. And then, as if to seal the deal, the text in v. 11 adds the great tag-word of rehabilitation: "Restore the fortunes." The promise is for return to something like normal, the measure of which is the singing, dancing, and laughter of wedding joy that every time is bet upon the future. It is no wonder that Jesus, in the wake of Jeremiah, appeals to the same imagery of wedding, bride, and bridegroom for the arrival of God's new future (Matt 25:1–13).

These four uses of the imagery of a wedding in Jeremiah—three negative and one positive—provide a screen through which to reread and reimagine our own pandemic with its *shut-down* and its *awaited reopening*. Beyond that, the imagery takes up this most treasured social practice of a wedding and lets it be a vehicle for articulation of God's steadfast love. The *silence and restoration* of wedding singing and dancing bespeak a regular feature of Israel's covenant faith, a faith practiced in *exile and homecoming*, a faith that in Christian parlance is reflected in *the shut-down of Good Friday* and *the opening of new life on Easter*. Judaism, and we Christians in its wake, can gladly attest:

> Weeping may linger for the night,
>> but joy comes in the morning. (Ps 30:5b)

The first two lines of this verse are awkward for us, because we do not readily speak of God's anger. But the Psalmist will give it voice:

> For his anger is for a moment;
> > his favor is for a lifetime. (Ps 30:5a)

The accent is on God's favor . . . for a lifetime, a very long time! There is, however, no denying the intense alienation from us that God knows. This is very hard to voice; we nonetheless observe it enacted in our empty social calendars.

Walter Brueggemann
March 27, 2021

18

The First Great Commandment

MATTHEW 22:37–38

Jesus' teaching of the "First Great "Commandment" is embedded in a series of disputes about the nature of faith and Jesus' capacity to articulate and enact that faith.

I.

The longer text of Matt 22:15–45 features four questions that constitute Jesus' "oral examination." The exchange is perhaps to test to see whether Jesus has a grasp of the tradition and can function as a reliable rabbi. But of course, in the hands of the Evangelist the question of being as reliable rabbi is transposed into the question of his being the Messiah (see Matt 16:16–20; 26:63; 27:17, 22).

The first three questions are put to him variously by his opponents, the Pharisees, the Sadducees, and the Herodians. It may be that the disputes were characteristic rabbinic conversations; in context, however, there is an adversarial edge to the questions. The first question concerns paying taxes to the empire (vv. 15–22). Here the issue is clearly adversarial because eventually he will be "no friend of "Caesar" (John 19:12). They "plot to entrap him." He offers, in response, his well-known enigmatic answer. And "they were amazed" (v. 22).

The second question is put to him by the Sadducees who were the imperial rationalists and concerned the resurrection that they were eager to deny (vv. 23–32). Again it is a trick question; again, Jesus will not be drawn. He delivers a theological maxim that voids the question (v. 32). Our "great commandment" comes in the third exchange, this time again the Pharisees (vv. 34–40). Though there is, in these verses, no hint of an adversarial tone, we may assume that the "plotted to entrap" in verse still pertains. They ask him to pick out, from the array of Torah commandments, the most important one. He does not hesitate. He answers promptly, as if he had anticipated the question. We do not know what his interrogators expected. Maybe there was a broad consensus among them on this commandment from Deuteronomy and they wanted to find out if he knew the answer and shared the consensus. But maybe not. Maybe there were diverse opinions. Maybe there were social conservatives among the Pharisees who wanted him to focus on sexuality. Or maybe there were some Pharisees who were fiscal conservatives and thought that the right answer was, "Tighten the money supply." Or perhaps there were social liberals who wanted him to respond with some word about government relief. Or perhaps there were rational liberals who wanted him to say, "God has no hands but our hands."

So they asked him. They held their breaths to find out which side he would take. As in the previous questions, however, he refused the temptation. He blew away the question with the quotation from Deut 6:5. How could he do better than Deuteronomy! He aligns himself with the most dynamic of interpretive traditions. He appeals back to the great Shema' text that the scribes would eventually mark as "WITNESS." He placed himself amid the first commandment of Sinai concerning the "God-monopoly" of the creator who freed the slaves (Exod 20:2–3). They must have leaned back stunned, because he had outflanked all their trickery. Except, of course, he must add an edge to it by following Deuteronomy with Leviticus on the neighbor (Lev 19:18). In Mark's memory, moreover, Jesus' teaching evokes a scribal endorsement, and Jesus responds with a commendation for the scribe (Mark 12:32–34). In Luke 10:25–28, it is Jesus who asks the question and the lawyer answers with "the two great commandments." In Mark 12:32, the scribe responds to Jesus' teaching, "You are right, teacher." In Luke 10:28, it is Jesus who answers, "You have given the right answer." But in Matthew, there is no such answer, no agreement, no affirmation, no response. His opponents are reduced to silence, no doubt avoiding eye contact!

When the stunned silence had gone on long enough and it was time to terminate the exchange, Jesus confronts his adversaries by asking them a question (vv. 41–45). He inverts the relationship, and now he is in charge. Foolish candidate, not to let it rest! But of course Jesus had been challenging the old teachers for a very long time (see Luke 2:46–47)! Here he riddles them a question about the Messiah; and "no one was able to give him an answer" (v. 46). No wonder there were no more questions. It turned out, of course, that not only did he get a "pass" from his examining committee. He overwhelmed them with his mastery of the tradition and his uncommon authority. It is no wonder that in Matthew 23 that follows, there is an assault on the scribes, the Pharisees, and hypocrites who had failed to probe or understand the tradition in all its radical contemporaneity.

So now we know. Now we know that Jesus understood, beyond his opponents, about the seductive possibilities about taxes (22:15–22), about the enigma of after-life (vv. 23–33), about Torah accents (vv. 34–40), and about kingship, divine and human (vv. 41–45). Now we know that his authority makes him master of all the traditions and institutions of his cultural religious world. He has evaded nothing. We know from him about the old city (Matt 23:37–39), the old temple (Matt 24:1–2), and the old tradition (23:1–36). All are in jeopardy!

Now we know that in the person of Jesus there are "birth pangs" that twist and turn against what was old (Matt 24:8). And we know, further, that what carries over from the old tradition is the core commandment that defines everything in the new age of the coming rule of God, as it has defined everything in the old age of Sinai. Jesus is a *rabbinic conservative* who enacts *revolutionary Messianic dimensions* of the Torah.

II.

We are of course pushed by the answer of Jesus in v. 37 back to the old tradition. He is not making this stuff up! Rather he invites his listeners to stand in the book of Deuteronomy at the brink of newness, at the edge of the Jordan River, ready to enter, yet again, the land of promise. That fraught moment of entry evoke Moses' most magisterial teaching. Israel is about to begin a new life in a new luxurious place, without manna (see Josh 5:12). The new land is permeated with temptation. At a surface level, it is the temptation of the Canaanites, as we used to talk about "Canaanite fertility religion." In fact "Canaanite" is a metaphor for the seduction of self-sufficiency that will come with the new land. The luxury to come will be extravagant:

> . . . a land with fine, large cities that you did not build, houses filled with all sorts of goods that you did not fill, hewn cisterns that you did not hew, vineyards and olive groves that you did not plant (Deut 6:10–11)

The temptation to come is self-made affluence that will invite Israel to think, "My power and the might of my hand have gotten me this wealth" (Deut 8:17). Such affluence, in time, will breed amnesia:

> Take care that you do not *forget* the LORD, who brought you out of the land of Egypt, out of the house of slavery. (Deut 6:12)

> Take care that you do not *forget* the LORD your God, by failing to keep his commandments, his ordinances, and his statues. (Deut 8:11)

> But remember the LORD your God, for it is he who gives you power to get wealth, so that he may confirm his covenant that he swore to your ancestors, as he is doing today. If you *forget* the LORD your God and follow other gods to serve and worship them, I solemnly warn you today that you shall surely perish. (Deut 8:18–19)

The risk of the new affluence to come in the land of promise is that you will forget where you came from. You will forget who you are. You will forget the giver of gifts. You will forget the conditionality of commandments. You will imagine autonomy that can be readily engraved in self-indulgent religious prattle about "chosenness."

Indeed, Hosea, a close child of Deuteronomy, sees that such amnesia is the primal seduction of Israel:

> She offered incense to them
>   and decked herself with her ring and jewelry,
> and went after her lovers,
>   and *forgot* me, says the LORD. (Hos 2:13)

> And since you have *forgotten* the Torah of your God,
>   I also will *forget* your children. (Hos 4:6)

> Israel has *forgotten* his Maker,
>> and built palaces;
> and Judah has multiplied fortified cities;
>> but I will send a fire upon his cities,
>> and it shall devour his strongholds. (Hos 8:14)

> When I fed them, they were satisfied;
>> they were satisfied, and their heart was proud;
>> therefore they *forgot* me. (Hos 13:6)

And Deuteronomy, mindful of the indictments of Hosea, adds urgency to the commandments with the imperative to remember:

> *Remember* that you were slaves in the land of Egypt, and the LORD your God redeemed you; for this reason I lay this command upon you. (Deut 15:15)

> *Remember* that you were a slave in Egypt, and diligently observe these statues. (Deut 16:12)

> *Remember* that you were a slave in Egypt and the LORD your God redeemed you from there; therefore I command you to do this. (Deut 24:18)

> *Remember* that you were a slave in the land of Egypt; therefore I am commanding you to do this. (Deut 24:22)

The summons of Deuteronomy turns on the issue of remembering and forgetting. Israel an remain rooted in the deep tradition of the God of the Exodus; or Israel can sign on for a less demanding, more readily embraced identity as a complacent, self-sufficient people whose horizon is one of control, management, and manipulation of the systems of life and death.

III.

All of that is inscribed in the "first great commandment." The commandment is dominated by the two big verbs, followed by provision for sacramental-educational reiteration. The first verb, the first verb of all biblical faith, is "listen." Israel has been addressed. Israel has been called by name. Israel has been summoned. Israel is on the receiving end of the purposes of God. The "Canaanite" temptation of the book or Deuteronomy is to imagine that "we" (Israel) hold the initiative, that we act first, that we define and decide and determine. "Shema'" places Israel in a receiving posture to accept what is given "from the other side," far out beyond our conjuring or knowing or controlling. It is clear, as in Exod 24:7 where "hear" has the force of "obey," that Israel is summoned to obey. To "listen" means, as we regularly communicate by tone to our children, to obey; "You don't listen" means you do not do what I say. Israel is identified as a listener!

The second great verb of the commandment is "love," a term that has of course been trivialized and cheapened in self-indulgent romanticism. We may identify two dimensions of "love" that are present in the commandment. It is beyond doubt that "love" is a covenant word that means to acknowledge the covenant Lord (covenant partner) and so to honor obligations that belong to the covenant.[1] Thus there is a solemn, juridical aspect to the term, a promise to obey. Thus in the book of Deuteronomy, both the ten commandments of 5:6–21 and the derivative corpus of (Deut 12–25) summon Israel to obey YHWH in every sphere of life. But second, as Jacqueline Lapsley has shown, "love" in this tradition is not exhausted by the juridical notion of covenant obligation.[2] There is also an affective element of emotional attachment and commitment. Thus Moses can twice use the powerful word $ḥšq$ (passionate desire) for YHWH's disposition toward Israel (Deut 7:7; 10:15), and surely Israel's love back to YHWH is with the same passionate affection, as in Ps 91:14. Thus Israel is not only commanded to love; Israel is bound to YHWH in compelling ways that are more elemental than mere obedience:

> The LORD your God you shall follow, him alone you shall fear,
> his commandment you shall keep, his voice you shall obey, him
> you shall serve, and to him you shall hold fast. (Deut 13:4)[3]

Israel is to be gladly preoccupied with the things that delight YHWH. The piling up of the imperative verbs attests to the emotional force of the

---

1. Moran, "The Ancient Near Eastern Background of the Love of God in Deuteronomy."

2. Lapsley, "Feeling Our Way: Love of God in Deuteronomy."

3. The final verb, "hold fast," is used in Gen 2:24 to characterize the man–woman relationship where it is often rendered as "cleave to." The same intent is in our usage in Deuteronomy 13, thus casting the intensity of the covenant as like a marriage relationship.

covenantal expectation. Or in the imagery of Jeremiah who lines out the honeymoon of covenantal faith:

> I remember the devotion of your youth,
> > your love as a bride,
> how you followed me in the wilderness,
> > in a land not sown. (Jer 2:2)

With such passionate devotion, Israel trailed after YHWH with glad eagerness, to do all that may please YHWH in the performance of fidelity.[4] Of this responding fidelity done with passion, Eberhard Busch concludes:

> [The first commandment] allows us and bids us to choose the God who graciously chooses us. We cannot do this on our own, but only in response to God's electing grace. And I give the response in that I "trust in God alone, humbly and patiently expect all good from God alone, and love, fear, and honor God with all my heart" (art. 94 [of the Heidelberg Catechism]). Love always also means choosing. Love means saying with all the passion of love in the action of my life: this one and no other! In this way we may and should on our side reflect the self-differentiation of God from the idols and take part in this differentiation. This means of one thing that we need to keep ourselves open to the fact that God—because God is not that motionless One behind and apart from all historical phenomena—deals with us and meets us in ever-new ways and changes, in bright and dark hours, as helper and as judge, as supporter and as challenger.[5]

The two great verbs, "hear" and "love," do not constitute a one-time utterance or a one-time embrace on the honeymoon of Israel. Moses provides for liturgical, didactic reiteration in what I have called "saturation education" (Deut 6:6–9).[6] The children are to be daily, visually, regularly reminded of the miracle and the obligation and the passion that belong to being YHWH's covenant partner and lover. The antidote to the threat of amnesia is the endless active reiteration of covenantal memory and obligation.

The outcome of such "hearing," "loving" and "reciting" is a conscious, intentional community of oddness, an oddness that touches all of

---

4. In Jer 2:2 the honeymoon is said to be one of *ḥesed*; the same term is used in Hos 6:6 where *ḥesed* is said to be YHWH's "desire."

5. Busch, *Drawn to Freedom*, 299–300.

6. Brueggemann, *Biblical Perspectives on Evangelism*, 103–9.

life. Thus the triad of "heart, life, might" in 6:5 intends to claim every part of Israel's life for a counter-cultural existence in the land of "Canaan." That counter-cultural existence is focused on the God of the Exodus with two concerns in this tradition. On the one hand, it warns, negatively, to resist the temptation of "Canaanite" religion and "Canaanite" economics that are anti-neighborly. Moses knows that the "Canaanite" regime of self-sufficiency is powerful and attractive, and Israel is to have none of it. On the other hand, the great commandment aims, positively, at transformative energy. The book of Deuteronomy clearly attests that the "land of Canaan" can be transformed into a neighborly community so that the institutions, policies, and practices of Israel in the land continue with the force of the Exodus, that is, they continue the work of neighborly emancipation. Israel's seduction is to be "like all the nations" (1 Sam 8:5, 19). But clearly Israel is otherwise. The first great commandment has the effect of de-absolutizing all other claims and goals and desires, and drawing Israel always back to the emancipatory force of the God of Exodus-Sinai. The "decrees, statutes, and ordinances" of YHWH are designed so that the children will ask and learn about the Exodus and the "lasting good" that comes from life with YHWH (Deut 6:24).[7]

IV.

Of the entire Torah that Jesus knew like the back of his hand, Jesus focuses—in his oral examination—on this one verse from the mouth of Moses. He intends, of course, that the urgency of Deuteronomy should pertain to his own contemporaries, for the pressure against the oddness of covenantal obedience is persistent and pervasive, then as now. In his context, the defining seductions away from covenantal obedience were the *absolutizing* of the commandments in a positivistic way without the agility of on-going interpretation, and *assimilation* to the empire of Rome. Indeed, the two temptations of absolutizing and assimilation work very well together, for the empire never objects to positivistic religious law. Perhaps the four-fold set of questions in Matthew 22 (three addressed to Jesus, one asked by Jesus) indicate the seductions against which the great commandment gives standing ground. The first question about "taxes to Caesar" concerns the empire. The second question

---

7. The phrase in Deut 6:24 reminds me of the mantra from Andrew Carnegie now used by the Carnegie Foundation to describe its work as doing "real and permanent good." The move from Deuteronomy to Carnegie surely requires some sense of irony.

on the resurrection suggests a Gnostic narcissism that always has an appeal. And the fourth question concerning the Messiah suggests a convergence of theological issue and political possibility among Jews. The cruciality of v. 37 relativizes all the questions and moves to the Holy Addressor who gives Judaism its grounding and *raison d'être*. "Heart, life, and mind" all belong to the Lord of the covenant. They do not belong to the empire of Rome or to the positivistic religious law. The response of the scribe in Mark 12:32–33 (with a probable allusion to Hos 6:6) agrees about the sacrificial practices of the temple cult. The temple cult, along with imperial authority and positivistic religious law, all may become instruments of self-serving and self-securing. The commandment is a summons away from self-securing. As the commandment calls away from self-securing to the covenant with YHWH, so the second great commandment calls toward the neighbor.

V.

Of course the hard part is the contemporaneity of the great commandment to our time and place and circumstance. Insofar as the great commandment has a critical function, it serves to destabilize our favorite loyalties:

> ... from each idol that would keep us,
>
> saying Christian, "Love me more than these."[8]

The "more than these" requires that we identify, as best we can, the seductive alternatives that seek to talk us out of our oddness in covenantal obedience. You, dear reader, might give different nuance to the idols that talk us out of our covenantal obedience; but the inventory has some constants that are pertinent in our time and place:

- The covenant anticipates that society—and the economy—are transformable to neighborliness. The temptation is whatever *talks us out of hope* and the energy to enact that transformative hope; dominant ideology specializes in the production of despair.

- The tradition of Deuteronomy warns about the seductions of "Canaanite religion and Canaanite economics" that turn our heads and

---

8. The lines are from the well-known hymn, "Jesus Calls Us, o'er the Tumult" by Cecil Frances Alexander.

our affections away from the neighborhood and toward the self. The covenant summons us to remember and the seduction is whatever *infects us with amnesia,* so that we lose our grounding and our identity. Dominant ideology prefers that we not remember.

- After recalling Pharaoh (in the book of Deuteronomy) and after "taxes to Caesar" (in the narrative of Jesus), the commandment witnesses against the absolutizing of the state, the empire, and in our own context *the ideology of militarism* that passes for patriotism. The reach of empire in our society extends to the control of markets, the mastery of "natural sources" (oil, water), and the "unnatural" sense of entitlement that comes with the thrill of the flag.

- On the list, according to the question of resurrection, is the "cult of the dead," and the cultural practice of denial, the desperate effort to prolong life and the deep individualism that leads to issues of personal survival and away from the rule of God.[9] The popular notion of "immortality" translates into a pursuit of youth (endless exercise) and beauty (cosmetic surgery) and power, as though to fend off death.

The amnesia prized in our society, given iconic force in the "delete button," makes erasure easy and credible. It is enough to erase the bad stuff of violence, oppression, and exploitation that has defined much of the church and much of our culture. But the more elemental erasure is the erasure of the gifts and miracles by which we live, so that the capacity for gratitude evaporates into an ocean of self-congratulations. It is this erasure that Moses warned against.

Michael Fishbane, in his exquisite little essay on Deuteronomy 6, suggests that the question of the child in v. 21 and the recitation for the child in v. 7 evidences a deep tension between generations in ancient Israel, "two generations' memories, sets of experiences, and commitments."[10] He judges that the fathers wanted to "transform their uninvolved sons from '*dis*temporaries' to *con*temporaries, i.e., time-life sharers" in the tradition.[11] That does not suggest for us, I judge, that the older generation among us remembers and that the younger does not. Matters do not divide that way. Rather what we face, in the new world of forgetting

---

9. See Becker, *The Denial of Death.*
10. Fishbane, *Text and Texture,* 81.
11. Fishbane, *Text and Texture,* 82.

amnesia, is a fresh "modern" way of being in the world that appeals to all, of every generation. The older generation is as vulnerable as the younger. Nor is it a matter of tradition vis a vis Enlightenment rationality, though that contest is worth pondering. I judge that the issue is more particular, namely, the *specificity* of an emancipatory narrative and a set of obligations that arise inescapably from that narrative and the seduction of the *generic*. The bid of the great commandment is to remember the miracles and the agent of the miracles, nameable miracles and namable agent, while our society wants to reduce everything— miracle and agent and memory— to the generic, because the generic neither offends nor demands. Thus the interpretive task is to move from that nameable agent and namable miracles to our practices of "heart, soul, and mind." With this triad one can easily line out the comprehensiveness of the claim of YHWH. If we focus on the triad, we may notice that the triad in the Hebrew of Deut 6:5 is somewhat different from the Greek of Matt 22:37. In the latter case the triad of "heart, soul, and mind" stays with the mental, emotional apparatus, thus a bid for a complete commitment. But in the Hebrew of Deut 6:5, the second element is *nephesh* (all of life, not *psyche*), and the third element is *me'od*, force, might, wealth, stuff. Perhaps it is not useful to parse the differences too closely because, in the end, both triads have in purview the totality of one's existence.[12] In passing I may note my conviction that I believe that a sermon that walks through the triad (either one) and tries to identity the "zones of life" that are addressed is both boring and unhelpful. The triad, either way, is about "everything":

> Were the whole realm of nature mine,
>
> that were a present far too small;
>
> love so amazing, so divine,
>
> demands my *soul*, my *life*, my *all*.[13]

It is the "all" that is required by the great commandment.

---

12. McBride, "The Yoke of the Kingdom," 303, has provided a compelling summary of the triad:

> heart—with an undivided loyalty, both good and evil impulses;
>
> soul/life—commitment even to the point of death or martyrdom;
>
> might—substance, wealth, property given in the service of God.

13. The lines are from the hymn of Isaac Watts, "When I Survey the Wondrous Cross."

Finally the great commandment will draw the preacher and the congregation into the deep contradiction that is palpable between covenantal obedience done with a glad heart and the self-serving of the modern Enlightenment individualized economy that receives its religious cover in a preoccupation with personal morality and private salvation.

But of course the commandment has not only a critical function against our dominant ideologies. It is also *an affirmative call* to an emancipated life with the God of the covenant. It invites us to see how our "heart soul, and mind" (or in the variant triad of Deuteronomy) may embrace God's liberating action. It is the deep claim of Sinai, transmitted by Deuteronomy, that life with YHWH is a life of unencumbered freedom, freedom from the demands of the state or of the corporate economy, freedom from endless production and consumption, freedom for an emancipated community that, unlike the scribes and Pharisees, can focus on "the weightier matters of the Torah, justice, mercy, and faith" (Matt 23:23).

In *The Evangelical Catechism,* the handbook of my pietistic tradition, the great commandment is taken up in questions 27–29:[14]

> How should you summarize the Ten Commandments?
>
> What does God declare concerning these Commandments?
>
> What does God mean by this declaration?

The answer to the second of these questions is:

> "God declares: You shall keep my statutes and my ordinances; by doing so you shall live."

The supportive citation references the narrative of Luke 10:25–28 wherein Jesus says to the layer, "Do this and you will live." Clearly that assurance from Jesus, the citation of it in the Catechism, and the tradition behind it have in mind a very different notion of life. It is not the onerous life of aggressive politics. It is not the life of fatiguing consumerism. It is not the life of acute personal preoccupation. It is rather a life in sync with the creator God who has gives gifts that preclude devouring anxiety (see Matt 6:25–33).

But it is the response to the third of these questions that strikes me as urgent and compelling for us:

---

14. *The Evangelical Catechism,* 51–52.

> By this declaration God means that we trust the Commandments and seek to live in accord with then. The Commandments are not given to us in order to put us down or to keep us from enjoying our lives, but rather to guide and help us make our way through life with faith, a sense of purpose, meaning, and joy. The Commandments offer us the freedom to live out the purposes of our creation.

This tradition knows that it is life lived in imagined but idolatrous autonomy that eventually "puts us down" and robs us of joy. Thus the commandment frontally contradicts the assumptions of modernist autonomy and insists that covenantal fidelity is the only way to freedom and joy. The outcome is freedom that is given only in a life of covenantal obedience.

It is not surprising that in the narrative of Matthew, his opponents do not speak after he enunciated the great commandments. They do not speak, because his teaching made no sense to them. They did not know what he meant, so inured were they to their several ideologies. But along with his utterance, he showed them what he intended! He showed them by act, by gesture, and by word. From that utterance the tradition keeps inviting to another way in the world, a way of freedom. With the emancipation of the first great commandment, his teaching rushes on to the neighbor. There is, however, plenty to chew on with the first great commandment, even before we get to the second.

May 26, 2010

19

A Little Evangelical Geography

MARK 7:24–30

I WANT TO OFFER you some instruction in evangelical geography, that is, reflection on how the good news is always context specific.

I.

In Mark 6:30–44 Jesus does his well-known feeding of 5,000. Remember that number, six! In 6:1, he is in Nazareth and after that he is "among the villages," all in Galilee. He has a quite extended ministry in Galilee, his home country. Except for a few Roman soldiers, Galilee was a place inhabited by small town and country Jews. It was a modest economy of a homogenous population, most of them living in subsistence, but making it, even while they paid taxes to the Jerusalem establishment that colluded with the Roman Empire. It was the kind of live-and-let-live of rural intimacy, all of one kind of people. They were economically vulnerable, but they were the religiously secure because they kept the commandments.

It does not surprise, in that peasant economy of Galilee, that some were not doing so well. It is no wonder that they chased after Jesus in hope. Even when he withdrew to a wilderness place for R and R, the crowd followed him, hoping for a wonder that would settle in well-being on their lives.

He of course does not disappoint them, because he has compassion for them. They are his own folks. In his compassion he taught them about an alternative way in the world that he called "the Kingdom of God." And then he brings his kingdom talk down to bodily reality as he always does. No use to have grandiose expectations unless it matters on the ground. In front of him were hungry people in that Galilee wilderness. He fed them! They were like sheep without a shepherd, and he fed them like a good shepherd. He started with a little, five and two, loaves and fish. It is what they had in that small economy of Galilee.

And then he committed his lordly action that has become our most elemental mantra: He took, he blessed, he broke, he gave. He multiplied. He performed the Eucharist. No explanation, just testimony. No rational thought that all the crowd whipped out their lunches and there was enough. It was not a slight of hand. It was not a trick to be figured out and explained. It was a wonder. It was a declaration of the power of holiness that he embodied right in the middle of Galilee. Loaves abounded and he shared them all around in that homogeneous Jewish population of his own kind. He assured that they had ample resources, 5,000 men! Add women and children who were also there but not recorded. And baskets and baskets of bread left over. It was in Galilee because in the next verse the disciples are out in a boat on the sea in a storm, the Sea of Galilee, his venue for obedience and abundance.

II.

A little more geography! At the end of chapter 7, we are told:

> Then he returned from the region of Tyre, and went by way of Sidon toward the Sea of Galilee, in the region of the Decapolis. (v. 31)

He was in the region of Tyre, Sidon, and the Decapolis, that is, out of Galilee. The Decapolis consists in ten cities that were built and inhabited by Greeks. We are not in Kansas anymore, or in Galilee. We are among non-Jews, Gentiles! He heals a deaf man there. Mark reports:

> Immediately his ears were opened, his tongue was released, and he spoke plainly. (v. 25)

He spoke plainly . . . in Greek!

And then, in chapter 8, there was again a crowd of hungry people. Hungry Greeks, hungry Gentiles, hungry people not of his own kind. Remember that number: **eight!** You know how the story goes. He was moved to compassion when he saw Greeks without food for three days. He quizzes his disciples about available provisions. Seven loaves; they do not even report a fish. But if we reckon five loaves and two fish, we get seven. Either way, **seven!** And then he reperformed our treasured mantra, with a slight variation: He took, he gave thanks (not "bless"), he broke, he gave. He gave thanks. Only then does Mark remember: Oh, there were also a few small fish. Add that to the seven. But they are few and small, so it does not really change the prospect for food.

They all ate. They were all full. There are abundant loaves. Four thousand people . . . this time not "men" but counting women and children. Well, maybe not just "men" because they are not Jews. Among Jews you count men as heads of households, but among Greeks, who knows whom to count? In any case, an abundance, an unexplained abundance . . . no explanation, only testimony, only testimony that the power of Jesus is at work among Gentiles. Because Gentiles, for all their difference, have this in common with Jews. They get hungry. They need to eat. They arrived in the wilderness without food. They are the target of the compassion of Jesus. They are participants in the wonder of Jesus; Greeks, in all regards, in this narrative, are just like Jews. The numbers vary, 5000 and then 4000, twelve baskets and then seven baskets. But it is all the same.

For Jews: He took, he blessed, he broke, he gave.

For Greeks: He took, he gave thanks, broke, he gave.

The power of Jesus and the wonder of God are underway for Jews in Galilee and for Greeks in the Decapolis. He is the lord of abundance for both populations!

III.

Don't you wonder how the narrative gets from chapter **six** to chapter **eight**? Well, it is by way of chapter 7. Remember that number, *seven*! Do you wonder how the venue for multiple loaves changed from Galilee to the Decapolis, from hungry Jews to hungry Gentiles?

Well, consider chapter 7. At the outset Jesus has an extended dispute with the Pharisees and the scribes about cleanness and defilement, about ritual contamination and social rejection. They differ. The Pharisees think you become unclean by what you eat and take in. Jesus insists, against that, that you become defiled from within, by attitude. Even given the dispute, however, both Jesus and his adversaries are preoccupied with defilement and cleanness, a very Jewish preoccupation. Indeed, Jesus has been nurtured in a Jewish community that had all kinds of commandments about purity and cleanness and holiness, and he knew how it was all parsed. The purpose of the purity regulations is to make a difference between "us" and "them," between the good people who have access to the goodies of God and those who have no admission to those goodies.

Every society has access laws. The difference between folks may be determined by your dress, or where you work, or where you went to school, or the accent in which you speak, or who your momma was, or how much money you have. Purity laws are articulated by the managers of the goodies in order to guard access to the goodies, to give some preferential treatment and to deny it to others.

In Mark 7, when Jesus finishes his long dispute about purity, he goes to Tyre. It is as if he has to get away from Jews, so he goes to Gentile geography. He is confronted immediately by a needy woman. Mark reports:

> Now the woman was a Gentile, of Syro-Phoenician origin. (v. 26)

She is a non-Jew. Just who you would expect in that region of Tyre! She was a non-Jew who is dangerous to the touch for a Jew. And she has a daughter who is occupied by an unclean spirit. She had heard of Jesus, and so she comes and asks him to do a healing wonder for her deeply distressed daughter.

But here is the rub. Jesus pushes her away. He says:

> Let the children be fed first, for it is not fair to take the children's food and throw it to the dogs. (v. 27)

In his code language, the "children" are the Jews, children of privilege, children of the chosen. The "dogs" are the Gentiles; by the label Jesus calls them by a bad name; he demeans them and diminishes their social significance. The chosen come first. The Jews are chosen and get first dibs. It would not be fair to take food that belongs to the chosen and give it to the Gentile dogs. Jesus is still embedded in the purity laws that the good people of God come first and get the goodies. He is a Jew and had not thought beyond his own Jewishness, his own racial-ethnic status. But his unreflective notion of Jewish chosenness is abruptly interrupted. This nobody of a disqualified woman confronts him:

> Sir, even the dogs under the table eat the children's crumbs. (v. 28)

Even the dogs—the Gentiles, the non-Jews of Tyre-should get a crumb, should get a gesture, should get a healing. They are also eligible for a transformative miracle, because the wonder of God cannot be monopolized by the chosen people.

Her words are a massive assault on Jesus and his idea of being privileged and chosen as Jews. He has to be reeducated. He has to move out of his naïve notion of purity and chosenness. He has to notice the world beyond his own kind. He has to accept that the others count as well. Amazingly, he accepts instruction from the woman. He does not refuse to grow. He says:

> For saying that you may go—the demon has left your daughter.
> (v. 29)

What a moment in the history of the world! This Jewish rabbi, perceived to be the Messiah, has to reach out to the others and has to engage his power for well-being to heal the other. He eradicates uncleanness for the Gentile girl. Does it take your breath away as it does mine, that Jesus had to be instructed about the power of God for those who are not my kind? It is this bold defiant mother who so cares for her daughter that she will not let old racist distinctions determine who will get healing. She insists on healing beyond the narrow sphere of privilege.

IV.

So here is the geography lesson of an evangelical kind. In chapter 6 Jesus does a food wonder *in Galilee for Jews*. In chapter 8, he does a food wonder for *Greeks in the Decapolis*. From chapter 6 to chapter 8, he has changed venues, and has distributed the goodies for people in a new region that until that moment, he did not think they should get, not even a crumb from the table of chosenness.

Jesus is able and ready to make this geographical move because of this instruction from a nobody of a woman who would not let him off the hook with his racial-ethnic bias that masqueraded as a religious scruple. She forces the issue. And Jesus exhibits his conversion by promptly going to the Decapolis; there he healed a deaf man and then he replicated his feeding miracle, this time for Greeks. She had forced the issue. That is how we get from Jews to Greeks, from Galilee to Decapolis. Who knew? Who knew that Jesus had to grow and give up old socio-religious conviction for the sake of God's way in the world? The geographical move is forced by a nobody who would not let the Messiah rest in his comfort zone.

V.

So consider this evangelical geography and how it might be narrated in Louisville. Imagine that the city of Louisville is divided into two zones as the old world was divided into two zones, Jews and Greeks. Imagine that there is a zone of privilege and purity and prosperity, like there was in Galilee, with the necessary purity codes. That part of Louisville, like the chosen of Galilee, manages all the goodies and has access, guarded by the purity requirements of the race, class, wealth, and influence of the ownership class.

And imagine that there is another zone of Louisville, out West. That zone is regarded by the leading opinion makers in the city, as impure, unworthy, undesirable, and dangerous to one's health and one's investments. It is for the opinion makers and the dispenser of goodies a no-fly zone, a no-go zone of disadvantage.

So imagine the two parts of Louisville, divided by rules of purity and defilement. In the proper part, miracles of abundance are performed all the time every day, by corporations and by government with good services and good schools, and even good grocery stores. It is not a surprise that the chosen should have such benefits . . . seven or twelve baskets of abundance left over all the time. The goodies properly belong to the prosperous ones, the chosen of privilege, never given to the "dogs" of defilement and uncleanness.

Well, as with Jesus, it is time to interrupt such uncritical assumptions and practices. It is time to move the festival of abundance from the zone of privilege to the zone of disadvantage, because all the loaves and fish of abundance cannot be kept in a zone of privilege that demotes all others to the status of dogs. Jesus had to reiterate his food wonder in the new zone where he had not, heretofore, thought to go.

That move from the zone of chosen privilege to the zone of disadvantage is not automatic. It is not ever done willingly. It is done only when this woman without pedigree, this woman and her allies, speak up and require a miracle of abundance for the dogs as for the chosen children.

Jesus, without this insistent woman, would never make that move. He is, however, glad and ready to make that move when he has his world map redrawn for him. He is recruited into evangelical geography.

As a result, I dare imagine that we today, in the wake of Martin, are on the move from chapter 6 (the zone of privilege) to chapter of 8 (the zone of disadvantage) by way of chapter 7, the episode of confrontation and reeducation that permits reimagining how the bread is to be managed differently. We dwell in her insistent protest:

> Sir, even the dogs under the table eat the children's crumbs. (v. 28)

And we insist until we get a reassuring answer:

> For saying that, you may go—-the demon has left your daughter. So she went home, found the child lying on the bed, and the demon gone. (vv. 29–30)

Nobody expected Jesus to be reinstructed, a converted Messiah. Nobody expects the leadership of privilege to be converted. But it happens! It happens because geography is not just settled into strict zones of abundance and disadvantage. Geography is an arena for Gospel transformation. It turns out that the Greeks of the Decapolis get their miracle of abundance. I have no doubt that such insistent instruction results in conversions and the redrawing of the maps of abundance. The future of West Louisville will be as recipient of abundance, much more than crumbs! Martin would expect us to interrupt settled geography. Martin would join us in the redistribution of bread and all manner of good things. God is the giver of many baskets of well-being, all that rich surplus that leads to well-being. This requires a gospel voice that recognizes that geography is not destiny. It is rather a matrix of abundance that depends on thanks and brokenness. Imagine, both *in Galilee among Jews* and *in the Decapolis among Greeks*, he took, he blessed, he broke, he gave. He still does!

Walter Brueggemann
MLK Day, 2016
Louisville, Kentucky

20

Toward Perfect Health

ON READING ACTS 3:1–16

You God who raises the dead;
You God who gives life;
You God who heals,

Dear Sir:
Here we are in the waiting room of your presence, hoping for an appointment. We come with our several diseases and disabilities,
> diseases of feet and arms and legs and digestive tracks,
> disabilities of body and of spirit,
>> lame in a thousand ways.

Here we sit and wait, with great expectation.
> We expect and hope for healing from you,
>> for transformation,
>> for forgiveness,
>> for emancipation.
> We expect . . . because we have heard tales of your healing capacity,

> old stories of lepers healed and women with bad backs,
>
> > new reports of beggars who ask for alms and receive healing.

Here we are, waiting for you:

But we do not wait alone:

> We bring as our companions in suffering,
>
> > the folk in this congregation who wait in need and in hope.
>
> We bring as our companions the wretched who wait,
>
> > diseased by economic disadvantage,
> >
> > disabled by political exclusionary power,
> >
> > immobilized by a thousand slaveries
> >
> > > and a dozen anxieties,
> > >
> > > alienated by failures and other open sores.
>
> We bring as our companions the complacent
>
> > who discover too late that they have grown numb in indifference,
> >
> > and cannot move their hands to help,
> >
> > or their hearts to connect.
>
> We bring as our companions
>
> > the nations of the world that are not healed,
> >
> > the frightened nations armed to their teeth,
> >
> > the old colonial powers that still want to control oil and markets,
> >
> > the erstwhile colonies that still lack viability,
> >
> > and our own nation-state with its pathologies of greed and hate and violence.
>
> We are all here before you,
>
> > not doubting your capacity,
> >
> > waiting for your readiness,
> >
> > open to your prescriptions,

>   ready immediately to leap and run in health,
>   to dance and sing in restoration,
>   to praise to you in our newness.
> Dear Doctor: deal with us soon,
>   bring your best arts of newness,
>   and make all things new,
>   even here,
>   even now,
>   even for us. Amen.

April 23, 2012

21

Peace—the Fruit of the Spirit

ANY STUDY OF GALATIANS in general and "fruits of the Spirit" in particular will be greatly illuminated by the recent work on Galatians by Brigitte Kahl.[1] She proposes that "Galatia" is not, as we were taught in seminary, a territory (northern or southern Asia Minor). The term is rather a sociological category for those who dissent from the dominant social order and who propose to live apart from that system of domination. Thus Paul addresses those who are ready to dissent and live otherwise. More specifically, Kahl argues—persuasively I judge—that the "law" that Paul castigates in that epistle is not the Jewish Torah (as much of our past discussion had assumed), but it is the law of the Roman Empire that is a law that enslaves in the service of domination and in an extractive economy: "The law and religion that Paul primarily criticizes are the law and religion not of Judaism but of the Roman Empire."[2] Thus Paul writes to address those who have opted to live under the rule of Christ as an alternative to the law of Rome; that alternative is an offer of freedom, so that *the emancipatory Gospel of Jesus* counters *the domination of Caesar*.

Specifically the "desires of the flesh" are attitudes and practices of self-indulgence and self-promotion that were crucial in an honor/shame society. Kahl, following Robert Jewett, sees these "desires" as a yearning to gain superiority in the context of Rome that was "the boasting champion

---

1. Kahl, *Galatians Re-Imagined*.
2. Kahl, *Galatians Re-Imagined*, 257.

of the ancient world.³ Paul's bid, against imperial seduction, is to live as a participant in a generative community rather than in the competitive rat-race of the dominant imperial culture.

I.

Because the "fruit of the Spirit" is the alternative to "the desires of the flesh," we may begin with the negative in order to see what Paul intended by way of contrast. The empire of Rome, like every empire, was a macho enterprise that celebrated and rewarded military prowess and that placed great accent on success and superiority in the ways that evidenced virility. This "virtue" was attached to self-promotion, self-indulgence, and self-exhibit at the expense of the other. Roman law was designed to reward those who could master the system and to diminish those who are "left behind" who could not compete. Thus Kahl can judge:

> Paul's entire argument from Gal. 3:28 through 5:15 is then not simply projecting an otherworldly freedom but is part of a coded discourse among the enslaved nations about the spirituality and practice of liberation from the Roman "yoke of slavery" (5:15).⁴

It is not surprising then that "strife" (*eris*) (that I take as the antithesis of "peace") should be prominent among the "desires of the flesh." Success according to Rome norms required "strife"; competition could be abrasive and would readily spill over into violence. In his more theologically programmatic statements, Paul will speak of strife that is practiced among those whom "God gave up" (Rom 1:24, 26, 28) to debasement:

> They are filled with every kind wickedness, evil, covetousness, malice. Full of envy, murder, strife, deceit, craftiness, they are gossips, slanderers, God-haters, insolent, haughty, boastful, inventors of evil, rebellious toward parents, foolish faithless, heartless, ruthless. (vv. 29–31)

In Romans 13, moreover, amid an argument about "governing authorities," Paul can say:

> Let us live honorably as in the day, not in reveling and drunkenness, and not in debauchery and licentiousness, not in quarreling and jealousy. (v. 13)

3. Kahl, *Galatians Re-Imagined*, 364 n64.
4. Kahl, *Galatians Re-Imagined*, 256.

According to Kahl, Paul has in purview the characteristic conduct of both those who dominated Roman social power and those who competed in an attempt to "catch up." The church that Paul has in purview in his admonition is a distinct contrast and alternative to that imperial model of well-being that is based on competition and individual, manly achievement that requires defeat of other competitors, all in a replication of the power and honor of "Caesar." Paul sees that the church cannot attest the gospel as long as it imitates those modes of life and social relationships.

II.

Paul is a pastoral theologian; while he has, according to Kahl, the big challenge of Rome on his horizon, his energy and passion are mostly devoted to the life of his beloved congregations. It is clear that the normative value system of Rome (self-advancement, self-promotion, self-exhibit) had effectively penetrated the life of the congregations that are themselves variously marked by strife, dissension, and quarrels.

—In the church in Corinth, Paul writes about the wisdom and power of the cross that contradicts the power and wisdom that evoke imperial norms:

> For it has been reported to me by Chloe's people that there are quarrels among you, my brothers and sisters. (1 Cor 1:11; see 3:3)

The quarrels arose from choosing up sides among apostolic leaders. In 2 Cor 12:20 Paul reprimands such conduct as a prelude to his lyrical exposition love as the gospel norm in chapter 13. The contrast he makes in chapters 12–13 is radical and complete.

—In his letter to the Philippians, Paul contrasts those who proclaim Christ "from good will" and "out of love" with those who do so for self-promoting reasons:

> Some proclaim Christ from envy and rivalry, but others from goodwill. These proclaim Christ out of love, knowing that I have been put here for the defense of the gospel; the others proclaim Christ out of selfish ambition, not sincerely, but intending to increase my suffering in my imprisonment. (Phil 1:15–17)

—The Pastoral Epistles utilize the same rhetoric concerning strife in the church. Those who depart from what the author regards as reliable apostolic teaching are self-promoting:

> Whoever teaches otherwise and does not agree with the sound words of our Lord Jesus Christ and the teaching that is in accordance with godliness, is conceited, understanding nothing, and has a morbid craving for controversy and for disputes about words. From these come envy, dissension, slander, base suspicions, and wrangling among those who are depraved in mind and bereft of the truth, imagining that godliness is a means of gain. (6:3–5)

In Titus, moreover, such strife leads to divisions in the church that are unacceptable to the author who has a passion for unity:

> But avoid stupid controversies, genealogies, dissensions, and quarrels about the law, for they are unprofitable and worthless. After a first and second admonition, have nothing more to do with anyone who causes divisions. (Titus 3:9–10)

In all of these references it is clear that the congregations have too readily imitated the way of the empire and abandoned the way of the cross that is a practical alternative to imperial domination.

III.

It is in the context of such societal seduction that we consider "the fruit of the Spirit" and specifically "peace" as a fruit of the spirit. Whereas the "virtues of empire" imitated by the church assure parsimony and competition for "scarce goods," (honor, recognition, achievement), the good news of the gospel is the generosity and abundance of God that summons to a corresponding generosity and abundance in the answering church. The generosity and abundance of the Gospel (that of God) and the responsive generosity of the community that embraces the gospel contradict the scarcity system of the empire and make the behavioral patterns of the empire irrelevant and obsolete. Thus "peace" in the life of the congregation (and in "Galatia" among those who refuse the rule of Rome) means to live in harmony and mutual respect, to "look after the interests of others" (Phil 2:4), and not to insist on the right and domination of one's own role or opinion.

"Peace" then belongs in the cluster of virtues (habits) that rely on the generosity and graciousness of God and on the guidance of the Spirit who will lead beyond where we are prepared to go. The implication of such communal solidarity is the recognition that one's own status and one's own opinion are in fact quite penultimate and must be submitted to the well-being of the congregation. Thus "peace" and its cognate attitudes and behaviors do not add up to a code of conduct. "Peace" is rather a vision of a life of gracefulness that is lived in response to the gracefulness of God. The interaction of God's initiatory and sustaining gracefulness and a responding gracefulness constitute is a profound contradiction to the way of the world that is the way of the dominant system of imperial Rome.

Paul's great manifesto of freedom means freedom from the lethal bondage to social relationships based on fear and domination:

> For freedom Christ has set us free. Stand firm therefore and do not submit again to a yoke of slavery . . . For you were called to freedom, brothers and sisters; only do not use your freedom as an opportunity for self-indulgence, but through love become slaves to one another. (5:1, 13)

Paul recognizes that the issue of freedom from self-indulgence of a combative society is freedom for the neighborhood:

> For the whole law is summed up in a single commandment: "You shall love your neighbor as yourself." If, however, you bite and devour one another, take care that you are not consumed by one another. (vv. 14–15)

"Love of neighbor" is the antithesis of self-promotion and self-indulgence that will lead to devouring appetites and policies. Thus,

> Bear one another's burdens, and in this way you will fulfill the law of Christ. (6:2)

This is the whole law! It is the law of the new rule of Christ that contradicts the rule of Caesar. Paul's horizon is closely upon the church; but it also stretches beyond the church to the "good of all," that is, to the common good:

> So then, whenever we have an opportunity, let us work for the good of all and especially for those of the family of faith. (6:10)

Paul sees that the alternative conduct of the church has indeed wide implications beyond the sphere of the congregation. The inclusiveness of the baptismal formula of 3:22 is reiterated at the close of his letter with a hope of "peace" for the church:

> For neither circumcision nor uncircumcision is anything, but a new creation is everything! As for those who will follow this rule—peace be upon them—and mercy, and upon the Israel of God. (6:15–16)

I am aware that all of this commentary on the life of the church amounts to a familiar recital of platitudes. The matter is nonetheless urgent in the church because the practice of domination in the church (in imitation of the empire) is such a recurring issue. The issue is joined sharply, for all of its familiarity, in a way that touches deeply into the reality of church life. Suppose, for example, that domination consists in the exercise of power that readily takes the form of knowledge, that is, power belongs to those who "know better." Over time the church has specialized in "knowledge as power," a theme voiced in I Corinthians 13. ("Knowledge puffs up.") Power—the capacity to control—depends on knowledge—control of data that conjugates as the truth. Knowledge takes many forms in the church:

- the capacity to manage and manipulate policy;
- expertise in things doctrinal in order to assert orthodoxy;
- the management of moral codes that approve or disapprove, exclude or include;
- a long memory that "we have always done it this way";
- the ability to shade gospel claims into social ideology, liberal or conservative;
- the ability to out-Bible, out-talk, out imagine, out-remember;
- the capacity to manage technological mysteries and electronic connections.

Every form of social knowledge may move toward absoluteness. Every form of absoluteness, moreover, leads to exclusiveness and eventually a readiness to minimize those who do not measure up, who do not conform or consent to such knowledge as truth. The process of *knowing* and *controlling* and then to *absoluteness* and then to *exclusion* and finally to *wounding* is a ready echo of the imperialism of the world that Paul occupies.

Against such a way of life Paul insists on "neighbor." What we know of "neighbor," moreover, does not envision control, power, or knowledge; it concerns rather faithfulness in relationship, to be found reliable even when not "correct." The gospel of fidelity has been, in Paul's time as our own, too much transposed into a gospel of certitude, and certitude has never saved anyone. Thus Paul, in his catalogue of the fruit of the spirit, urges that the church remember and practice gospel faith that is about reliable social relationships, and not about being right, knowing better, having control, or advancing one's self. Indeed such faithful social relationships entail a certain loss of control for the sake of those whom God has put in front of us. It is impossible to imagine "Caesar" losing control and thereby ceasing to be Caesar. But we have this the declaration that God, in God's self-giving love, has for the sake of love, given up conventional divine control in the cross in order to create new possibilities for creation (Phil 2:5–11). It is no wonder that the apostolic preaching of the cross and resurrection caused the empire in the book of Acts to tremble. Indeed, the radicality of the fruit of the Spirit that entails loss of control for the sake of neighborliness causes the conventional church to tremble. For such self-giving abandonment might lead to all manner of "objectionable" connections for the sake of neighborliness.

IV.

"Peace" is not simply a Rodney King bid that "we all get along." "Peace" is not settling for the golden mean or the lowest common denominator. "Peace" is not the avoidance of issues that may cause conflict. "Peace" rather is the offer of the self in fidelity for the sake of the community. There can hardly be any doubt that the "imperial" ways of the world have impinged powerfully upon the contemporary church. The readiness of the church to divide into "red" and "blue" congregations, judicatories, and denominations is simply a sign that the gospel has been transposed into categories that offer "win-lose" options with losers being excluded. Indeed that the Church Growth Movement proposed forming communities of "like-minded" folk is a reflection of ideological passion that cannot welcome neighbors who are of a different mind. The "fruit of the spirit" is easy (or irrelevant) within communities of the like-minded. It is, of course, more demanding and more costly in a community of the "other-minded" who parse the gospel in ways different from our own.

Paul, however, is relentless. He will not compromise this defining point. He believes that the *The Big Sort* according to opinion, or interest, or ideology in no way to build a church.[5] "Peace" is the recognition that

---

5. See Bishop, with Cushing, *The Big Sort*.

all of our best convictions are penultimate and finally must yield to the presence of the neighbor.

The wonder of "Word and Sacrament" is urgently to the point. The sacrament is a performance of an open cluster of symbols that give great room for different opinions. As a consequence the church cannot impose too much on the thickness of sacramental symbols. It honors a mystery that is beyond explanation.[6] But sacrament comes with word. Sacrament comes with interpretation of Scripture. Our usual assumption is that the sermon "explains" something of the sacrament. But what if the process is in fact reversed? What if the sacrament illumes the sermon? What if all of our words of proclamation are regularly and knowingly passed through the filter of "blessed and broken," "blessed" as infused with power beyond us, "broken" as the shattering of our best certitudes. It is such utterance and gesture of "blessed and broken" that permits a genuine festival of life-giving surplus!

If we contrast the "desires of the flesh" with the "fruit of the spirit," we are promptly plunged into the vortex of scarcity and abundance, or better, into *parsimony and surplus*. The way of the empire, in contrast to the festival of surplus, is a way of scarcity. The empire never intends to distribute "freely," but always arranges that scarce goods are kept for the powerfully privileged. It is the way of the empire and so the way of the parsimonious church to make sure that entitled people have surplus with cost to the rest. Such a way allows for no peace at all. The gospel way, that Paul champions, is a way of abundance, of a community that need not quarrel because there is enough for all of honor, status, and valorization from which follows enough for all of material requirements. The fact that "loaves abound" in surplus means that there can be love, joy, peace, and patience!

Those who practice such neighborliness are grounded in abundance that emancipates, while the empire of market ideology intends that we will always strive, always be in strife for scarce goods. In the gospel of Mark, after Jesus has fed 5000 with twelve baskets of surplus and fed 4000 with seven baskets of surplus, the disciples still cannot compute the surplus of abundance. Jesus says to them in exasperation:

> Do you not yet understand? (Mark 8:21)

---

6. See Schwartz, *Sacramental Poetics at the Dawn of Secularism*, concerning the mystery of the sacrament and its ready distortion for the sake of power.

Mark, in his wisdom, can tell us why the disciples did not get it about gospel abundance:

> They did not understand about the loaves, but their hearts were hardened. (Mark 6:52)

The disciples are astonished because Jesus' actions fit none of their categories of explanation. They could not compute the surplus of bread; they could not connect the dots of abundance. And the reason they could not is because "their hearts are hardened." That is, they are a living replication of Pharaoh, the great master of scarcity who lived with a hardened heart. They trusted scarcity and could not fit the abundance of Jesus into that purview. Thus it is a contest of *scarcity* (that makes for competitive acrimony) and *abundance* (that makes peace possible). It is an easy move from *remembered Pharaoh* to *present-tense Caesar* who remains still the master of administered scarcity that requires strife, jealousy, and competition. Contra Pharaoh and Caesar is the Lord of abundance, offering a world where peace among neighbors is permitted, expected, and plausible.

It is important to recognize that among us market ideology with its passion for commoditization, backed by an immense military investment, marked by an endlessly escalated fear of terrorism that relentlessly calls attention to violence in the neighborhoods wants to keep us on edge, fearful, anxious, on guard, and exclusionary. We can see this fearful anxiety being acted out in society and much too often in the church that imitates society. But all of that is Caesar's big lie! And our kids are seduced in powerful ways into Caesar's big lie.

As I write this Nick Bilton reports on his nephew, ten years old, who is "obsessed" with "Clash of Clans, a super popular game played on smart phones."[7] He reports on the way in which his nephew had advanced enough in the clan to be able to exclude some others from his "clan." But then in a narrative reversal, his nephew found he in turn had been excluded from the clan he led; he was preoccupied in anxious ways with his own exclusion. Bilton suggests that such exclusionary action comes "naturally to 10-year-old boys, whether online or in the real world." Such exclusionary action, however, is much more than that. The game is a school for the empire through which our young are inducted into a world of scarcity and violent competition that make peace impossible.

---

7. Bilton, "Lord of the Screens."

Against such specious world-construction, the real world entrusted to us is a world of abundance where the practice of peace among neighbors is not only mandated but is fully appropriate. The movement of our lives from the "desires of the flesh" (funded the empire) to "the fruit of the spirit" (gifts given in the gospel) requires a) escaping the grip of Caesar and b) witnessing that loaves abound, fully enough for the neighbor. Such a reality makes a different life possible, a life lived in joy and generosity. As Paul asserts, "There is no law against such things (5:23). Well, the only law against neighborly generosity is the law of Caesar. But this law of Christ that Paul articulates is alternative to the law of Caesar who sponsors and insists upon on-going strife. We in the church are constantly being talked out of the law of neighborliness, and then we decide yet again for that gospel counter-law. The force of Caesar is powerful; but the "Galatians" knew better!

June 5, 2015

22

Three Key Moves toward White Extremism

CHRISTIAN EXTREMISM, A.K.A. "WHITE extremism," is widespread in our society. It comes in two forms. On the one hand white Christian extremism is of the thuggish popular variety that tilts toward and is tempted by violence (with the rhetoric of anger and hate). This variety was on full exhibit in the capitol on January 6. On the other hand it is of a legal variety that operates by regressive measures concerning voting rights and immigration policy (with the rhetoric of "The Constitution.") Both forms of Christian extremism aim at protecting white Christian privilege and excluding non-whites (non-Christians) by circumscribing rights, privileges, and entitlements of US citizenship. Mythic propulsion of this extremist is the imagined threat of being "replaced." Both forms of Christian white extremism have long depended on white supremacy that requires exclusion by both *legal means* and by *means of thuggish intimidation*.[1] It happens that such Christian white extremism is currently aimed at Islam ("radical Islam") and Asian-Americans, but it is the same force and energy that have been directed toward other populations that constitute a threat of "the other." The combination of thuggish and legal action has served to protect and maintain or recover white Christian monopoly. It is my judgment that we cannot fully understand white

---

1. See Cone, *The Cross and the Lynching Tree*, and the astonishing work of Ida B. Wells in Giddings, *Ida: A Sword among Lions*.

Christian extremism if we do not consider white Christian supremacy, that is, white Christian superiority. Here I will consider three important historical moments in the long-term emergence of superiority and supremacy that regularly issue in extremism.

I.

At the outset the early Christian movement was a Jewish sect within Judaism. The early highly contested decision to open the Christian community to Gentiles opened the way for growth and expansion beyond the confines of a Jewish sect (Acts 15). The transport of Christian faith and Christian community west from Jerusalem to Rome is laid out in the career and epistles of the apostle Paul, in the book of the Acts of the Apostles (see Acts 28:11–14), and in the legends of St. Peter. It was inevitable that this early movement would be transposed into a Gentile phenomenon.

Even given the rapid expansion and growth of the movement, the Christian Church remained an illicit, subversive movement in the Roman Empire that was subject to abuse by imperial authorities.[2] All of that was changed by the Edict of Milan in 313 CE. The exact details of that historical turn are unclear; what is clear is that in these years Emperor Constantine encouraged a policy and practice of toleration toward the Christian movement that was confirmed and sealed by Licinius, emperor in the East. While the grant of Milan in 313 was of a general confirmation of religious freedom, its clear intent was to make space for the Christian movement to which Emperor Constantine became an adherent.

While the "Edict of Milan" only gave "toleration" for the freedom the Christian movement, it did not of itself confirm Christianity as the religion of the empire. But it did not, on the other hand, preclude the political effect whereby the "religion of the Emperor Constantine" became "the religion of the empire." That is, making space for its *legitimacy* promptly led to the *establishment* of Christianity as the imperial religion in the West. Thus a ready case can be made that this moment of legitimation established Christian domination that took a long while to implement in practice. The effect was to join *power* to *chosenness*, this replicating the practice of ancient Israel that joined *chosenness* to *power* in the Davidic–Solomonic dynasty, a joining that was only terminated by the end of the dynasty with the destruction of Jerusalem. In Jewish

---

2. See Stark, *The Triumph of Christianity*.

tradition the convergence of *chosenness* and *power* has come to belated expression in the Zionist doctrine of the state of Israel. From the outset the Christian movement understood itself as "the chosen of God," but that chosenness did not until now convert to power (see John 15:16; 1 Cor 1:27–28; 1 Pet 2:9–10). When chosenness is linked to power, however, it is predictable that a sense of superiority and supremacy would soon follow.[3] Christians (white Christians in the west) were on their way to being both supreme and superior.

II.

The long term development of the new Christian West solidified into the domination of the Roman Church through the authority of the Pope, coupled with the establishment of a variety of "Christian princes." While the relationship between and interaction among the Vatican and these several princes were complex and endlessly contested, the growing assumption of dominant Christian tradition, Christian authority, and Christian power as settled, established, and unquestioned. The tacit assumption is that these established powers (church and states) by right and by obligation should extend their authority to the entire known world so that Christendom should be conterminous with the known world. The ground for such a claim is that Christian truth was without challenge or rival, and that truth could be extended and expanded by Christian governance and the combination of business expansion, missionary effort, and where necessary coercive military action.

It was of course inevitable that such universal claims would collide with other theo-political claims, notably those of Islam in the East. Alexios I, emperor in Constantinople, appealed at the end of the eleventh century to Rome for assistance and relief from Islamic political pressure. In 1095 Pope Urban II responded to that urgent appeal for help by proclaiming a crusade that would mobilize a political military force of Christian powers in the West against Muslim power in the East, and specifically in the context of Jerusalem:

> Urban now proclaimed the Crusade in an appeal of almost unexampled consequence. The enterprise had magnified in his

---

3. Brown, *Through the Eye of the Needle*, has traced the dramatic altering of Christianity in the fourth and fifth centuries when wealthy persons joined and came to dominate the church.

conception from that of aid to the hard-pressed Alexius to a general rescue of the holy places from Moslem hands ... The real work of the First Crusade was accomplished by the feudal nobility of Europe ... The complete defeat of an Egyptian relieving army near Ascalon on August 12, 1099, crowned the success of the Crusade.[4]

Thus the barbaric assignment of the First Crusade consisted in a military assault on Muslims in the East propelled by the religious authorization of the pope as the final authority of Christendom. While the venture played out in political military ways, it implied at every step the duty and obligation of Christendom to extend its reach to the East and the right to eliminate Islamic power. It is highly ironic that Saladin, Islamic ruler in Syria and Egypt, a primary adversary for the Crusaders, conducted himself with generosity that was in sharp contrast to the ruthlessness of the Christian crusaders.

For our purpose it is sufficient to notice that the Pope and the Christian princes simply assumed the legitimacy of Christian military force to extend the presence, influence, and political power of Christendom to the East. Those who opposed the Crusaders, on religious grounds, were dismissed as illegitimate agents who were rightly eliminated by whatever means necessary. Thus the superiority of the Christian West, the primacy of Christian theological claims, and the propriety of Christian power were all treated as settled legitimacies.

Remarkably the great historian, Williston Walker, can celebrate the gains of the Crusades as contributing to the "highest theological development," yielding "great popular religious movements," and evoking "great artistic development," that for him allow the verdict: "Admitting that the Crusades were but one factor in this result, they were worth all their cost."[5]

Such a remarkably myopic verdict is fully contained within the rights and privileges of white Western Christians without any notice of the blatant dismissal of the claims of Islam, or the residue of resentment that would continue to fester for foreseeable futures. That verdict is an example of the sheer disregard of the "other" when evaluating and appreciating the gains made for the "superior" historical reality of Christendom.

The Crusades performed white Western Christian superiority toward the external "other" of Islam. Within a century of the proclamation of the

4. Walker, *A History of the Christian Church*, 220–21.
5. Walker, *A History of the Christian Church*, 224.

First Crusade (1095) the same performance of superiority was offered toward the internal "other" by the Synod of Toulouse in 1229. That Synod initiated an investigative Inquisition into a variety of "heterodoxies" that departed from the teaching of the Catholic Church and that challenged the monopoly of faith taught by the Roman Church. Thus *the Inquisition* can be seen as the internal expression of the same impulse to which *the Crusades* gave external expression. Both externally in the Crusades and internally in the Inquisition, the unquestioned authority of the church provided the warrant for aggressive action. In order to maintain that unchallenged authority, the church via the Inquisition did not hesitate to enact harsh violent measures against heterodox tendencies.

The history of the Crusades and the Inquisition is, to be sure, enormously complicated. It is not complicated, however, to discern the singular claim that is championed through all of the complexity, namely, that Christian faith of a particular kind, codified in a particular form, deserves to be dominant and justifies the use of violence to enforce and maintain that claim. We have here come a very long way from the "Edict of Milan" in 313. That edict only *allowed* Christian faith; it did not *establish* it. From the first, however, that "toleration" was tied to the power of the empire. As a result what was allowed at Milan was de facto established and soon placed beyond question or challenge. When tied to power as it was in the horizon of the Christian princes, it was an easy step toward exclusive legitimacy that would not and could not tolerate the "other," not the "other" of Islam and not the "other" of heterodox Christian teaching.

III.

The modern world arrived with the theological revolution of Martin Luther and the scientific reasoning of René Descartes. In that same moment, with the work of Columbus, Balboa, Magellan, Pizzaro, de Soto, and Cortés, the princes of the Christian empire readily "deserved" a whole new world of the Western hemisphere that was filled with both compelling resources and a population of the "other" who fit none of the categories of imperial Christendom. That "discovery" of the New World by these daring explorers, backed by the rights, greed, and legitimacy of nations states, led to enormous energy in the claim and occupation of western lands and, not surprisingly, to intense competition for control among the European powers.

In order to adjudicate such competing claims and in order to assert the authoritative reach of Christendom into "the new lands," the Vatican in 1493 issued its decree, "The Doctrine of Discovery."[6] It is impossible to overstate the importance and long-term impact of this papal edict. It declared, in tight and comprehensive legal reasoning, the right and duty of the Spanish king to control and administer vast lands in "the new world," the freedom to occupy the land, to possess its rich resources, and to convert or eliminate its indigenous populations. While the decree was to the immense advantage of the Spanish state that was closely allied with the papacy, we should not miss the astonishing assumption of authority by the pope and the high-handed reasoning that the "new lands" were waiting to be "discovered," occupied, and exploited by European princes. The entire project smacks of an assumption of cultural-political superiority and of religious supremacy.

The Doctrine of Discovery served to dispossess native peoples of their lands and resources, and it was especially important in the colonial practices of the English-speaking world. The doctrine illuminates our theme of superiority and supremacy, for as Ruru, Lindberg, and Miller can assert:

> The Doctrine of Discovery has it origin the notion of superiority. The Doctrine is built upon this largely racialized philosophy: those who were superior had superior rights to those who were inferior. "Infidel" inferiority was predicated upon notions of correspondence with the imperialist defined notions of humanity. Finding the basis in religious theology, the Old World was understood to exist by virtue of the theology which defined colonizing nation inhabitants as possessing direct relationship to the Supreme Power through his representatives on earth. Those who were unrelated to the representatives were understood to be opposed to and conflicting with the authority. They were also understood to possess less humanity. This understanding led, further, to the supremist understanding that those who did not share imperialist religious beliefs and who did act in accordance with those beliefs, were lesser humans. Lesser humans had, as well, lesser rights: to liberty, to property, to life. This list of infidels included Indigenous peoples within the "New World."[7]

---

6. For a contemporary critical assessment of the doctrine of discovery (*Inter Caetera*), see Wolk and Heinrichs, eds., *Yours, Mine, Ours: Unravelling the Doctrine of Discovery*, a special edition of *Intotemak* published by the Mennonite Church Canada.

7. Ruru, Lindberg, and Miller, *Discovering Indigenous Lands*, 94.

As we draw our attentions closer to the superiority and supremacy in the United States, we are able to see how the Doctrine of Discovery has come to serve white supremacy. Thus Lindsay Robertson has traced the way in which the Doctrine was incorporated into US law by Chief Justice John Marshall, and how the Doctrine became the basis for Andrew Jackson's displacement of the Cherokee Indians in order that whites in Georgia could secure the land as their own.[8] Thus the land is claimed not by conquest but by "discovery."

A recent echo of possession "by discovery" is narrated by Patrick Phillips, *Blood at the Root,* who reports on the way in which African Americans were forcibly dispatched out of Forsythe County Georgia in the twentieth century.[9] The displacement of the black population of the county featured a combination of white extremism in both thuggish and legal types. The thuggish way consists in forcibly removing all blacks under pain of death. The legal aspect was that when blacks had abandoned their homes and property in fear, whites paid tax on the property for seven years and thereby became the new owners. The dramatic expulsion from Forsythe County is only a recent example of the long term enactment of Christian white superiority and supremacy that eventuates in extremism in both thuggish and legal modes. It takes no imagination at all to see the linkage between this displacement and the ancient displacement of the Canaanites by the chosen who were entitled to the land.

We come now, in the wake of Donald Trump, to the mantra, "Make America Great Again." The phrase is shot through with racist nostalgia for the occupation of the land by those who are superior and supreme. I am bound to conclude that President Trump himself is only the point person and means of expression of that misguided sense of supremacy and superiority. That sense of superiority now receives legal expression in immigration restrictions, voter repression, and militarization of police authority, all of which aim to delegitimate the "other" that embodies threat and alternative to white domination. Thus the adrenalin behind the mantra is yet another expression of a superiority and supremacy that are deep and long-standing in white Western Christendom. Trump's own deep and defining commitment to this ideology is evident, for example, in his dismissal of congresswomen with whom he disagrees, that

---

8. See Robertson, *Conquest by Law*; and Newcomb, *Pagans in the Promised Land.*
9. Phillips, *Blood at the Root.*

they should all "go back to where they belong." This, even though they are all and each a US citizen!

IV.

The matter is much more complex than this simple enumeration. I suggest, however, that when we read backward, we are able to see the long line of development that has eventuated in Christian white extremism. One recent articulation of such extremism, of course, is the current anti-Muslim fad that concerns both a new "crusade" against Islam and an exclusion of Muslims from the United States on religious grounds. That anti-Muslim white extremism is of a piece with long-term, anti-black extremism that yields harsh reaction against any black gain in politics or economics.[10]

But behind that extremism toward blacks and toward Muslims and Asian-Americans (or toward any other challenging group) is deeply rooted in the "doctrine of discovery" that assumes the legitimacy of white Western European control over native peoples who are incapable of self-governance. The action of "discovery" has given ground for endless land appropriation. But that "doctrine" would not have been possible had not the authority of the church and its administration of all Christendom been articulated and performed in the Crusades and the Inquisition. That enormous ecclesial assumption of authority, in turn, would not have been possible without the establishment of Christian faith as the true religion of imperial Europe and of the entire known world. The thuggish and legal means of extremism are only possible because of the long term claim of supremacy and superiority that has no capacity for positive engagement with "the other."

I may add a coda that will indicate that such extremism is not simply the work of thuggery but in fact is a compelling conviction of much of the intellectual class as well. Tomoko Masuzawa has detailed the way in which "world religions" developed as a nineteenth-century project in Europe.[11] While the project was concerned with the five world religions (Judaism, Christianity, Islam, Hinduism, Buddhism), the hidden but powerful agenda was to exhibit the superiority of Western Christianity. Masuzawa shows that for all of its urbane scholarship, in fact "world

---

10. See Anderson, *White Rage*.
11. Masuzawa, *The Invention of World Religions*.

religions" was shot through with racist assumptions. Davis Hankins and I, moreover, have shown how this assertion of white European superiority was bootlegged into our discipline of Old Testament study in the form of "the Documentary Hypothesis" that purported to trace "religious evolution" in the Bible from "primitive Semitism" to the sophistication that culminated in Western categories of faith.[12]

I cite this remarkable insight from Masuzuwa to indicate how racist proclivity has permeated into the domain of critical scholarship that makes a pretense of objectivity. The current fruit of this long-term trajectory of racial superiority is the war on "radical Islam" that is readily taken to be characteristic of all Islam. This articulation of cultural reality has been given classic and effective formulation by Samuel Huntington in *The Coming Clash of Civilizations*.[13] That model of cultural reality now appeals with great weight not only in popular US opinion but in the high councils of learned experts. It is clear enough, in my judgment, that this current preoccupation with "radical Islam" is simply another manifestation of Western white supremacy that has shown up in opposition to Muslims in the Crusades and more broadly in the Doctrine of Discovery with the extravagance of colonial exploitation.

It is of immense importance that Huntington's well-known thesis has been effectively answered by Martha Nussbaum who has shown that it is the inability to honor the other that is the key issue in Huntington's formulation and in the doctrine of discovery.[14] (Nussbaum offers a close reading of the Hindu–Muslim conflict in India as a case study for her compelling thesis.) It is clear that "the other"—non-Christian, non-white, non-Westerner—does not need to be honored if and when Christian white Westerners are in all cases and circumstances superior. The entire trajectory of superiority serves to diminish and dismiss "the other" as an important and defining presence in the world.[15] Nussbaum has proposed, to the contrary, that the "clash" of which Huntington writes is in fact a "clash within." She sees that in each of us there is a clash between *fear of the other* and *welcome of the other*. How we work that clash

---

12. Brueggemann and Hankins, "The Invention and Persistence of Wellhausen's World."

13. Huntington, *The Clash of Civilizations and the Remaking of World Order*.

14. Nussbaum, *The Clash Within*.

15. Even in the Edict of Milan, the language was only the rhetoric of "tolerance" that regularly turns out to be patronizing and condescending. Significant honoring of the "other" requires much more engagement than what is indicated by "tolerance."

is decisive for our common human future. Because the clash is "within," it is clear that pastors have important and quite distinctive work to do in making that clash available to our own awareness and then providing processes and venues in which the clash can be appropriately dealt with. Without such processing it is no wonder that demagogues find it easy to mobilize that great fear of the "other" in popular, violent, and dangerous ways. It is not likely that there is much thuggish supremacy among our church constituency. But it is for sure that there is much legal, polite white supremacy within the confines of the church. For that reason this is an urgent task for pastors. We will do well to let people in on this long term history of supremacy and how we ourselves are on the receiving end of that trajectory, much to the betrayal of evangelical faith.

There is, I judge, a straight line from the Edit of Milan through the Crusades, through the Doctrine of Discovery to the violence of January 6 that sought to block the proper functioning of our multi-racial democracy. All of this cannot be blamed on or credited to President Trump because it is thick, deep, and systemic among us. There is no doubt, nevertheless, that Donald Trump has served to legitimate that long lingering destructive sentiment. It is evident, of course, that the gospel contradicts this trajectory of fear. But the undoing of its power among us will require careful, intentional, sustained teaching in order to *unlearn our dominant historical-political-theological tradition.*

May 6, 2021

23

A Retrospect

It has been a long run for me with the *Journal of Preacher*—both as an editor and as a contributor. Here are some of my reflections on my investment in the *Journal*.

I.

The *Journal* has been, beyond my expectation, a most important matrix for my own scholarly work as a biblical interpreter. According to my not-fully-reliable records, I submitted my first article to the *Journal* in 1985, the year before I joined the faculty of Columbia Seminary. That article in the Easter issue was titled, "The Family as World-Maker" (pp. 8–15). Beginning in 1987, my first full year at the seminary, I began to contribute regularly to the *Journal* almost every year, largely at the invitation of Erskine Clarke. The slow year-by-year accumulation of these scribbles led me to republish them in book form. My friend, K. C. Hanson, editor in chief at Cascade Books, graciously agreed to the republishing, and did so in four small books:

- *Truth-Telling as Subversive Obedience* (2011)
- *Remember You are Dust* (2012)
- *Embracing the Transformation* (2014)
- *The Practice of Homefulness* (2014)

After some time I also became an associate editor of the *Journal*. That work included the writing of a foreword for several issues each year. The first of these was in Easter 1991. After that I wrote forewords regularly, for the most part alternating with Erskine Clarke.

The willingness of Erskine Clarke and the *Journal* to accept and publish my several articles over time was a very happy chance for me to write short pieces that sought to make telling connections between the Bible and contemporary practices of the church and, more specifically, the practices of preaching. Over time this process helped me in decisive ways to become unambiguously clear about my proper work. While I have always worked to maintain credible membership in the academic guild of Old Testament studies, I was able to see that my proper work was in and for the church. More specifically, the most important constituency for my research and writing have been the pastors of the church who themselves labor relentlessly to articulate the kinds of links and connections I have tried to make. While I think I have contributed significantly to the *Journal*, the *Journal* itself has had a significant impact on my vocational identity and focus. As a result I have been able to keep clearly in purview the kinds of readers for whom I have wanted to do my work.

II.

Erskine Clarke has developed and supported a reliable cadre of writer-preachers who have filled our pages with thoughtful, bold, and suggestive materials. On the one hand, this company of contributors has consisted in "celebrity preachers," the folk who have immediate and widespread name recognition. This amazing company includes, among others, William Barber, Tom Long, Barbara Brown Taylor, Sam Wells, and Will Willimon. It has been a special privilege for me, as an editor, to communicate with and be taught by such luminaries in our common work. These "all star" preachers have enabled the *Journal* to maintain consistently high standards for our regular readers. After all, these notable preacher-writers have not arrived at such status and recognition by happenstance or by accident, but as an outcome of hard work that has come via their uncommon gifts. Such preachers have set high standards for the rest of us and invited us and, by their example, empowered us to greater artistic imagination and to boldness in proclamation. To be sure, such preachers over time have benefited in their work with various support systems other preachers may not have, plus the luxury of travel and mobility that permit a good sermon to be sounded more than once. A good journal on preaching must offer the best preachers with the best sermons; happily we have been able to do that in a consistent way.

III.

On the other hand, most of the work of the *Journal* has not been done by celebrity preachers. It has been done, rather, by working parish pastors who do the daily, demanding work of pastoral care and administration, who live with endless conflict and challenge, and yet find time and energy to do the bold, thoughtful work of preaching. I am regularly astonished by the way in which Erskine Clarke has continued to recruit good preacher-writers from many places and many traditions, pastors who labor in relative obscurity, but who relentlessly hang in for the sake of the Gospel.

The large number of writer-preachers represented in our pages attests to the continuing importance and vitality of preaching, and to the large capacity among us to mobilize serious thought, vivid imagination, risky courage, and careful reading for that hard work. When one considers these work-a-day preachers in their localities, one comes to two fresh appreciations. First, we freshly appreciate the missional vitality of local congregations in their several contexts. Such congregations do not spend time reading op-ed pieces about the demise of the church; rather, they engage in missional ways in the Gospel issues in their contexts. A bit ago Tia and I happily participated in a lovely dinner party to welcome our new associate pastor. I did not know everyone there. But I knew three couples, all somewhat older. One couple had devised a long-running program of breakfast seven days a week for many of our homeless community's population. One couple gives its energy to a church garden that produces great quantities of vegetables for our homeless shelters. The third couple had adopted an unwanted child with Down's syndrome and brought her to adulthood. None of these folk gloated over their missional work. But all of them did it; and surely all of them have been sustained in the missional work by good preaching and worship. These are the kind of folk who *evoke* good preaching and who, at the same time, deeply *depend* upon it. Their pastors (and a myriad like them) are the ones who have evoked and sustained such missional passion.

Second, we become freshly aware of how pivotal good preaching is for the experience of and mobilization of a missional congregation. After all the rhetorical fads and homiletical cleverness, what still counts in the local congregation is *truth-telling* about the pain of the world, and then *hope-telling* that evokes passionate investment. My faithful reading of *Journal* articles and sermons regularly fills me with immense wonder and immense gratitude for the steadfast ways in which preachers do their work, hanging in despite all kinds of resistance and conflictual behavior in their midst.

IV.

The accent of the *Journal*, of course, is not on its preacher-writers, celebrity or otherwise. Our accent is unambiguously upon our readers. That readership is somewhat small. (We are hopeful that we will increase circulation with new prospects for marketing with our new leadership.) But it nonetheless includes a broad base of ecumenical interest that attracts not only preachers but other church leaders and folk who value the act and art of preaching. But the focus is upon working preachers who must and may regularly do the work of the proclamation of the Gospel. Every preacher I know who has not "gone to seed" is alert for new ideas, for fresh angle on a text, or a new image or metaphor to open reality differently. It is our hope and expectation that the *Journal* should respond to this requirement for preachers.

Beyond that, we are alert to the social context most preachers among us share. That context is variously marked by an erosion of pastoral authority, a loss of institutional credibility, the force of ideologies that sound true but are in fact inimical to the Gospel, and the seduction of the mantra, "spiritual but not religious," all reinforced by the losses dictated by the pandemic. The convergence of these several factors makes preaching a most demanding exercise. Indeed, give or take a bit, one could imagine that very many preachers can readily identify with Paul's lyrical self-description:

> We are afflicted in every way, but not crushed; perplexed, but not driven to despair, persecuted, but not forsaken; struck down, but not destroyed. (2 Cor 4:8–9)

A convergence of the social realities mentioned above can indeed cause a preacher to be *afflicted, perplexed, persecuted,* and *struck down.* Every preacher lives with such social realities in the process of sermon preparation and delivery. But of course what strikes one most forcefully in Paul's statement is the resolve and reality beyond these negations. Given all of that with none of it denied or sugarcoated, Paul nonetheless is *not crushed, not driven to despair, not forsaken, not destroyed*. It is that series of refusals (*"not, not, not, not"*) that carries the day. What makes that great refusal possible, for Paul and for many of our readers, is the deep conviction,

> That this extraordinary power belongs to God and does not come from us (v. 7).

Such preachers, like Paul, are,

> Always carrying in the body the death of Jesus, so that the life of Jesus may also be made visible in our bodies. (v. 10)

The risks and dangers are instanced by social context; the assurances on which we rely lie beyond social reality and yield an unaccommodating vocation. That is my sense of our readership, a company of called, convicted, determined folk. In various precarious social circumstances they fall back on that "extraordinary power" that is on offer for those with eyes to see and hearts to receive.

Given that shared circumstance of our readers, I reckon that the *Journal* can serve such preacher-readers in two ways. First, our pages offer a rich attentiveness to fresh angles and images. Beyond that, second, the preacher-writers and preacher-readers of the *Journal* constitute a goodly band of sisters and brothers who, through a variety of connections, constitute a collegium who can say:

> We share our mutual woes, our mutual burdens bear,
> And often for each other flows the sympathizing tear.[1]

It is my hope and assumption that the *Journal* functions as a tool for solidarity so that our preacher-readers are not alone in facing *affliction, perplexity, persecution*, and being *struck down*, but belong to a company that knows, in solidarity, about that "extraordinary power that belongs to God." At our most subversive risk-taking for the sake of the Gospel, it matters that we belong, together, to that great cloud of witnesses who "run with perseverance the race that is set before us" (Heb 12:1–2).

It is my hope and expectation that on both counts, as a source for *fresh thinking* and as means of *collegial solidarity*, the *Journal* may support

---

1. "Blest Be the Tie That Binds."

the faithful preaching of the church. At our best we may hope that our preaching is fully marked, as it is at the end reported of Paul. He was,

> Proclaiming the kingdom of God and teaching about the Lord Jesus Christ with all boldness and without hindrance. (Acts 28:31)

I love that final phrase in the book of Acts, "without hindrance." Who knew? Who knew as we read of the several tribulations of Paul in the book of Acts or in his own epistles? Who knew that in spite of such risk and danger (2 Cor 11:25–28!), he would persist and end up "without hindrance"? This narrative in the book of Acts is a summary report of a preacher who did not waver or give up in the face of deep challenge. The names of preachers who go on "without hindrance" is *"Legion."* Happily, many of these are among our readers!

V.

In retrospect, I am grateful on all counts for my time with the *Journal*:

- Pleased to have an opportunity to write and to be published in the *Journal*;
- Glad to have interacted with the celebrity preachers who occupy our pages;
- Rewarded by my contact with the company of on-the-job preacher-writers; and
- Encouraged by the host of our readers who do the day-to-day work of pastoral ministry.

Beyond all of that, however, the best and most singular blessing for me over this period of time has been my engagement with Erskine Clarke, with a chance to observe his work up close. The *Journal* is an outcome of Erskine's imaginative will to support and encourage pastors, the product of his patient tenacity that has not only sustained the *Journal*, but has maintained the very high standards that he intended at the outset. There has been, to be sure, an important supporting cast of writers, editors, and nearly invisible staff to maintain the *Journal*. But it is Erskine who single-handedly has provided the energy and resolve for these many years of quality publication.

It strikes me, as I am informed by Paul's Easter lyric, that Erskine is exactly an "Easter guy." As every reader will know, Paul concludes his moving Easter doxology in his characteristic way, with an ethical imperative that arises from the news:

> Therefore, my beloved, be steadfast, immovable, always excelling in the work of the Lord, because you know that in the Lord our labor is not in vain. (1 Cor 15:58)

The marks of those who receive the new reality of Easter are to be *steadfast, immovable, excelling in the work of the Lord*. Over the years of the *Journal*, Erskine has been relentlessly steadfast in his vision for the *Journal*. And once he has set his course, he is indeed immovable. As for the "work of the Lord," he and Nan do many things to contribute to the wellbeing of the neighborhood. But I reckon that Erskine's primary "work of the Lord" in which he excels is to be a truth-teller through his singular historical research. He has not let us escape from the deep reality of injustice that occupies our common past. Such truth-telling is hard work, and Erskine has stayed at it through the many volumes of research and narration. Paul assures that such good work is "not in vain." For sure Erskine's truth-telling work has not been in vain. Nor has his deep investment in the *Journal* been in vain, for it has over this long run given support, encouragement, guidance, and sustenance for the faithful preaching of the Word.

I finish then with my great thanks to Erskine for his generous friendship and reliable colleagueship. On behalf of our many readers, moreover, I voice our common thanks for the work of the *Journal* that has been Erskine's great work that at its best has been "the work of the Lord."

August 27, 2021

Bibliography

Adams, Marilyn McCord. *Horrendous Evils and the Goodness of God*. Ithaca: Cornell University Press, 1999.
Alexander, Cecil Frances. "Jesus Calls Us O'er the Tumult." In *Glory to God*, 720. Louisville: Westminster John Knox, 2013.
Anderson, Carol. *White Rage: The Unspoken Truth of Our Racial Divide*. New York: Bloomsbury, 2016.
Barth, Karl. *Commentary on the Epistle to the Romans*. Translated by Edwyn C. Hoskyns. 6th ed. Oxford: Oxford University Press, 1977.
Bauman, Zygmunt. *Modernity and the Holocaust*. Cambridge: Polity Press, 1989.
Becker, Ernest. *The Denial of Death*. New York: Free Press, 1973.
Berry, Wendell. "Local Knowledge in an Age of Information." In *The Way of Ignorance and Other Essays*, 113–26. Emeryville, CA: Shoemaker & Hoard, 2005.
Bilton, Nick. "Lord of the Screens." *The New York Times*, May 20, 2015.
Bishop, Bill, with Robert G. Cushing. *The Big Sort: Why the Clustering of Like-Minded Americans Is Tearing Us Apart*. Boston: Mariner, 2009.
Boer, Roland. *The Sacred Economy of Ancient Israel*. Library of Ancient Israel. Louisville: Westminster John Knox, 2015.
Bordo, Susan. *The Flight to Objectivity: Essays on Cartesianism and Culture*. SUNY Series in Philosophy. Albany: SUNY Press, 1987.
Brown, Peter. *Through the Eye of the Needle: Wealth, the Fall of Rome and the Making of Christianity in the West, 350–550 AD*. Princeton: Princeton University Press, 2012.
Brueggemann, Walter. *Biblical Perspectives on Evangelism: Living in a Three-Storied Universe*. Nashville: Abingdon, 1993.
———. *Embracing the Transformation*. Edited by K. C. Hanson. Eugene, OR: Cascade Books, 2014.
———. "The Family as World-Maker" *Journal of Preachers* 8.3 (1985) 8–15.
———. "The Formfulness of Grief." In *The Psalms and the Life of Faith*, edited by Patrick D. Miller, 84–97. Minneapolis: Fortress, 1995.

———. *Journey to the Common Good*. Louisville: Westminster John Knox, 2010.

———. *The Practice of Homefulness*. Edited by K. C. Hanson. Eugene, OR: Cascade Books, 2014.

———. "Psalms and the Life of Faith: A Suggested Typology of Function." In *The Psalms and the Life of Faith*, edited by Patrick D. Miller, 3–32. Minneapolis: Fortress, 1995.

———. *Remember You are Dust*. Edited by K. C. Hanson. Eugene, OR: Cascade Books, 2012.

———. *Solomon: Israel's Ironic Icon of Human Achievement*. Columbia: University of South Carolina Press, 2005.

———. *Truth-Telling as Subversive Obedience*. Edited by K. C. Hanson. Eugene, OR: Cascade Books, 2011.

Brueggemann, Walter, and Davis Hankins. "The Invention and Persistence of Wellhausen's World." *CBQ* 75 (2013) 15–31.

Buber, Martin. *Between Man & Man*. Translated by Ronald Gregor Smith. Afterword translated by Maurice Friedman. New York: Macmillan, 1965.

———. *I and Thou*. Translated by Ronald Gregor Smith. Edinburgh: T. & T. Clark, 1937.

Buckley, Michael J. *At the Origins of Modern Atheism*. New Haven: Yale University Press, 1987.

Busch, Eberhard. *Drawn to Freedom: Christian Faith Today in Conversation with the Heidelberg Catechism*. Translated by William H. Rader. Grand Rapids: Eerdmans, 2010.

Byassee, Jason. *Praise Seeking Understanding: Reading the Psalms with Augustine*. Grand Rapids; Eerdmans, 2007.

Calvin, John. *Commentary on the Book of Psalms Volume First*. Grand Rapids: Baker, 1979.

Childs, Brevard S. *Introduction to the Old Testament as Scripture*. Philadelphia: Fortress, 1979.

———. "Psalm Titles and Midrashic Exegesis." *Journal of Semitic Studies* 16 (1971) 137–50.

Claudius, Matthias. "We Plow the Fields and Scatter." In *The Presbyterian Hymnal: Hymns, Psalms and Spiritual Songs*, 560. Translated by Jane M. Campbell. Louisville: Westminster John Knox, 1990.

Coates, Ta-Nehisi. *Between the World and Me*. New York: Spiegel & Grau, 2015.

Cone, James H. *The Cross and the Lynching Tree*. Maryknoll, NY: Orbis, 2011.

Eagleton, Terry. *Reason, Faith, and Revolution: Reflections on the God Debate*. The Terry Lectures. New Haven: Yale University Press, 2009.

Eichrodt, Walther. "The Holy One in Your Midst: The Theology of Hosea." *Interpretation* 15 (1961) 259–73.

The Evangelical Catechism: A New Translation for the 21st Century. Translated by Frederick R. Trost. Cleveland: Pilgrim, 2010.

Fawcett, John. "Blest Be the Tie That Binds." In *Glory to God*, 306. Louisville: Westminster John Knox, 2013.

Fishbane, Michael. *Text and Texture: Close Readings of Selected Biblical Texts*. New York: Schocken, 1979.

Fosdick, Harry Emerson. "God of Grace and God of Glory." In *Glory to God*, 307. Louisville: Westminster John Knox, 2013.

Friedman, Milton. *Capitalism and Freedom*. Chicago: University of Chicago Press, 1962.
Fukuyama, Francis. *Truth: The Social Virtues and the Creation of Prosperity*. New York: Free Press, 1996.
Gerstenberger, Erhard S. *Der Bittende Mensch: Bittritual und Klagelied des Einzelnen im Alten Testament*. Wissenschaftliche Monographien zum Alten und Neuen Testament 51. Neukirchen-Vluyn: Neukirchener, 1980. Reprint, Eugene, OR: Wipf & Stock, 2010.
Giddings, Paula J. *Ida: A Sword among Lions: Ida B. Wells and the Campaign against Lynching*. New York: Amistad, 2008.
Gilkey, Langdon. "Cosmology, Ontology, and the Travail of Biblical Language." *Journal of Religion* 41 (1961) 194–205.
Glory to God. Louisville: Westminster John Knox, 2013.
Goodchild, Philip. *Theology of Money*. Durham: Duke University Press, 2009.
Goodwin, Doris Kearns. *Leadership in Turbulent Times*. New York: Simon & Schuster, 2018.
Graeber, David. *Debt: The First 5000 Years*. New York; Melville House, 2011.
Hays, Richard B. *Echoes of Scripture in the Gospels*. Waco: Baylor University Press, 2016.
Horkheimer, Max, and Theodor A. Adorno. *The Dialectic of Enlightenment: Philosophical Fragments*. Stanford: Stanford University Press, 2002.
Huntington, Samuel P. *The Clash of Civilizations and the Remaking of World Order* (New York: Simon & Schuster, 2011.
Janowski, Bernd. *Arguing with God: A Theological Anthropology of the Psalms*. Translated by Armin Siedlecki. Louisville: Westminster John Knox, 2013.
Jenson, Robert W. *Canon and Creed*. Interpretation: Resources for the Use of Scripture in the Church. Louisville: Westminster John Knox, 2010.
Kahl, Brigitte. *Galatians Reimagined: Reading with the Eyes of the Vanquished*. Minneapolis: Fortress Press, 2010.
Kearney, Richard. *Anatheism: Returning to God after God*. Insurrections. New York: Columbia University Press, 2010.
———. *The God Who May Be: A Hermeneutics of Religion*. Bloomington: Indiana University Press 2001.
Koch, Klaus. "Is There a Doctrine of Retribution in the Old Testament?" In *Theodicy in the Old Testament*, edited by James L. Crenshaw, 57–87. Issues in Religion and Theology Philadelphia: Fortress, 1983) 57–87.
Langer, Susanne K. *Philosophy in a New Key: A Study in the Symbolism of Reason, Rite, and Art*. Cambridge: Harvard University Press, 1942, 1957.
Lapsley, Jacqueline E. "Feeling Our Way: Love of God in Deuteronomy." *CBQ* 65 (2003) 350–69.
Lerner, Alan J., and Frederick Loewe. "If Ever I Would Leave You." *Camelot*, 1960.
Lewis, Alan E. *Between Cross and Resurrection: A Theology of Holy Saturday*. Grand Rapids: Eerdmans, 2001.
Lifton, Robert Jay. *Witness to an Extreme Century: A Memoir*. New York: Free Press, 2011.
Linafelt, Tod. *Surviving Lamentations: Catastrophe, Lament, and Protest in the Afterlife of a Biblical Book*. Chicago: University of Chicago Press, 2000.
Lindbeck, George. *The Nature of Doctrine: Religion and Theology in a Postliberal Age*. Philadelphia: Westminster, 1984.

Lindstrom, Fredrik. *Suffering and Sin: Interpretations of Illness in the Individual Complaint Psalms.* Coniectanea biblica: Old Testament Series 37. Stockholm: Almqvist & Wiksell, 1994.

Lomax, Eric. *The Railway Man: A True Story of War, Remembrance, and Forgiveness.* New York: Ballantine, 1996.

Macpherson, C. B. *The Political Theory of Possessive Individualism: Hobbes to Locke.* Oxford: Clarendon, 1962.

Masuzawa, Tomoko. *The Invention of World Religions: Or, How European Universalism Was Preserved in the Language of Pluralism.* Chicago: University of Chicago Press, 2005.

Mays, James Luther. "The Place of the Torah-Psalms in the Psalter." *JBL* 106 (1987) 3–12.

McBride, S. Dean, Jr. "The Yoke of the Kingdom: An Exposition of Deuteronomy 6:4–5." *Interpretation* 27 (1973) 273–306.

Miller, Patrick D. *Sin and Judgment in the Prophets: A Stylistic and Theological Analysis.* SBL Monograph Series 27. Chico, CA: Scholars, 1982.

———. *They Cried to the Lord: The Form and Theology of Biblical Prayer.* Minneapolis: Fortress, 1994.

Moltmann, Jürgen. *Theology of Hope: On the Ground and the Implications of a Christian Eschatology.* Translated by John Bowden. New York: Harper & Row, 1965.

Moran, William L. "The Ancient Near Eastern Background of the Love of God in Deuteronomy." *CBQ* 25 (1963) 77–87.

Newcomb, Steven T. *Pagans in the Promised Land: Decoding the Doctrine of Christian Discovery.* Golden, CO: Fulcrum, 2008.

Nussbaum, Martha C. *The Clash Within: Democracy, Religious Violence and India's Future.* Cambridge, MA: Belnap, 2007.

Otto, Rudolf. *The Idea of the Holy: An Inquiry into the Non-rational Factor in the Idea of the Divine and Its Relation to the Rational.* Translated by John W. Harvey. 2nd ed. New York: Oxford University Press, 1950.

Perronet, Edward. "All Hail the Power of Jesus' Name." In *Glory to God*, 263. Louisville: Westminster John Knox, 2013.

Phillips, Patrick. *Blood at the Root: A Racial Cleansing in America.* New York: Norton, 2016.

Polanyi, Karl. *Personal Knowledge: Toward a Post-Critical Philosophy.* New York: Harper & Row, 1958, 1962.

The Presbyterian Hymnal: Hymns, Psalms and Spiritual Songs. Louisville: Westminster John Knox, 1990.

Rad, Gerhard von. "The Levitical Sermons in I and II Chronicles." In *The Problem of the Hexateuch and Other Studies*, 267–80. Translated by E. W. Trueman Dicken. New York: McGraw-Hill, 1966.

———. *Studies in Deuteronomy.* Translated by David Stalker. Studies in Biblical Theology 1/9. London: SCM, 1961.

———. *Wisdom in Israel.* Translated by James D. Martin. Nashville: Abingdon, 1972.

Ricoeur, Paul. *The Conflict of Interpretations: Essays in Hermeneutics.* Edited by Don Ihde. Evanston: Northwestern University Press, 1974.

Robertson, Lindsay G. *Conquest by Law: How the Discovery of America Dispossessed Indigenous Peoples of Their Lands.* Oxford; Oxford University Press, 2015.

Ruru, Jacinta, Tracey Lindberg, and Robert J. Miller. *Discovering Indigenous Lands: The Doctrine of Discovery in the English Colonies*. Oxford: Oxford University Press, 2010.

Sapir, Edward. "Language." In *Encyclopedia of the Social Sciences*, edited by Edwin R. A. Seligman, 9:155–69. 15 vols. New York: Macmillan, 1933.

Schwartz, Regina M. *Sacramental Poetics at the Dawn of Secularism: When God Left the World*. Cultural Memory in the Present. Stanford: Stanford University Press, 2008.

Scott, James C. *Against the Grain: A Deep History of the Earliest States*. New Haven: Yale University Press, 2017.

Stark, Rodney. *The Triumph of Christianity: How the Jesus Movement Became the World's Largest Religion*. New York: HarperOne, 2011.

Stone, S. J. "The Church's One Foundation." In *Glory to God*, 321. Louisville: Westminster John Knox, 2013.

Stroup, George W. *Before God*. Grand Rapids: Eerdmans, 2004.

Tutu, Desmond, and Mpho Tutu. *The Book of Forgiving: The Fourfold Path for Healing Ourselves and Our World*. New York: HarperOne, 2014.

Walker, Williston. *A History of the Christian Church*. Rev. ed. New York: Scribner, 1959.

Watts, Isaac. "When I Survey the Wondrous Cross." In *Glory to God*, 223. Louisville: Westminster John Knox, 2013.

Westermann, Claus. *The Living Psalms*. Translated by J. R. Porter. Grand Rapids: Eerdmans, 1989.

———. *Praise and Lament in the Psalms*. Translated by Keith R. Crim and Richard N. Soulen. Atlanta: John Knox, 1981.

———. *The Psalms: Structure, Content & Message*. Translated by Ralph D. Gehrke. Minneapolis: Augsburg, 1980.

Woelk, Cheryl, and Steve Heinrichs, eds. *Yours, Mine, Ours: Unravelling the Doctrine of Discovery*. Special ed. of *Intotemak* (2016).

Wybrow, Cameron. *The Bible, Baconism, and Mastery over Nature: The Old Testament and Its Modern Misreading*. American University Studies, Series 7, 112. New York: Lang, 1991.

Zenger, Erich. *A God of Vengeance? Understanding the Psalms of Divine Wrath*. Translated by Linda Maloney. Louisville: Westminster John Knox, 1996.

The New York Times (April 21, 2020) A15

Name Index

Adams, Marilyn McCord, 77
Adorno, Theodor A., 73n
Alexander, Cecil Frances, 176n
Alexios I, (Emperor), 203
Anderson, Carol, 208n

Balboa, Vasco Núñez de, 205
Barber, William, 212
Barth, Karl, xv, 75
Bauman, Zygmunt, 73
Becker, Ernest, 177n
Berry, Wendell, 31, 32n
Bilton, Nick, 199
Bishop, Bill, 197n
Boer, Roland, 31n
Bordo, Susan, 69n
Brown, Peter, 203n
Brueggemann, Ed, xiii
Brueggemann, Tia, ix, 213
Brueggemann, Walter, ix–xii, 8n, 10n, 47n, 116n, 174n, 209n
Buber, Martin, 58, 135
Buckley, Michael J., 69
Busch, Eberhard, 174
Byassee, Jason, 54n

Calvin, John, 7, 9, 11
Campolo, Tony, x, xiii, 125

Carlin, George, 118–19, 121–23
Carnegie, Andrew, 175
Childs, Brevard S., 14n, 15, 48n
Clarke, Erskine, xvi, 211–13, 216–17
Claudius, Matthias, 51n
Coates, Ta-Nehisi, 153
Columbus, Christopher, 205
Cone, James H., 201n
Constantine, (Emperor), 202
Cortés, Hernán, 205
Cushing, Robert G., 197

Descartes, René, 205
de Soto, Hernando, 205

Eagleton, Terry, 79
Eichrodt, Walther, 74n

Fawcett, John, 13
Federer, Roger, 150
Fishbane, Michael, 177
Forbes, Jim, x, xiii, 125
Fosdick, Harry Emerson, 39
Freud, Sigmund, xv
Friedman, Milton, 40–41
Fukuyama, Francis, 74

Gerstenberger, Erhard S., 9

NAME INDEX

Giddings, Paula J., 201
Gilkey, Langdon, 70, 74
Goodchild, Philip, 72n, 77n
Goodwin, Doris Kearns, 55
Graeber, David, 45n

Hankins, Davis, 209
Harper, Jet, xvi
Hays, Richard B., 54
Heinrichs, Steve, 206n
Horkheimer, Max, 73n
Huntington, Samuel P., 209

Jackson, Andrew, 207
Janowski, Bernd, 10n
Jenson, Robert W., 75
Jewett, Robert, 191
Joyce, James, 108, 113

Kahl, Brigitte, 40, 191–93
Kearney, Richard, 76n, 81n, 108n
Koch, Edwin J., xiii
Koch, Klaus, 105

Langer, Susanne K., 75–76
Lapsley, Jacqueline E., 173
Lerner, Alan Jay, 26n
Lewis, Alan E., 32
Licinius (Emperor), 202
Lifton, Robert Jay, 78
Linafelt, Tod, 35–36, 91
Lindbeck, George, 8
Lindberg, Tracey, 206
Lindstrom, Fredrik, 56
Loewe, Frederick, 26n
Lomax, Eric, 104n
Long, Tom, x, xiii, 212

Macpherson, C. B., 74n
Magellan, Ferdinand, 205
Marshall, John, 207
Masuzawa, Tomoko, 208
Mays, James Luther, 48n
McBride, S. Dean, Jr., 178n
McEnroe, John, 150, 158
Miller, Patrick D., 58n, 105n
Miller, Robert J., 206
Moltmann, Jürgen, 70n

Moran, William L., 173

Nadal, Rafael, 150
Newcomb, Steven T., 207n
Nussbaum, Martha C., 209

Otto, Rudolf, 91

Perronet, Edward, 153
Phillips, Patrick, 207
Pizzaro, Francisco, 205
Polanyi, Karl, 76

Rad, Gerhard von, xiv, 70, 92, 106n
Raynal, Rosemary, xvi
Ricoeur, Paul, 57
Robertson, Lindsay, G., 207
Ruru, Jacinta, 206

Sapir, Edward, 76
Schwartz, Regina M., 198n
Scott, James C., 21
Song, C. S., 123
Stark, Rodney, 202n
Stone, S. J., 153
Stroup, George W., 8n

Taylor, Barbara Brown, x, xiii, 212
Tennyson, Alfred Lord, 82, 95
Toynbee, Arnold, 119
Trump, Donald J., 82, 95, 165, 207, 210
Tutu, Desmond, 113
Tutu, Mpho, 113

Urban II, (Pope), 203–4

Walker, Williston, 204
Watts, Isaac, 178
Wells, Ida B., 201
Wells, Sam, 212
Westermann, Claus, 10–11, 58
Williams, Serena, 150
Willimon, Will, x, xiii, 212
Woelk, Cheryl, 206
Wright, G. Ernest, 70
Wybrow, Cameron, 72

Zenger, Erich, 16

Scripture Index

OLD TESTAMENT

Genesis

1:11	28
1:22	28
1:29–30	28
2:24	173

Exodus

1:16	23
1:22	23
2:23	22
3:3	78
3:14	76
4:22	25, 87, 152
5:4	22
5:9	22
5:13	22
5:17	22
5:19	22
6:6	86
6:7	86
7:5	86
7:17	86
8:10	86
8:22	86
8:23	23
9:4	87
9:23–26	87
9:29–30	86
10:2	86
10:8	23
10:9	21, 23
10:24	24
10:26	24
11:5–7	87
11:7	86
12:28	79
14:4	64, 86
14:17	64, 86
14:18	6
14:30	86
15:13	28
16	28, 34
16:3	32
16:14	28
16:15	29
16:17–18	4, 29
17:6	28
19:6	152
20:2–3	169
24:7	173
34	109
34:9	109
34:10	109

Leviticus

	115, 169
19:18	169
26	84
26:23–26	83

Numbers

11:4	33
11:5	33
11:11–14	33–34
11:18–20	34
11:18	34
11:23	34
11:31–32	34
14:2–4	33
14:9	33
14:20	33
14:22–23	33

Deuteronomy

	xiv, 46–48, 50, 84–85, 105–6, 115, 152, 169–73, 175–77, 179
5:6–21	173
6	177
6:5	169, 178
6:6–9	174
6:7	177
6:10–11	171
6:12	171
6:21	177
6:24	175
7:6	152
7:7	173
8:11	171
8:15–18	29
8:17	171
8:18–19	171
10:15	173
12–25	173
13	173
13:4	173
14:1–21	91
14:2	152
15:4	45
15:11	45
15:5	172
16:3	1
16:11	37
16:12	172
17:18–19	52
24:18	172
24:22	172
28	105
28:1–68	105
28:20	84
28:21–34	84
28:21	84
28:25	84
28:30–33	84
30:15–18	105
30:15	50
30:19	50

Joshua

5:12	170

Judges

12:1–6	126–27

1 Samuel

6:19–20	91
8:5	175
8:19	175

2 Samuel

6:6–11	91
11–12	14
24	89
24:12–13	83

2 Kings

6:8–23	42, 137
6:16	42, 137
6:17	42, 137
6:24	137
24:13—25:21	108

2 Chronicles

20:9	83
36:22–23	xiv

Nehemiah

9:6–37	108
13:3	79

Job

	91, 107
1:9	107
21:7	55
28	93
28:11	93
28:12	93
28:20	93
28:23–27	93–94
28:28	94
38:4–11	89–90
38:31–33	90
39:1–2	90
39:9–12	90
40:4	90
40:14	90
41:1–7	90
42:2	90
42:6	90

Psalms

1	48–52, 56
1:6	49, 83
2	48, 52, 56
2:1–3	52
2:4–5	52
2:6–7	52
2:7	48, 54
2:10	52
2:12	52
3	14
3:7	61
6:1–5	61
7:1	61–62
7:6	61–62
9:4–6	62
9:19	62, 80
10:12	62, 80
18:1	58
19	51
19:7–8	51
19:10	51
22	140
23	15
30	10
30:1–3	58
30:1	79
30:5a	167
30:5b	166
30:6–7a	10
30:7b	10
30:8	10
30:9	10
30:10	10
30:11	10, 58
30:12	10
31	10
33:6	xv
34	14
35:1–3	62
40	10
40:9–10	60
44:9–17	19
44:17–19	55
51	14, 15
52	14
54	14
57	14
59	14
60	14
63	14
65:9–13	17
66	10
66:10–12	59
72	13, 54
72:3–4	53
78:24–25	29
85:10–11	17
88	60
88:1–2	19–20
88:6–8	60–61
88:8	20
88:9	19–20
88:13	19–20

Psalms (continued)

88:14–18	60–61
88:18	20
89:3–4	47
89:19–20	47
89:28–29	47
89:49	56
96–99	53
96	54
96:10–12	53
102:12–13	59
105:26–36	87
105:37	87
105:40–41	30
106	108
107:4–9	30
109:9–13	15
109:21b	16
109:31	16
110:1	53
110:5	53
112	13
115:4–7	71
115:5	71
115:8	71
116	10
119	48
132	47
132:11–12	47
138	10
138:1–4	60
138:1–2	80
145:14–20	59
145:15–16	17–18
145:20b	18
146:7–9	59

Proverbs

	92, 107
10:4	106
10:16	106
10:27	106
10:30	107
16:2	92
16:9	92
19:21	92
20:24	92
21:2	92
21:30–31	92
25:2	94

Isaiah

	x, 89, 100
2	100
2:4	99–100
2:6–8	88
2:10	87
2:12–17	87
2:19	87
2:22	88
5:6–7	110
5:8–24	110
9:7	53
11	100
11:1–9	98
11:6–7	101
11:9	102
14:27	91
19:22	89
30:20	1
40:27	133
41:17–20	63
41:18	80
42:14	134
43:11–13	63
44:24–26	63–64
45:1	154
45:9–10	92, 154
45:12a	154
46:10–11	64
49:14	133
49:15	25, 134
52:7	xiv
52:13—53:12	140
53:2–3	144
54:7a	68
54:7b	68
54:8a	68
54:8b	68
55	x, 1
55:1–2	30, 36
55:1	3

55:2	4	51:20–23	65
55:6–9	114	52:12–30	108
55:6–7	110		
55:6a	6	## Lamentations	
55:8a	6		
55:10	27	1:4–5	109
55:12–13	110, 114	2:12	35
55:12	4	3:18	109
56	114	3:21–23	109
56:7	114	3:22–23	67
58:6–7	114	4:4–5	35
65	100	5:22	35
65:17–18	100		
65:20a	100	## Ezekiel	
65:22a	100		
65:25	100		84
		6:11	84
## Jeremiah		7:15	84
		9–10	115
2:2	174	12:16	84
2:4	71	16:41b–42	65
5:14–17	65	18:5	111
11:10	115	18:9	111
12:1	55	18:21	111
14:13	84	29:3	22
15:3	84	32:2	22
19:11	111	34:15–16	115
20:8–9	120	34:16	66
20:13	125	36:24–27	111
21:9	84	36:29	66
23:23	20	37:11	134
23:29–32	120	37:12–14	66
24:10	84	40–48	115
29:18	84		
30–31	111		
31:2	111	## Daniel	
31:3	111		
31:20	25, 66	4:35	92
31:31–34	111		
31:34	111	## Hosea	
32:36	84		
33:7–8	111	2:9–13	65
34:17	84	2:9	80
38:2	84	2:13	171
42:17	84	4:1–3	106
42:22	84	4:6	171
44:13	84	6:6	176

SCRIPTURE INDEX

Hosea (continued)

8:14	172
9:10	71
11:1	25
11:5–7	110
11:8–9	66
11:8	25, 80, 110
11:8b–9	110
11:9	74
13:6	172

Amos

4:6–11	65
8:9–10	65

Micah

3:11–12	106

Zephaniah

1:12	71

NEW TESTAMENT

Matthew

3:1–12	98
3:8	102
3:10	102
6:24	37
6:25–33	179
16:16–20	168
22:15–45	168
22:15–22	168, 170
22:22	168
22:23–32	169, 170
22:34–40	169, 170
22:37–38	168
22:37	170, 178
22:41–45	170
22:46	170
23	170
23:1–36	170
23:12	143
23:23	179
23:37–39	170
24:1–2	170
24:8	170
25:1–13	166
26:11	37
26:63	168
27:17	168
27:22	168
27:51–54	134
28:18	52

Mark

1:11	54
1:14–15	xvi
6	185, 187
6:1	181
6:30–44	181
6:31	30
6:34	137
6:38	137
6:41–43	4
6:52	139, 199
7	184, 187
7:24–30	181
7:26	184
7:27	184
7:28	185, 187
7:29–30	187
7:29	185
7:31	182
8	30, 185, 187
8:2	30, 137
8:5–7	137
8:21	198
12:32–34	169
12:32–33	176
12:32	169
14:7	37

Luke

2:46–47	170
5:30	79
7:34	79
10:25–28	169, 179
10:28	169

15	25	1:28	192
16:13	37	4:17	135
18:4	40	10:14–15	xiv
21:9–19	118, 123	13	192
21:12–13	123	13:3	192
21:14–15	123		
21:16–17	124		
21:18–19	124		
23:44–45	134		
24:21	134		

1 Corinthians

1:11	193
1:27–28	152, 203
3:3	193
15:58	217

John

9:2	105
10:10	28
12:8	37
15:16	152, 203
18:1—19:42	140
18:36	141
18:38	142
19:10	141

2 Corinthians

4:8–9	214
8	129
8:9	31
9:8–10	27–28
11:25–28	216
12–13	193
12:20	193
13	193

Acts

	123, 128, 154, 197, 202, 216
3:1–16	188
10:14	155
10:15	155
10:34–43	151
10:34–35	155
10:34	156
10:36	156
10:38	156
10:40	156
10:43	156
13:33	48
15	202
28:11–14	202
28:30–31	xvi
28:31	216

Galatians

3:28–29	155
3:28	192
5:6	40
5:14	44
5:15	192
5:19–21	39, 44
5:21	41
5:22–23	44
6:2	40, 44

Ephesians

4:19	40
5:3–5	40

Philippians

1:15–17	193
2:4	194
2:5–11	197

Romans

1:24	192
1:26	192

Colossians

3:3–8 — 40

Hebrews

11:11–12 — 135
12:1–2 — 215

1 Peter

2:9–10 — 152, 203

Revelation

6:8 — 83
11:15 — x, xvii

www.ingramcontent.com/pod-product-compliance
Lightning Source LLC
Chambersburg PA
CBHW031354230426
43670CB00006B/540